Epworth Commentaries

General Editors
Harold F. Guite and Ivor H. Jones

The Gospel of John

Epworth Commentaries

The Gospel of
JOHN

KENNETH GRAYSTON

EPWORTH PRESS

Extracts from the Revised English Bible are © 1989
by the Delegates of the Oxford University Press and the
Syndics of the Cambridge University Press, and are used by
permission.

British Library Cataloguing in Publication Data

Grayston, Kenneth
  The Gospel of John.
  1. Bible. N. T. John – Critical studies
  I Title
  226.506

  ISBN 0–7162–0467–3

First published 1990
by Epworth Press
Room 195 1 Central Buildings Westminster
London SW1H 9NR

Phototypeset by Input Typesetting Ltd, London
and printed in Great Britain by
Billing & Sons Ltd, Worcester

CONTENTS

Contents

GENERAL INTRODUCTION

The *Epworth Preacher's Commentaries* that Greville P. Lewis edited so successfully in the 1950s and 1960s having now served their turn, the Epworth Press has commissioned a team of distinguished academics who are also preachers and teachers to create a new series of commentaries that will serve the 1990s and beyond. We have seized the opportunity offered by the publication in 1989 of the Revised English Bible to use this very readable and scholarly version as the basis of our commentaries, and we are grateful to the Oxford and Cambridge University Presses for the requisite license and for granting our authors pre-publication access. They will nevertheless be free to cite and discuss other translations wherever they think that these will illuminate the original text.

Just as the books that make up the Bible differ in their provenance and purpose, so our authors will necessarily differ in the structure and bearing of their commentaries. But they will all strive to get as close as possible to the intention of the original writers, expounding their texts in the light of the place, time, circumstance, and culture that gave them birth, and showing why each work was received by Jews and Christians into their respective Canons of Holy Scripture. They will seek to make full use of the dramatic advance in biblical scholarship world-wide but at the same time to explain technical terms in the language of the common reader, and to suggest ways in which Scripture can help towards the living of a Christian life today. They will endeavour to produce commentaries that can be used with confidence in ecumenical, multiracial, and multifaith situations, and not by scholars only but by preachers, teachers, students, church members, and anyone who wants to improve his or her understanding of the Bible.

Spring, 1990   Harold F. Guite

PREFACE

In this commentary I have tried to allow the Gospel to speak in its own terms. Anyone reading the Fourth Gospel must constantly be making comparisons with the other three; but those comparisons are best made when a reader has first given a sympathetic hearing to the evangelist. Presumably he thought he was putting forward a coherent and plausible account. He has a right to be heard in the terms he has chosen.

Much more can be expected from a full-scale, technical commentary. During the writing of this one I have diligently consulted seven (listed on p. xiii).

The shortest is 650 pages long, the longest 1,700. Readers who are encouraged by this commentary to read further are advised to make a quantum jump to that size of commentary, beginning with Lindars. There they will find what I have not included, namely: (a) a great deal of technical information e.g. on the variations in the Greek text (on which I comment only when familiar versions may cause readers to puzzle over the REB rendering); (b) literary analysis of each passage to distinguish between the evangelist's source and his own contribution; (c) enquiries about the historical reliability of Johannine statements in comparison with other evidence, sometimes assuming that synoptic statements can remedy or supplement John; and (d) intensive debate with the great number of scholars who have written learnedly on Johannine matters.

What I have written arises from many years of professional study, from teaching college and university students, from preaching to local congregations and contributing to study groups. I have tried to keep in mind at every point the receiving community, for I believe that the evangelist did his best for us when he addressed the precise needs of his own Christian group (and was not giving way to the individualism of which he has been suspected). I have written long paragraphs on leading terms in the Gospel, chiefly because terminology is notably important in this Gospel, and Johannine words do not always carry the meaning we ourselves associate with them or the meaning that standard theologies fix on them. In the notes I have tried to make it possible for readers to verify what I say, for I am offering not simply my opinion but a defensible interpretation of known facts.

This commentary does not pretend to be a conscientious summary of what everybody is saying, though it is certainly in touch with mainstream interpretation. It is an attempt to convey a sense of theological excitement and discovery, in the hope that St John's Gospel will do for others what my most recent study of it has done for me.

Almost always I have quoted from the REB translation of Old Testament, Apocrypha and New Testament, though of course I have used the Greek text[1] of John in preparing my exegesis. For reasons of space the full text of the Gospel is not printed, but if readers will match my exposition to their own text of the Gospel I think the argument should be easy to follow.

I am grateful to Roger Coleman, lately of the Cambridge University Press, for making available before publication the text of the Revised English Bible; and to Sarah Baird-Smith, the Editorial Director of Darton, Longman and Todd, for allowing me to use some material from ch. 8 of my book *Dying, We Live* (London 1990). It is a pleasure to record that the copy for this book was typed and set out by Margaret Hardwidge, BA (Theol.); and that my wife gave shrewd and detailed care in checking the typed and printed text.

---

[1] Usually that of Nestle, 26th ed. by K. and B. Aland, Stuttgart 1987.

BIBLIOGRAPHY

Commentaries

R. Bultmann, *The Gospel of John: A Commentary*, Oxford and Philadelphia 1971 (German 1964/66)

R. E. Brown, *The Gospel according to John* (Anchor Bible), 2 vols., New York 1966

L. Morris, *The Gospel according to John* (New International Commentary on the New Testament), London and Grand Rapids 1971

B. Lindars, *The Gospel of John* (New Century Bible), London and Grand Rapids 1972

R. Schnackenburg, *The Gospel according to St John* (Herder's Theological Commentary on the New Testament), 3 vols., London and New York 1968–82 (German 1965–75)

C. K. Barrett, *The Gospel according to St John*, Introduction with Commentary and Notes on the Greek text, 2nd ed., London and Philadelphia 1978

E. Haenchen, *John* (Hermeneia), 2 vols., Philadelphia 1984 (German 1980)

Other books frequently cited

The Mishnah, ed. and trans. by H. Danby, Oxford 1933

The Dead Sea Scrolls in English, ed. and trans. G. Vermes, 3rd ed., Harmondsworth 1987 (cited as *DSSE*)

K. Grayston, *The Johannine Epistles* (New Century Bible), London and Grand Rapids 1984

J. H. Charlesworth, *The Old Testament Pseudepigrapha*, 2 vols., London and New York 1983–85 (cited as *OTP*)

E. Schürer, *The History of the Jewish People in the Age of Jesus Christ*, rev. ed. of English trans. by G. Vermes and others, 3 vols. in 4, Edinburgh 1973–87

Theological Dictionary of the New Testament, ed. G. Kittel and G. Friedrich, English trans. ed. G. W. Bromiley, 10 vols., London and Grand Rapids 1964–74 (cited as *TDNT*)

Bibliography

Philo and Josephus are cited from the Loeb Classical Library, London and Cambridge, Mass.

English versions of the Bible
(cited by their initials)

Authorised Version, 1611
Revised Version 1884
Revised Standard Version 1952
New English Bible 1970
Good News Bible 1976
New International Version 1979
Revised English Bible 1989

INTRODUCTION

The Gospel begins by drawing attention to *logos* (1.1) which means at very least 'communication by speech'. Hence it is sensible to examine the methods of communication used in the Gospel itself.

The *language* of the Gospel is a simple Greek, highly characteristic (shared only with the Johannine Epistles) and easily recognisable even in translation. It is simple because it employs a small stock of words, some of which are repeatedly used, e.g. the prologue alone produces life, light, witness, world, know, and truth; and the same passage illustrates the repetitive style by which so often the Gospel creates its striking and serious impression on the reader. Further, the writer uses a limited range of grammatical constructions. He constantly puts short statements side by side, with or without a linking 'and'. This feature is obscured in REB, but is plain in earlier translations, e.g. 'The two disciples heard him say this, and they followed Jesus. Jesus turned and saw them following and said to them, 'What do you seek?' And they said to him, 'Rabbi' (which means Teacher), 'Where are you staying?' He said to them, 'Come and see' (1.37–39 RSV). This simple narrative method, used also in the teaching sections, is more characteristic of Jewish style than of Greek. Indeed detailed examination of John's correct but individual style shows evidence of Greek influenced by a Jewish background. But attempts to show that the Gospel, or even part of it, was first written in Aramaic (the common language of Jewish people) have not proved convincing. It is more likely that the writer used a language carefully devised to communicate his subject matter, a language made possible by the culture of Greek-speaking Judaism which drew its inspiration from the Greek Old Testament and some of its modes of expression from Greek mystical writings.

The *literary structure* depends on the arrangement of a few written forms, namely brief narratives usually containing dialogue, short or extended dialogues (often provided with a kind of dramatic setting), instructive monologues, and short passages of information linking one section of the Gospel to the next. These forms are written with a remarkable uniformity of style. As the Gospel stands it is impossible by using stylistic tests to distinguish one speaker from another, or even to decide where a speech of Jesus ends and where the writer's comment continues the discourse. But the writing is preserved from monotony by the ingenious variety with which the basic forms are handled.

It is instructive to consider these forms a little further – first the narratives (*a*, *b*, *c*) and then the speech units (*d*, *e*). (*a*) A few narratives are related without elaboration: the walking on the water (6.16–21), the entry into Jerusalem (12.12–15), the twofold denial by Peter (18.15–18, 25–27), the crucifixion, death and burial (19.17–42), the discovery of the empty tomb (20.1–10) and the first appearance to the disciples (20.19–23). These narratives have parallels in the synoptic gospels but are written in an independent manner. For example, the Johannine passion narrative corresponds fairly well with the synoptic account apart from numerous additional touches and rearrangements; yet, in John, Jesus carries the cross himself, there are different witnesses to the crucifixion, Jesus speaks different words, and the burial is otherwise managed than in the synoptic gospels. Hence narratives of this type are units of old tradition which the writer was not inclined to elaborate. He no doubt used them more or less in the form already familiar to his community, and indicated their significance by the way he placed them and the links he provided with the surrounding material.

(*b*) Rather more narratives are accompanied by dialogue which is as significant as the events related. The disturbance in the temple (2.13–22) and the anointing (12.1–8) differ from type (*a*) narratives only in the greater importance of the included dialogue; otherwise they show the same kind of relation to the corresponding synoptic narratives. All four accounts of the feeding miracle (6.1–15) are very similar; but the healing miracle (4.46–54) is related only in barest outline to the centurion's boy in Matthew and Luke. The healing at the pool of Bethesda (5.1–9) cannot be paired with any synoptic healing, though the story concludes with a command for the man to take up his bed and walk – which belongs in Mark to the healing in quite different circumstances of the paralytic in Mark 2.1–12. Hence narratives of this type are also units of old tradition which have been preserved chiefly for the dialogue attached to them, and for that reason they have had a formative influence on the composition of the Fourth Gospel.

(*c*) In other narratives the dialogue influence is even stronger. The giving of sight to a man born blind (9.1–41) has no comparable synoptic parallel (though in Mark 8.22–26 the restoration of sight to a blind man also makes use of spittle and manual actions). But the healing is less prominent than the dialogues prompted by it. The exchanges between the newly sighted man, his neighbours and parents, the Pharisees, and finally Jesus himself stand at the central point of the Gospel. They display essential teaching about one of John's few major themes: the coming of illumination. Another major theme, the renewal of life, is similarly dealt with in the long account of the raising of Lazarus (11.1–44), though here the complex dramatic dialogue precedes the act of power instead of following it. Although there is no synoptic parallel to the full narrative, there are less explicit raisings of the dead in Mark 5.38–43 (Jairus' daughter) and Luke 7.11–17 (the widow's son at Nain). Outside the Fourth Gospel the name Lazarus (common enough in its Hebrew form Eleazar) occurs only in the popular story of the beggar and the rich man (Luke 16.19–31) which ends with a reference to resurrection. The sisters Martha and Mary appear (without mention of a brother) in Luke 10.38–42. These contacts between John and Luke are strengthened by the appearance of the risen Lord at the sea of Tiberias (21.1–14) which seems to belong to the same tradition as the miraculous draught of fish in Luke 5.1–11. The turning of water into wine at Cana (2.1–11) perhaps calls to mind the Markan parables of the bridegroom and wedding guests, the wine and wineskins (Mark 2.19–22); but the footwashing (13.1–11) is a purely Johannine way of introducing the final supper of Jesus with his disciples. Such narratives as these scarcely come from the common stock of old tradition; within the tradition of the Johannine community they bring out the significance of important themes by means of dramatic narrative and explanatory dialogue.

Now we leave narratives, and turn to the speech units. (*d*) Very common throughout the Gospel is the dialogue with a dramatic setting, though the setting may have little importance. For example, the circumstances and location of the Bethesda healing are irrelevant to the subsequent discussion (5.9b–18) which is introduced by a new theme: healing on sabbath. The long dialogue on the Bread from heaven (6.25–59) is separated from the feeding miracle and largely independent of it. Sometimes the dialogue in a dramatic setting is a formal variant of a monologue (as 14.1–31 with formal interpositions at vv. 5, 8 and 22). Elsewhere we find a monologue contained within opening and closing dialogues (16.16–18, 19–28, 29–33). Thus dialogue and monologue cannot always be distinguished; but dialogues are clearly present in every section of chs. 1–12 and they take up more than half the total space. Few have more than a general parallel in the synoptic gospels, and most have none at all. Hence it is evident that for the Evangelist dialogue is a very important method of communication and that these dialogues convey themes significant to his community.

(*e*) There remain the instructive monologues, which have no more than reminiscences of synoptic sayings. The most striking example is the imagery of the sheepfold and the description of the good shepherd (10.1–18) which reflects images from several synoptic parables (the lost sheep, the thief, the man who fell among robbers, the sheep among wolves, the door and the doorkeeper). The explanation of the footwashing (13.12–20) includes variants of synoptic sayings. The Baptist's testimony to Jesus (1.29–34) contains clear echoes of synoptic sayings, but what appears in the synoptic gospels as a narrative of Jesus' baptism has become a monologue by the Baptist – who may have another monologue in 3.31–36. Otherwise all the monologues are spoken by Jesus: in his first hostile conflict with the Jews (5.19–47), in the conclusion of his public testimony (12.44–50), in his final intercourse with his disciples (13.31–35; (14.1–31); 15.1–16.15, 19–28), and in the presentation of his account to the Father (17.1–26). So then, even when dialogue is so important, it is necessary that Christians should hear Jesus addressing them, and should hear him addressing his Father – not only speaking *to* them but also speaking *for* them.

So much for the main narrative and speech components of the Gospel. How then does John dispose them? It may rightly be said that he follows the sequence of events common to the synoptic gospels, from the work of John Baptist, a departure to Galilee (4.3) and return to Jerusalem (7.10–14), to the arrest, trial, crucifixion, death, and resurrection of Jesus. But it is a mistake to assume, both for Mark and for John, that sequence in time and sequence in location are of overriding importance. Both evangelists select material from a traditional stock, and so arrange it as to display theological convictions. No contempt for historical fact is implied by displaying particular episodes in such contexts as bring out their significance for the writer. John's method of constructing a Gospel should first be studied and understood in its own right, and then comparison with the synoptic traditions will indeed be fruitful.

The Johannine *scheme* is in principle simple:

1.1–18 the prologue.

1.19–12.50 Jesus and the *kosmos*.
This section contains numerous encounters, conversations, and disputes between Jesus and followers of John Baptist, temple authorities, Pharisees, Samaritans, the inhabitants of Judaea and of Galilee. It may perhaps be subdivided:
1.19–4.54 containing a series of 'recognitions' which introduce leading themes of the Gospel;
5.1–12.50, full of provocation and dispute, a trial of strength between Jesus and 'the Jews'.
The whole section is held together by two interlocking systems, one of miracles (which John calls 'actions' or 'signs'), one of Jewish festivals.

13–17 Jesus and the disciples.

18–20 the passion and resurrection.
In effect: Jesus, the Jewish authorities and the Roman state.

21 a resurrection supplement.

That orderly analysis, however, overlooks the evidences of disorder which any reader can detect. For instance, the final chapter is attached only loosely as an appendix after the formal conclusion has apparently been reached in 20.30–31. The prologue, although referring to themes common elsewhere in John, is distinguished by its rhythmical style and distinctive *logos* teaching. In chs. 13–17, the farewell discourse seems to be brought to an end by 'come, let us go' in 14.31; yet in fact it continues throughout chs. 15–17; and ch. 16 works over themes of departure and return already dealt with in 13.31–14.31. Chapters 11 and 12 raise a suspicion that they are an addition to an earlier account of the ministry that ended with ch. 10. This is not to overlook the significance of the raising of Lazarus, but to ask whether it was part of the original structure. The striking sayings about the 'advocate' in chs. 14–16 can be read as additions to an earlier draft. In other words, the compositional seams are showing.

Elsewhere the present order of material has more obvious problems. For instance, at the end of ch. 4 Jesus is for the second time at Cana in Galilee. In ch. 5 he goes to Jerusalem for one of the festivals, performs a miracle, and gives a long discourse; but, without any warning to the reader, at the beginning of ch. 6 he is again active in Galilee and remains there through two miracles and a long discourse.

Yet the beginning of ch. 7 belatedly explains that Jesus travelled about in Galilee and avoided Judaea because the Jews wanted to kill him, referring back to the plot mentioned in 5.18. He is immediately urged by his unbelieving brothers to visit Jerusalem for Tabernacles, but says, 'I am not going to this festival because the right time for me has not yet come.' But two verses later he goes up, not openly but in secret. The oddity of this arrangement (at least to modern readers who expect continuity) can mostly be removed by reversing chs. 5 and 6. In that case Jesus begins in Cana (ch. 4), then crosses the sea of Galilee for the multiplication of the loaves, the walking on the water, and the discourse on the bread (ch. 6). Thereafter he goes to Jerusalem, cures the paralysed man on the sabbath and becomes the object of a Jewish plot (ch. 5). Therefore he returns to Galilee and avoids Judaea (ch. 7) – and all is well (except for the obstinately contradictory statements in 7.8–10). When Jesus turns up in Jerusalem, halfway through the festival, and publicly addresses the Jews (despite going up 'not openly but in secret') he speaks in justification of the sabbath healing performed at the *previous* festival. A more satisfying sequence would be obtained if 7.15–24 were placed after 5.47, and the resultant gap between 7.14 and 25 would close up without leaving a trace. Thus encouraged, we could remove 8.13–20 from its present position and place it after 7.24 as an appropriate conclusion to the dispute that began with the sabbath healing. And in this way the satisfaction of re-arrangement becomes addictive.

These *literary problems* of the Gospel at least suggest that it is not an indivisible historical account or a theological dissertation, coherently planned from the first and issued in a carefully edited form. Some take the view that the original material of the Gospel became disordered (though plausible accounts of how that happened are hard to find), and was put into its present form by a careless or uncomprehending compiler. But those who re-arrange the material to their own satisfaction import assumptions of their own without giving themselves a distinct advantage over commentators who take the material as it comes and use liberal cross-references.

Another view suggests that the writer used various *sources* in composing the Gospel, sources which sometimes escaped his control and so caused uneven passages and discontinuities. It may indeed be so. It seems clear that the writer was intent on composing a Gospel, and it is most likely that he learnt the form of a Gospel from Mark. The literary relations between John and Mark are not sufficiently close to demand the conclusion that John directly drew material from

Mark (though he may have done); but it is likely that he would have learnt from Mark that a Gospel begins with John Baptist and ends with the death and resurrection of Jesus, that the scene changes from Galilee to Judaea, and that it contains miracles, parables and wisdom teaching, conflict with the Jews, instruction of disciples and a farewell speech. The Fourth Gospel begins and ends in the proper way. It preserves the main locations but varies the proportions. It transforms the conflict with Jews and Romans into two highly dramatic trials. From a larger stock of miracles (which it calls *signs* or *deeds*) it presents seven, and provides four of them with explanatory discourses. These explanations, together with the controversial dialogues and the lengthy farewell discourses, replace the expected parables and wisdom teaching.

Granted that John went his own way in constructing a Gospel, where did he find his material and learn his manner of presenting it? The *material* very likely came from an oral tradition of the words and actions of Jesus; the *manner* may derive (as some suggest) from a collection of stories portraying Jesus as a miracle-worker and a collection of Hellenistic discourses in which the heavenly redeemer discloses himself. These would be the so-called 'signs-source' and 'discourse-source': they might do something for the exegesis of the Gospel but little to explain its literary oddities.

The most defensible and fruitful view is that the Gospel was composed in stages out of various components.

(*a*) A traditional passion narrative retold to display the dominating role of Jesus, with one explanatory passage (18.34–35) in typically Johannine style.

(*b*) A collection of narratives from various backgrounds: the Jewish Christians of Judaea and some from Galilee, former followers of John Baptist, and Samaritan converts. Flexible use is made of this material in order to display the earliest recognition of Jesus and then the fuller recognition that should be given him when his glory is disclosed and his self-revealing words are understood. Here the issue of faith and unbelief is repeatedly explored, and is written up as a trial of strength between Christian and Jewish perceptions. There may be signs in this long section (1.19–12.50) that what we now read is the end result of earlier attempts to arrange the material in various ways; and it can be argued that some features were added to guard against unsatisfactory attitudes inside the Johannine community for which the Gospel was composed.

(*c*) At an early stage of composition, the end of ch. 14 may have moved at once to the beginning of ch. 18. John 13–14 is the final gathering of Jesus with 'his own who were in the world', and this is the necessary farewell discourse. All that needs to be said has been said, and indeed rather more than is necessary (for the promise of the 'advocate' in 14.16–17 and 26 sits uncomfortably alongside the promise that he and the Father will come and make their dwelling with the believer (14.23)).

(*d*) John 17 is written as a report of the Son to the Father in which he hands back his commission and prays for the believers whom he has sent into the world. This chapter therefore indicates how the work of Jesus should be understood, taking up the indication in the prologue (1.1–18) of how the Gospel should be read. Spirit is absent from both.

(*e*) But all was not well in the Johannine community: it needed help to maintain itself against hostility from outside and controversy within, especially from those who set Jesus aside, claimed the gift of the Spirit and went confidently into the world. Hence chs. 15 and 16 were provided, statements about the 'advocate' were added to ch. 14, and references to the Spirit in 1.19–12.50 were carefully subordinated to Jesus.

(*f*) A lively resurrection narrative in John 20 leads to the immediate inbreathing of the Holy Spirit by Jesus; and to the proper obstinacy of Thomas who will not make his great confession until he is assured by the marks of crucifixion.

(*g*) John 21 contains supplementary stories and instruction (2–19) which might equally well have appeared earlier in the Gospel. They are accommodated here by turning them into resurrection appearances. The chapter concludes with an attempt to clear up a misunderstanding about the beloved disciple, and a half-hearted apology from a group of Christians for having ventured to add material from the oral stock to the written record.

That account, which hints at the process of *composition*, suggests that the writer was constructing his Gospel with fidelity to early Christian tradition and in response to pressing questions in the community. The literary problems are not caused by accident or by inept use of sources, but by the need to try first this way, then that way to communicate the truth of the Gospel to Christians in need of help.

The sometimes rough and unfinished state of the Gospel as we now read it is not evidence that the final editor overlooked necessary revisions, but that any edition of the Gospel must be responsive to the needs of its readers.

Finally, therefore, what needs were in mind when the Fourth Gospel was being composed? Why did the community require (or create) its own distinctive version of the Jesus-story?

1. Not because it was interested in the long history of God's covenant with the Jewish people. The Gospel draws freely on convictions and imagery from the Jewish scriptures. Jesus is acclaimed as king of Israel by Nathanael and by the crowd (1.49; 12.13), and condemned as king of the Jews by Pilate; but in fact the Jews become a body of people hostile to Jesus and his disciples. In the synoptic gospels the announcement of the kingdom of God is the critical point in the relation of God with the Jews; but in John after mention in one early episode (3.3, 5), 'kingdom of God' disappears. In the synoptic gospels, the fight against demons is evidence that God is exercising his kingly power at the hands of Jesus; but in John there are no exorcisms. Matthew's Gospel shows great interest in the reapplication of the law of Moses; but John's Gospel is devoid of interest in specific moral or cultic instruction. Luke, at the beginning of his Gospel and of Acts, shows devotion to the temple as a virtue; John parades the destruction of the temple and the ending of the festivals. John's community knows that 'it is from the Jews that salvation comes' (4.22) but it has no interest in the question whether the Lord would restore the kingdom to Israel (Acts 1.6).

2. A different way of viewing a Gospel would be to take it as a story-telling supplement to a credal formula. For example, Philippians 2 presents Christ Jesus by means of the imagery of humiliation and exaltation: he who exchanged the form of God for the form of a slave, and was crucified, thereafter to be exalted and to bear the supreme lordship. There is something similar in John 17:5: 'Father, glorify me in your own presence with the glory which I had with you before the world began.' If the formula of descent and ascent is a focus for worship and devotion, it can be filled out by stories which tell how the Lord demonstrated his hidden glory when a slave, how he came to be crucified, and how he triumphed over death. Thus a Gospel would be providing information about Jesus so that the Lord of the community could be reverenced in the proper way; and that presumably was what Luke thought he was doing in writing his Gospel. Now John (who perhaps made use of the Lukan tradition)

may indeed provide selected information about Jesus (selected, because a good deal of available information is left out); but that cannot have been his chief aim. His community needed not more information but discussion of what they already knew, and authoritative interpretation of it (hence the dialogues and monologues). They needed not more stories about Jesus but assurance that Jesus was God's representative and could act on their behalf.

3. The most pressing concern of the Johannine community is indicated by the remarkably frequent use of 'world' in the Gospel. The Greek word *kosmos*, meaning all that was created or the social organisation of human life, entered the speech of Greek-speaking Jews (in the Wisdom of Solomon and IV Maccabees) round about the beginning of the Common Era. In the synoptic gospels its use is popular and conventional, but in the Fourth Gospel it is technical and distinctive. Unlike the heroic Maccabean brothers who, even when threatened by torture and death, discussed why they should deprive themselves of 'this sweet world' (IV Macc. 8.23), the Johannine community considered that 'the whole world lies in the power of the evil one' (I John 5.19). The prologue to the Gospel indicates that much will be said about a world which does not recognise its creator. Although 'the light has come into the world . . . people preferred darkness to light because their deeds were evil' (3.19). Although the *kosmos* is God's creation, and so is loved by God and the object of his saving action, it hates Jesus and his disciples. For them it is hateful. It constitutes 'this world below', hostile to 'the world above' (8.23), 'earthly things' against 'the things of heaven' (3.12). It is darkness as opposed to light, blindness versus sight, death against eternal life. How is it possible, in such a world as this, to experience joy, healing, mobility, nourishment, reassurance, sight and resurrection – to oversimplify the meaning of the signs in the Gospel (see also pp. 31–33)?

That kind of question was constantly asked in late antiquity. There were many answers, it may be mystical or gnostic. Some of them included a fanciful kind of creation story to account for and characterise the evils of the world (very different from the modest prologue of the Gospel). Most of them offered means for coming to terms with the world below while claiming kinship with the world above; and some of them may have spoken of a redeemer from the world above who descends to the world below, there identifies the lost and alienated exiles from the world above, reveals to them their true origin, and returns above to prepare a place for them.

The redeemer's descent and ascent is centrally important in the Gospel. Hence rescue from alienation in this world is a possible way of defining John's aim in writing. Two methods characteristic of Hellenistic religion are presented and discussed as ways of escape: one is by rebirth, the other is by coming to knowledge. (*a*) Rebirth is expressed by the frequent use of 'born of God' in I John, e.g. 'Whatever is born of God overcomes the world' (I John 5.4). It is a Hellenistic rather than a Jewish image. In John 3 it is discussed with Nicodemus, probably linked with baptism, and joined with the Son of Man's descent from and ascent to heaven. (*b*) In the gnostic systems, 'knowledge' is not so much information as awareness. In accordance with the famous instruction from the temple at Delphi – namely 'Know thyself' – it means awareness of your own true being. John never uses the noun (possibly to avoid the gnostic meaning) but he gives importance to the verb. In the Gospel it is only Jesus who can say 'I know where I come from and where I am going' (8.14). For the rest of us it is sufficient that he says 'I know my own and my own know me' (10.14), with the consequence that 'if you knew me you would know my Father too' (14.7).

Thus it appears that the evangelist goes beyond the intention of the synoptic gospels in order to meet needs that were strongly felt in his community. To do that he goes into the Hellenistic world for forms that correspond to those needs, and which can be adapted so that they both contain the old tradition without destroying it and also develop its inherent strengths.

The Prologue
1.1–18

The prologue is written in a markedly rhythmical style. That suggests that it is to be learnt by heart and kept in mind when the Gospel is read. It is a kind of bookmark for whatever passage is under consideration.

It falls into two parts: vv. 1–13 speak of the Word, John Baptist, and the world; vv. 14–18 add 'we' and 'us'. Thus it contains not only theological instruction but also testimony. Here we have the first indication that the Gospel offers not dispassionate information about the Son of God but information corresponding to the interests of the Christian community (for people testify about what concerns them and their neighbours). Both parts begin with the word *logos*, used with a meaning that is unknown elsewhere in the Gospel; and both parts refer to the witness of John Baptist. But otherwise the two parts differ in wording. Part 1 introduces a string of common Johannine words: *life, light, darkness, sent, believe, world, know* and *born*; part 2 has the common words *glory, father* and *truth*, but also a string of words that are otherwise non-Johannine (*made his home, grace, fullness, made known*) or very uncommon (*only Son, nearest to the heart, even Jesus Christ*). Thus part 1 is an introductory evocation of the *logos*, in line with central Johannine teaching, displaying the conviction that illumination is possible in an unresponsive world, and raising questions of belief and witness. Part 2 looks like the response of a we-group of leaders (such as are found in I John) who stress the flesh of the *logos*, by means of which they have beheld his glory and shared in the fulness of his grace. Both parts are held together by variations on the Greek verb 'to receive' in vv. 5 (*master*), 11, 12 and 16.

Part 2 of the prologue explicitly speaks of the *Father's only Son, Jesus Christ*. But who or what is referred to by *the Word* in part 1? The capital letter and the use of he and him in vv. 1–4 and 10–12 suggest the Son, before and after his entry into *the world*. But if so, why is *The Word became flesh* delayed till v. 14? The word *logos* in Greek is masculine, but in English would more naturally be referred to as 'it'. How you translate depends on what image you have in mind when beginning the prologue. If you have an image of two heavenly beings, you will choose 'he'; if an image of God speaking, you will choose 'it'. One meaning of *logos* is 'command' (*hoi deka logoi*, the Ten Commandments in Exod. 34.28; cf. John 8.55 'I obey his word'): so in the beginning was God's command which created all that is, gave life and light, entered the world and was rejected by most but not all of mankind.

Anyone familiar with Jewish writings circulating in the NT period will at once recognize that pattern: it corresponds to the divine Wisdom. Hellenistic Judaism drew a distinction between God's actions and the wisdom with which he planned them. Thought comes before action: so (it can be said) thought mediates between somebody and what he does. Hence Wisdom could be represented as a person (female because the Hebrew and Greek words are feminine) acting as God's assistant in the creation of the world (Prov. 8.22–31) and offering necessary instruction to mankind. How is Wisdom received? Two diverse views are expressed. In one, Wisdom sought a resting place, found it in Israel, and established herself as the law which Moses commanded (Ecclus. 24.7–34). In the other, Wisdom cried aloud in the street, but people refused to listen and ignored her counsel (Prov. 1.20–33; Bar. 3.11–13). According to I Enoch 42 (which may have been written at the end of the first century CE) 'Wisdom went out in order to dwell among the sons of men, but did not find a dwelling; Wisdom returned to her place and took her seat in the midst of the angels.' The best that could be said is that 'age after age she enters into holy souls, and makes them friends of God and prophets' (Wisd. 7.27). Put like that, it is very similar to the prologue, especially if Word and Wisdom are reciprocal in meaning: 'You made all things by your word, and in your wisdom fashioned man' (Wisd. 9.1).

It can be suspected, therefore, that the writer of the prologue composed (or made use of) a traditional Wisdom-psalm, but changed the feminine Wisdom to the masculine Word. In that case, why does John Baptist appear in the middle of the psalm – somewhat intrusively perhaps, for v. 6 sounds not like part of a psalm but like the beginning of a story? And, in v. 15 of part 2, John appears so awkwardly as to disturb the connexion of thought. The writer presumes that the reader already knows about John, for v. 15 refers to what John says in v. 30. Is it possible (it has been asked) that some members of the community gave too much importance to John, so that he had to be put firmly in his place at the beginning of the Gospel? But to introduce him at all into the initial Logos-psalm gives him outstanding importance. That must imply that historically disciples of John were a formative element in the Johannine community. Origins are not everything, but they are important. So also is disturbance. The intrusion of John into both parts of the prologue is not to be treated as the writer's clumsiness: it suggests that the operation of the Word is not like a steady stream of divine energy but, like cosmic radiation, is subject to major disturbances.

Nevertheless, the intrusiveness of John suggests that the prologue was written in stages. A reasonable possibility can be explained if a more literal translation of the Greek is used:

(i) The original Logos-psalm ran thus:

1. In the beginning there was the Word,
    and the Word was directed towards God;
    indeed the Word was God.
2. There it was in the beginning directed towards God.

(4 lines)

3. Through it all things came to be.
    Without it nothing came to be.
4. By it what came to be was life.
    That life was light for mankind.
5. That light shines in darkness,
    and darkness did not grasp it (*katelaben*).

(6 lines)

9. There was the true light,
    which gives light to everyone,
    coming into the world.
10. It was in the world,
    and the world through it came to be,
    but the world did not receive the Word.
11. It came to its own,
    but its own people did not accept it (*parelabon*).

(8 lines)

12. But to all who did accept it (*elabon*)
    it gave the right to become children of God.

(2 lines)

That would be an impressive psalm, with stanzas of 4, 6 and 8 lines leading to the striking conclusion (of only 2 lines) that the reader can become a child of God. It is entirely possible to read the psalm as referring throughout to the Word as the divine command (hence the use of 'it'); but it is difficult for Christian readers to avoid the impression that 'he' is equally appropriate, and that the Word is the Divine Son, entering the world at v. 9 (or even at v. 5).

(ii) The next stage is the addition of vv. 14 and 16–18 when community leaders add their testimony. This array of close-knit statements is linked to the foregoing psalm by the repetition of Word in 14 and the use of received (*elabomen*) in 16.

(iii) Then were added the references to John Baptist in vv. 6–8 (possibly the original beginning of a first draft of the Gospel, on the model of Mark) and 15.

(iv) Finally, the last line of v. 12 'to those who believe on his name' and the whole of v. 13 were added, in order to present believing and rebirth as the sources of divine sonship.

It is now possible to ask two questions about the prologue: how does it function? and what was its intended purpose?

It functions by outlining the relation between the unseen divine being and human existence. The statement may be read as referring either to the divine Wisdom or to the human Agent. It is qualified by reference to the historic biblical tradition represented by John, and completed by testimony from the Christian community to the benefits of divine sonship.

Its intended purpose is to display the problem, namely the rejection of divine Wisdom, for which the Gospel is the definitive solution.

1.1–2 The first sentence asserts the primacy of intelligible speech. *In the beginning* obviously copies Gen. 1.1 but the prologue carries the thought back beyond creation (which appears in v. 3) to the inherent nature of divine existence. When the word *God* presents itself to the mind, the primary impression is not irresistible power or ecstatic confusion, but *logos*. And this *logos* existed (only) in relation to God. The addition 'only' is justified by the emphatic repetition of this second statement in v. 2. Cf. the similar statement about life in I John 1.2. The point is not so much that a secondary divine being enjoyed companionship with the deity (as REB suggests) but that the primacy of *logos* is regarded entirely in terms of God's intentions. Correspondingly the perception of deity is primarily in terms of intelligible speech: *what God was, the Word was* (a translation devised to represent the possible grammatical force of calling the *logos theos* but not – with definite article – *ho theos*). Hence God is not the incommunicable divine being who may perhaps be sought but never attained; he is in his own being the one who communicates and discloses himself.

THE WORD

The word *logos* occurs many times in the Gospel. It may refer to (i) the word of God, in scripture and in the message given to Jesus; (ii) a statement or a familiar saying; (iii) the comprehensive teaching of Jesus; and (iv) the testimony which disciples offered to the world. In other parts of the NT, also, 'the word' means the missionary proclamation; and that is one reason why it appears in the prologue. As 'the word of God' it was already familiar from the OT in God's creative action ('The word of the Lord created the heavens' Ps. 33.6), his renewing power ('He sent his word to heal them' Ps. 107.20) and his gift of Torah ('Your word is a lamp to my feet' Ps. 119.105). As I John 1.1 says, it was the life-giving word. That becomes very plain when it refers to the comprehensive teaching of Jesus: those who hear his word and believe on God who sent him pass from death to life, and are assured of the love and the presence of God (5.24; 14.23).

In all these examples 'the word' is what somebody says or commands. But it is customary (and perhaps proper) to think of the *logos* as having an existence related to but distinguishable from God. If so, has the writer adopted, from the Greek world of his time, a habit of using *logos* to signify a kind of divine being? Even though making such use of *logos* only in the prologue, he may have implied that Jesus, throughout the Gospel, is to be interpreted in that fashion. Since the words and actions of the Johannine Jesus are sometimes strikingly different from those of the synoptic Jesus, the possibility must be explored. There are two kinds of writing which (like John) presume upper and lower levels of existence and use *logos* to link them: Philo and the gnostics.

Philo, who lived in Alexandria from about 20 BCE to 50 CE, was a Jewish mystic, philosopher, and composer of allegories on the Pentateuch. He appropriated and adapted the teaching of Plato and the Stoics and (in a wayward and unsystematic manner) talked frequently of the divine *Logos* as an emissary of the unknowable deity. For human beings there are two worlds: the material world known by the senses, and the immaterial world by the mind. God's *Logos* reaches down to the immaterial world, and our *logos* reaches upwards to it; but God's *Logos* never descends into our material world.[1] The prologue might have been written to oppose Philo's main conviction.

[1] S. Sandmel, *Philo of Alexandria*, New York and Oxford 1979, p. 95.

5

The so-called gnostic sources are difficult to assess. They vary greatly in quality (from impressive spiritual meditations to a farrago of mystifying nonsense) and in their share of gnostic assumptions and figures of speech (or, as some would say, myths). The surviving documents were mostly written after the Gospel and some were even influenced by it. Yet effective comparisons can sometimes be made, e.g. between the Gospel and the so-called Odes of Solomon[2] which are a set of forty-three Christian hymns, probably composed in Aramaic, at Antioch about 100 CE – the very time and place for the possible composition of the Gospel. In both the Odes and the Gospel parallels of a kind have been noted with the Thanksgiving Hymns of Qumran. From the very different character of the Odes and the Gospel it can be deduced that neither had direct influence on the other, but both drew upon the assumptions of a particular kind of Jewish-Christian thinking about the upper and lower worlds and the significance of *Logos*. To give one example from Ode 41:

> And his Word is with us in all our way,
> the Saviour who gives life and does not reject ourselves.
> The Man who humbled himself,
> but was raised because of his own righteousness.
> The Son of the Most High appeared
> in the perfection of his Father.
> And light dawned from the Word
> that was before time in him.
> The Messiah in truth is one.
> And he was known before the foundation of the world,
> that he might give life to persons forever by the truth
>   of his name.

1.3–5   Through the intelligible self-disclosure of God *all things came to be*. Immediately there is a distinction between that which comes into existence and that which exists eternally. When God utters his command to the primeval chaos he calls into being that which he addresses, as (by analogy) the actor calls into being an audience attentive to the play and the preacher a congregation responsive to the sermon. The insistence that *no created thing came into being* without the *Logos* effectively blocks a common gnostic belief that the physical world was created by an inferior and hostile deity, and strictly limits

[2] *OTP* II, pp. 725–771.

the independence of Satan, the devil, and the prince of this world. If therefore Christians are distressed by the world and harassed by the devil, they must address their complaints to God and seek redress from him.

The *Logos* comprises *life* – naturally, since God is the source of all life and 'has life in himself' (5.26). When God uttered his self-disclosing command, the animate universe came into being; and when he breathed into Adam's nostrils the breath of life (Gen. 2.7), *that life was light* for *mankind* (amending REB). As regards human beings, life is defined as light. Life is heir to such qualities as have already been attributed to the *Logos* – intelligibility, self-disclosure, the power to communicate. To live is to receive illumination, whether that means understanding what is being said, grasping it with imaginative insight, experiencing an enlargement of awareness through religious knowledge, or perceiving the right course of action. It is the opposite of misunderstanding, confusion, spiritual blindness, and moral error. The excellence of light is emphasised by reference to its opposite: *darkness*; and so the first mention of Johannine dualism is made. It is based on Gen. 1.3 where God 'separated light from darkness' and is therefore a qualified, not a strict, dualism. Light and dark are not two competing, independent powers; for darkness, however alarming and dangerous it may be, is not more than the absence of light. What can be said about the relation of light and dark appears in v. 5, viz. the *light* goes on shining (continuous present tense) *in the darkness, and the darkness has never* at any time (aorist tense) *mastered it*, i.e. learnt the meaning of what if offers. (The verb could also mean 'exercised mastery over it', but nowhere else does John suggest that darkness fights for victory over the light.) This is the bleak diagnosis of the human condition: people fail to grasp the benefits of light and prefer darkness (so 3.19).

LIFE, LIGHT AND DARKNESS

These were very familiar themes in the religions of the ancient world. In Judaism: Ps. 36.9 'for with you is the fountain of life, and by your light we are enlightened'; Prov. 6.23 'for a commandment is a lamp, and teaching a light, reproof and correction point the way of life.' In Christian Hellenism: Odes of Solomon 10 'The Lord has directed my mouth by his Word, and has opened my heart by his Light. And he has caused to dwell in me his immortal life.' In pagan gnostic Hellenism: Hermetic Tractate 13 (which explains

7

the conviction that no one can be saved before rebirth) 'Holy
knowledge, since I have been illumined by you, while praising
through you the intellectual light, I rejoice with intellectual
joy . . . Life, save! Light, illumine!' The predictable contrast
between light and darkness was strikingly present in the Community Rule of Qumran where he who created man to govern the
world 'appointed for him two spirits in which to walk until the
time of His visitation: the spirits of truth and falsehood. Those
born of truth spring from a fountain of light, but those born of
falsehood spring from a source of darkness.'[3]

Thus John used language sanctioned by scripture, and familiar
to all his readers. What he made of such language is disclosed in
the course of the Gospel which is intended to arouse belief in Jesus
as the Christ and Son of God, and to convey life by his name
(20.31). For this purpose use is made of symbolic language (living
water, bread and light of life, raising the dead), of the sign of
Lazarus, and of explicit statements about eternal life which is
finally described as knowing the only true God (17.2–3). The chief
references are in chs. 3–8 and 11. Thus 'life' dominates the Gospel;
'light' is equally important but less dominant. Jesus is light for the
world (8.12; 9.5; 12.46), in the sense indicated by the richly symbolic
story of sight for the man born blind. Hence when he is present it
is day-time, after which comes the night (11.9–10; 12.35–50). When
therefore the world prefers darkness to light, the judgment goes
against it (3.19–21).

1.6–8   As Jesus later remarks, 'John was a brightly burning lamp,
and for a time you were ready to exult in his light' (5.35). The high
generalities of vv. 1–5 are interrupted by a man with a name, for that
in fact is how the light had always come to Israel, by the prophetic
voice of a person *sent from God*. In agreement with early tradition, John
appears indispensably at the beginning of the Gospel. Commissioned
by God, he represents the prophetic voice of scripture: he is given a
place, important and defined, in the Christian community – *not
himself the light*, but witness to it (described in 1.19–3.36). It was not
John's mission to make disciples for himself but to allow those who
heard his testimony to the light to *become believers*. The Gospel never
uses the noun 'faith', but the verb 'to believe' appears some ninety
times (contrast Mark where noun and verb are used theologically

---

[3] Community Rule iii.17–19 (*DSSE* pp. 64–65).

thirteen times). 'Sent' and 'witness' are also key words of the Gospel. (For 'believing' see p. 37, and for 'sent' p. 59.)

1.9–11 The prologue now returns to the *logos* (shown in the Greek by *auton*, masc., not *auto*, neuter, which would have to refer to *phōs* in vv. 10–11) and describes it as the light that genuinely makes human social life possible: *the true light . . . was* all the time (rather than REB *even then*) *coming into the world*. The keyword *world* is best considered at 3.16. It does not here refer to the great universe (for John was indifferent to cosmic speculation, and probably ignorant of the verbal constructions of gnostic myths); it refers to the social world of mankind. What converts a primeval *chaos* into a habitable *kosmos*, and so preserves it, is the divine *logos*. Only if it *gives light to everyone* is a workable *kosmos* possible. (The Greek of v. 9 can be translated as in REB mg. 'The true light was in being, which gives light to everyone entering the world'; but the first phrase is pointless, and the second would be a poor rendering of an unsuitable rabbinic idiom.)

Thus the divine illumination was present in the social institutions which owed their very existence to the *logos*, but the world made no answering response. The world *did not recognise* and acknowledge that which kept it in being. On any doctrine of *logos* – whether Jewish (the commandment of God), or Stoic (the rational principle in the universe) – that must be incomprehensible and tragic. If we now remember that mankind includes a chosen people who are familiar with the Word of the Lord and are taught to obey it, then surely they should welcome the true light, but *he came to his own, and his own people would not accept him*.

That statement can properly be regarded as summing up the long history of God's dealings with his people, if *logos* means prophetic instruction from Moses to John. But Christian readers can scarcely fail to mark its ironic suitability to the *logos* who became flesh. He too 'came into the world as a light' (12.46) 'but people preferred darkness to light because their deeds were evil' (3.19). This is to be a story of misunderstanding and rejection by those who are dearest to God, who devoutly and passionately believe they are acting in God's name.

1.12–13 But not everyone rejected the *logos*, for to some *he gave the right to become children of God*. Right which renders *exousia* is too juridical here, and 'ability' is better. The word can also mean 'freedom of choice' (10.18), 'warrant' (5.27; 17.2) and 'absolute power' (19.10,

11). What being children of God implies is not directly discoverable from the Gospel; but the Epistle indicates that they are born of God whose seed remains in them, that they love fellow Christians and keep God's commandments, and that when Jesus is disclosed they will be like him (I John 3.1–2, 9–10; 5.1–2). It can therefore be stated rather insistently that they become children of God not by any act arising from blood relationships, or from human intentions, or from a husband's desire for children, but solely from the life-giving act of God. That act is not arbitrary. It is done for *those who put their trust in him*, or (as the older translation had it) 'believed in his name'. In the Gospel 'believing' means much more than the conventional sense of holding views and convictions: putting one's trust in someone is a large part of its meaning (see also p. 37). But putting trust in whose name? and what does 'name' imply?

NAME

In scripture a name is never to be taken for granted. (1) It may seem no more than an identifier, like *a man named John* in v. 6; but in fact it carries the whole weight of the Baptist's testimony, and signifies the existence of John's disciples and their influence in the Johannine community. 'There was a man named Wesley' conveys much more than an eighteenth-century English clergyman. (2) Name can mean reputation and power to prove it. The Welsh have a name for singing: their choirs and football crowds prove it. To believe in his name means to entrust oneself to his reputation and power (with consequent disabilities if he has a bad name, 15.21[4]). This meaning is pushed into the areas of magic and fantasy in Hellenistic and gnostic religion. (3) Name can mean authorisation, backing – as a university Vice-Chancellor is authorised to speak in the name of the Chancellor. So Jesus came, not in his own name, but in the name of his Father (5.43), and he acted in his Father's name (10.25). Christians are encouraged to ask in the name of Jesus (14.13, 14; 15.16; 16.23, 24, 26). 'To believe in the name of Jesus' (2.23; 3.18) is very common in the shortened form 'to believe in him'.

Jesus is chiefly concerned with the reputation and power of God. When he says 'Father, glorify your name' (12.28) he directs

---

[4] In 15.21 a literal rendering would be 'All this they will do to you on account of my name', i.e. my bad reputation with them.

attention to the name in which he came. At the end he claims to
have made known God's name to the people with whom he had
worked (17.6, 26). As in Isa. 52.6 'my people will know my name',
it includes support now and promise for the future. So then the
logos rewarded those who put their trust in God by giving them
the ability to become children of God.

Born . . . of God is considered at 3.3–8. There is a little early Latin
evidence in v. 13 for a different phrasing; *who put their trust in him
who was born, not of human stock, by the physical desire of a human father,
but of God*. That was intended as a reference to the virgin birth of
Jesus. It is not original, but the verse as we have it may imply that
children of God share the mysterious origin of the *logos*. The doctrine
of the virgin birth might be more important for spiritual than for
physical birth.

1.14   The community leaders now add their testimony as fellow-
citizens who have seen the consequences of the *logos* having become
flesh. The word *flesh* does not play a prominent part in the Gospel,
and its significance is best considered in ch. 6. At this point it is
sufficient to look ahead to 3.6 where *flesh* and spirit are sharply
distinguished. They are two opposed manners of existence (not two
substances): spirit is free and spontaneous, flesh is dependent and
constricted. The one belongs to God, the other to mankind. Thus
when it is said that the *logos became flesh*, it is equally implied that it
did not become spirit. In so far as God is knowable, it is because he
makes himself known in his *logos*. His Word is heard *through* such
prophetic voices as John's, but now it is perceived *in* the flesh (that
is, the dependent and constricted life) of one who *made his home among
us*. Although Spirit is very important in the Gospel, our direct
access to the self-communicating deity is not via spirit but via
flesh. According to the Epistle, some spirit-inspired members of the
community were unwilling to acknowledge 'Jesus Christ come in the
flesh', because they preferred spontaneous access to God in the Spirit
and despised constricted access in the flesh of Jesus Christ. But the
community leaders testify that the *logos* through whom *all things came
to be* was known to them in creaturely *flesh*.

And they *saw his glory*. In the Gospel glory is used in the common
Greek sense of 'good repute' (e.g. 5.41–44), often with the special
sense of the outward signs of the power and presence of God: Isaiah
saw his glory in the temple (12.41, referring to Isa. 6; and see Exod.

16.10; 24.17; 40.34–38). The illness of Lazarus was an occasion for displaying the power and presence of God (11.4, 40). The whole Gospel is concerned with the question whether the words and actions of Jesus permitted people to see the glory of God or prevented them from seeing it. Whatever the contemporaries of Jesus may have thought, the later community leaders had no doubt: they saw *such glory as befits the Father's only Son*.

Thus is introduced the image which lies behind almost all that Jesus does and says in the Gospel: he is the only Son carrying out his Father's wishes and doing his work. As the Gospel tells the story and displays the teaching, it will be found that he does nothing on his own initiative and yet is empowered to act with the full authority of the Father who sent him. If we ask why the Father did not come himself, the answer is that by the agency of Jesus he did. The Son was *full of grace and truth*.

The word *grace* is not common in Johannine writings. Here therefore it will bear the meaning familiar to Hellenistic life, namely 'generosity'. Aristotle defined it as 'helpfulness towards someone in need, not in return for anything, nor that the helper may get anything, but for the sake of the person who is helped'.[5] In John's day it was a fixed term (especially in inscriptions) for the favours bestowed by rulers, and in popular religion it indicated power that comes from the world above. On first thoughts, *truth* is a strange companion for generosity, for it belongs so often to conflict or misunderstanding. Truth is what we, not our opponents, say: it corrects their inadequate, or perverse, or lying words. This will be discussed at v. 17.[6] Here it indicates that the generosity that fills the word-become-flesh is neither delusive nor corrupting but belongs to the integrity of the Father.

1.15   John's testimony is again invoked (not exactly as in REB): *John* bears *witness to him and* has *proclaimed: 'This* was *the man of whom I said'* (1.30), and so on. The use of tenses suggests that John's testimony was still active in the community. *He comes after me* may imply that Jesus appeared at first as a disciple of John but then was ranked ahead of him. According to the ancient rule, 'No pupil ranks above his teacher' (Matt. 10.24; cf. John 13.16). He may develop what his teacher said and draw out its implications, but he does not supersede

---

[5] *Rhetoric* ii.7.
[6] See also p. 78.

his teacher's wisdom unless he can draw upon more ancient wisdom. John's testimony (which implies what is vulgarly called Christ's pre-existence) concedes that whatever Jesus says and does has inherent priority over anything John can say and do. Since John may be taken as representing the whole prophetic tradition right back to Moses, his testimony gives Jesus priority over the law.

1.16–18 Having enlisted John as a witness on behalf of Jesus, the prologue now recruits Moses and formally speaks of the incarnate *logos* by his human name. Verse 16 picks up the stress on *full* in v. 14, not with the semi-technical sense it bears in Ephesians and Colossians but with the implication that what was *given through Moses* in part is now given *through Jesus Christ* in full. In Exod. 34.6 God appeared to Moses 'abundant in goodness and truth' (AV). But in Jesus Christ there came the true generosity of God (which is the meaning of *grace and truth*). It is not denied that the law was a gift of God's generosity, through the prophet Moses; but it is asserted that the community had *received grace upon grace* – the comprehensive grace of God foreshadowed in the law.

MOSES AND THE LAW

According to Deut. 18.18–20 the Lord said to Moses, 'I shall raise up for them a prophet like you, one of their own people and I shall put my words into his mouth. He will declare to them whatever I command him; if anyone refuses to listen to the words which he will speak in my name I shall call that person to account. But the prophet who presumes to utter in my name what I have not commanded him . . . that prophet must be put to death.' How shall they know? 'When a word spoken by the prophet in the name of the Lord is not fulfilled and does not come true, it is not a word spoken by the Lord.' On two occasions this promise is recalled in the Gospel: when people saw the sign of the bread that Jesus had performed (6.14) and heard his words about living water (7.40) – as Moses had obtained manna in the wilderness and water from the flinty rock – they said, 'Surely this must be the Prophet.' The questions at issue throughout the Gospel are whether Jesus fulfils that promise, whether he speaks in the manner of Moses and with his authority, or whether he has a wholly different authority and a name greater than prophet – or indeed whether he does not speak in the name of God at all.

References to Moses and the law are therefore samples of conflict between Jesus and his opponents. Apart from that, the Gospel has little interest in the moral law (except for community love) and a certain disapproval of the temple and its festivals. Jesus offered sight to the blind, especially those Pharisees who (as disciples of Moses) could not identify the source of Jesus' teaching (9.28–29). For his part, Moses was their accuser, for he wrote concerning Jesus (5.45–46), and Moses in the wilderness provided Jesus with necessary imagery and argument: when Moses lifted up the serpent (3.14–15), gave bread from heaven (though it is the Father who gives true bread from heaven, 6.32), gave the law (which his opponents had the murderous intention of breaking, 7.19), and gave the law of circumcision (originating with the patriarchs) which could take precedence of sabbath (7.22–23). There are indications of an interest in the time *before* Moses – hence the discussion in John 8 about Abraham – and of the Father's intention which underlies Mosaic law.

The conflict between Jesus and his opponents becomes sharpened when it seems to reflect the feeling of Christians in dispute with the synagogue at the end of the century. Jesus advances his argument by appeal to the law of two witnesses (8.17) and to the striking use of 'gods' in Ps. 82 (10.34) though calling it *'your* law'; and he shows acceptance of his rejection by quoting Ps. 35 which he calls *'their* law'. He talks as if he were a Gentile or a renegade Jew. Elsewhere Jesus accepts the law as witness on his own side. Hence these three references are plausible on the lips of Jesus only if they imply 'the law which you claim as your own property'.

According to Exod. 33.18–23, Moses prayed to God, 'Show me thy glory.' In response God agreed to disclose his goodness, his name, his graciousness and compassion – but not his face. 'You will see my back, but my face must not be seen.' The Gospel goes further: *No one has ever seen God* (also 6.46 and I John 4.12, 20). But, on the principle that only God can reveal God, *God's only Son . . . has made him known*. Unlike Moses, who at best could see only the back of God – God as he departed and disappeared from view – the *only Son* could see him face to face (v. 1), in the closest intimacy (lit. 'in the Father's bosom'; cf. 13.23 where the beloved disciple was reclining in the bosom of Jesus). Hence the Son could indeed disclose the divine secret (for the verb was a standard term in Hellenistic religion for explaining omens and other sacred matters).

God's only Son picks up *the Father's only Son* of v. 14, and comes
again in 3.16, 18 and I John 4.12, 20. It is entirely appropriate to the
context, but it may be an alteration of the original wording. Instead
of *monogenēs huios* (only Son) an impressive array of witnesses,
including the two oldest Greek manuscripts, have *monogenēs theos*
which can be translated 'God the only [Son]' (NIV). That might well
reflect a Greek use of *theos*, more flexible than the Jewish, returning
in fact to the description of the *logos* as *theos* in v. 1. However that
may be, the reader is reminded that the words and actions of the Son
of God are not those of a secondary deity but of God himself.

AWARENESS OF GOD

An explanatory remark in 17.3 describes eternal life as knowing
the only true God and Jesus Christ whom he has sent. It is therefore
instructive to discover how God is perceived in the Gospel. When
Paul offered the gospel to pagans he urged them to turn from idols
and become servants of the true and living God (I Thess. 1.9). So
in the Gospel, the only true God 'has life in himself' (5.26) and is
called 'the living Father' (6.57). He is ceaselessly at work (5.17, 19)
in the world he loves (3.16), he gives sight to the blind (9.3), and
raises the dead (5.21). Chiefly, he speaks (8.47; 9.29; 10.35), and
sends messengers to utter his words (3.34), so that in his Word
there is life and light for mankind (1.1–4). In traditional Jewish
fashion he is pictured as a reigning monarch (3.3, 5), the 'righteous
Father' (17.25) whose wrath is to be feared (3.36). Hence he is to
be loved (i.e. obeyed), offered service (16.2), and worshipped
(4.21, 23). He is of course unseen (1.18) – except by one alone, 'who
has come from God and seen the Father' (6.46), who discloses
what he has seen in the Father's presence (8.38). Hence he is able
to say 'Anyone who has seen me has seen the Father' (14.9).
Otherwise God himself cannot be seen, only his glory when the
Father is glorified in the Son (14.13). Why can God not be seen?
because God is Spirit (4.24) which is like the wind: you can hear
the sound of it but you can neither see nor know whence it comes
or where it goes (3.8). Aside from one departure, this whole
perception of God is entirely faithful to the old Jewish understanding of God.

The one departure: God's activity is mainly defined by reference
to Jesus who is *the Father's only Son* (1.14; 3.18). That is confirmed
by John's testimony (1.34), Nathanael's admission (1.49), his own

disclosure (9.35–36; 10.36), Martha's confession (11.27), and the purpose of the Gospel (20.31). He called God his own Father, so (in the view of his opponents) claiming equality with God (5.18). 'As the Father has life in himself, so by his gift the Son also has life in himself' (5.26). He came from God (6.46; 8.42; 13.3; 16.27), and he returns to God (13.3; 14.12, 28; 16.10, 28; 20.17). Even more significant: *God sent him* (3.17; 5.36–37; 6.44, 57; 8.16, 18, 26; 10.36; 14.24; 17.18; 20.21) to do the Father's work (10.37–38) and to say what the Father teaches him (8.28). 'The Father loves the Son and has entrusted him with complete authority' (3.35) and full jurisdiction. 'It is his will that all should pay the same honour to the Son as to the Father. To deny honour to the Son is to deny it to the Father who sent him' (5.22–23).

This important theme is insistently repeated. Anyone familiar with Jewish law knows at once what has happened: God has appointed an Agent to carry out his wishes. The Agent is to be accepted as carrying, in the area to which he is assigned, the full power of God himself. His decisions are God's decisions, his promises are God's promises. Hence Jesus can say 'The Father and I are one' (10.30). But they are not identical: it is the Father who *sends* him and Jesus who *is sent*. Hence Jesus must also say 'the Father is greater than I am' (14.28). Jesus' work as Agent of God is perfectly expressed in another variation of the central theme: 'Do you not believe that I am in the Father, and the Father in me? I am not myself the source of the words I speak to you: it is the Father who dwells in me doing his work' (14.10).

Jesus and the kosmos
1.19–12.50

This long section of the Gospel describes the complex action that precedes the passion. It is necessary to understand the meanings of *kosmos*, conventionally translated 'world', if the purpose of the story-telling is to be grasped.

KOSMOS (see also pp. xxiii–xxv)

1. In an inclusive sense, *kosmos* may mean the totality of created things: hence the relation of God to Jesus 'before the world began' (17.5, 24).

2. In a spatial sense it means the great world in which we live (21.25).

3. In a local sense it may mean the people of the neighbourhood: 'Show yourself to the world' (7.4) means 'act publicly'; 'all the world has gone after him' (12.19) means 'everybody within reach'; and similarly 14.22; 16.21; 18.20.

4. In a hostile sense it means the social world from which the Christian community has withdrawn. In general it is implied that the followers of Jesus are a band of people selected from the *kosmos* so that their loyalty lies outside it, trained by Jesus and then sent back into the *kosmos* to be a task-force working in his name. This theme is insistently developed in the Farewell Discourses (13–17) but is announced as early as 8.23 when Jesus says to the Jews: 'You belong to this world below, I to the world above. Your home is in this world, mine is not'; and it is finally stated when Jesus says to Pilate: 'My kingdom does not belong to this world' (18.36). The disciples of Jesus are selected from the *kosmos* (15.18–19), given to him by God (17.6), and then sent back (17.16–18). They will experience hatred, misery, and suffering (17.14; 16.20); but they will be protected from the evil one, experience Christ's peace such as the world cannot give, and realize that he has conquered the

world (17.15; 14.27; 16.33). This of course is largely drawn from John 17, a prayer intended to disclose the inmost intention of Jesus' conflict with the *kosmos* and the consequent nature of the Christian community. What that is, however, depends not solely on withdrawal from the *kosmos* but also on engagement with it.

5. In an accepting sense *kosmos* means structured human society, created by the *logos* and loved by God who provides it with food and life (6.33). It is, of course, true that the world fails to recognise its maker (1.10; 17.25), that people prefer darkness to light because their deeds are evil (3.19), and that the world is wrong about sin, justice and judgment (16.8). Even more: the world is so ruled that its structures can be operated in hostility to God ('the prince of this world', 12.31; 14.30; 16.11). Nevertheless, God is moved not by anger at defiance of his power but by love for the world. 'God so loved the world that he gave his only Son, that everyone who has faith in him may not perish but have eternal life. It was not to judge the world that God sent his Son into the world, but that through him the world might be saved' (3.16–17; 12.47) – and he is promptly recognised by the Samaritans as 'Saviour of the world' (4.42); and by John as 'the Lamb of God who takes away the sin of the world' (1.29). He gives his flesh for the life of the world (6.51), he is light for the world (8.12; 9.5) – in his definitive statement to Pilate: 'For this I was born; for this I came into the world: to bear witness to the truth' (18.37). His aim is to give sight to the blind, with the predictable consequence that some who are sure that they already see the truth will become blind (9.39).

As Jesus was consecrated in the service of the truth, so also are the disciples (10.36; 17.17) that others may believe through their words. And not only by their words: by their unity and participation in the life of the Father and the Son, the world may come to acknowledge God's sending and love (14.31; 17.20–23). The world, it is true, cannot of itself accept the Spirit of truth, but the disciples can, and they are his witnesses to the world (14.17; 15.26–27).

This is very different from the gnostic scheme. Though the Gospel may address the same spiritual problem, viz. mankind's true home and its alienation from the *kosmos*, its assumptions are different. The *kosmos* is not created by an inferior deity but by the command of God. Alienation occurs not because mankind are ignorant of their true nature but because they fail to recognise their maker. Salvation is not recovering their lost status by a minority of spiritual persons, but becoming children of God by trusting themselves to the Saviour sent from heaven. The Saviour did not enter the world to seek out his own and remove them to the heavenly world, but to open the way of ascent by his own death and to send back his disciples, guaranteed a place in his Father's house, to be responsible witnesses to the world and bearers of the Spirit.

Recognitions of Jesus
1.19–4.54

These initial chapters take up a stance towards questions that must have disturbed the community, namely: first, what understanding of Jesus had groups brought into the community from their former allegiance? and second, what was the necessity and significance of baptism?

It is well known that the Evangelist places the disciples' discovery of the identity of Jesus, as well as the aggressive Temple episode, early in the Gospel instead of late as in Mark. This is distressing to any who think that history demands chronology, that events are believable only if they are told in actual sequence. Let them try rewriting 1.29–34, and then ask why the Evangelist did not so write. In fact the writer dips into the traditional memories of the community and finds information about events (marked as such by the stock storytelling phrase the next day) which he places in the order best suited to his purpose. It is characteristic of group memories (of a family or a clan) that they are tenacious of events and what was said, and of the context in which they happened, but not necessarily of reliable sequences.

In 1.19–2.12 the contribution of John and the Galilean disciples is described; in 2.13–3.21 the cautious adherence of such Jerusalem Pharisees as were not offended by the action in the temple; in 3.22–4.2 the additional support of John is recorded; in 4.3–42 the qualified and then enthusiastic adherence of Samaritans is explained; and in 4.43–54 an explicit Galilean sign is provided.

Testimony of the Baptist
1.19–34

1.19–28 John, already introduced in 1.6–8, 15 as a man sent from God, who bore testimony to Jesus and announced his priority, now appears in his (already known) role as a baptiser. But it is not known why he baptises. Since spontaneous religious movements are likely to be dangerous, the authorities (*priests and Levites* conventionally representing the temple hierarchy, *Pharisees* representing serious lay devotion) naturally want to know what was John's intention. If he claimed warrant as one of God's anointed agents (or messiahs – the Qumran sect expected at least two), or as returning Elijah (as promised by Mal. 4, 5–6), or as the Mosaic prophet (as promised in Deut. 18.18–20) then they knew ways of containing John's movement. But he denied all three. Instead, he found his warrant in Isa. 40.3: his was *a voice crying in the wilderness*, making direct access possible for the Lord to come and reveal his glory to all flesh (as Isaiah further explains). In a different way, the same words of Isaiah had prompted the Qumran sect (whose members had been admitted by being 'sprinkled with purifying water and sanctified by cleansing water') to go into the wilderness and, by their study and exact practice of the law, to prepare the way for God.[1] Since that was obviously not John's intention, why (they asked) was he baptising? Surely he must present his baptism as a call to repentance or as an act of purification, no doubt modelled on the promise that 'I shall sprinkle pure water over you, and you will be purified from everything that defiles you . . . I shall give you a new heart and put a new spirit within you' (Ezek. 36.25–26).

John's reply was indirect: *I baptise* [only] *in water* – implying that there was another and more important baptism, about which they should be asking questions. This is the first indication that the necessity and significance of baptism must be thought about, especially as the imagery of immersion in water has more than one meaning: water can be threatening (as in the flood that sweeps everything away), or purifying, or life-giving. But John's baptism had the special function of creating conditions in which the presence of 'the unknown person' could be announced and his identity could be recognised – a person so high in dignity that even a prophet sent

---

[1] Community Rule iii.4–9, viii.13–16 (*DSSE* pp. 64, 73).

from God was *not worthy* (in a formal Semitic expression of deference) *to unfasten the strap of his sandal*. (It was general rabbinic opinion that a disciple owed the duty of a slave to his master.)

This took place at Bethany beyond Jordan which has not been identified and was unknown in 200 CE; it is obviously different from the Bethany two miles from Jerusalem (11.18). What follows concerns Jews from Bethsaida in Gaulanitis (north-east of the Sea of Galilee) and Cana in central Galilee. These indications of topography are not unimportant, since the work of Jesus will have two main areas, one in Jerusalem and one in the north with somewhat different theological responses.

1.29–34 In the other Gospels John proclaimed 'a baptism in token of repentance, for the forgiveness of sins' (Mark 1.4); but not in this Gospel where the word 'repentance' nowhere occurs, and 'forgiving' only once in the post-resurrection community (20.23). Dealing with sin is not the business of John but of Jesus, the successor to John who is really his predecessor. John baptised in order that Jesus, the Word become flesh, *might be revealed to Israel*. Hence Jesus, representing the eternity of God, comes later on the scene than John but *ranks ahead of him* and deals, not with failures to keep the law, but with the world's failure to recognise the source of its being. In the Gospel sin is characteristically the opposite of truth; it is unbelief (16.8–9). And according to John, Jesus *is the Lamb of God who takes away the sin of the world*. In the Gospel it is not a matter of having sins expiated (contrast the First Epistle where sin is lawlessness, and expiation is explicitly mentioned: I John 3.4; 2.2) but of removing the condition of *sin* (i.e. wilful ignorance of the *logos*) by transfer to a new *kosmos* (see pp. 17–19). John's duty was to *make a way for the Lord* into the hearts and minds of the Jewish people. He therefore used the well-tried way of baptising[2] in order to give sight to the blind: his baptism made it possible to recognise Jesus.

Lamb of God is a unique phrase. Presumably among John's disciples it was meaningful, but to others it is puzzling. The words *of God* could mean 'belonging to or suitable for God', but probably 'provided by God'. Does that refer to (i) God's promise to Abraham to provide a lamb (*probaton*) for a burnt offering as a substitute for Isaac? In fact he provides a ram (*krios*). It seems unlikely that the Gospel's word for lamb (*amnos*) would suggest to Greek readers the elaborate Jewish

---

[2] J. Thomas, *Le Mouvement Baptiste en Palestine et Syrie (150 av. J.-C.–300 ap. J.-C.)*, Gembloux 1935.

speculations about the binding of Isaac. Or to (ii) the lamb that becomes leader of the flock, the slain lamb (called *arnion*) of Rev. 5.6; 6.1; 7.17 who protects, guides and fights for the flock? Possibly in v. 36, but scarcely here. Or (iii) to the lamb without mark or blemish of I Peter 1.19 by whose precious blood Christians were set free? That might be an exodus reference, though Exod. 12.5 simply requires an animal in good condition; or a reference (as in I Peter 2.21–25 and Acts 8.32–33) to the suffering servant of Isa. 53 who indeed 'bore the sin of many'. But he bore the painful consequence of their sins, rather than removing them; and of course I Peter 2.25 calls Jesus not the Lamb but 'the Shepherd and Guardian of our souls'. It would be odd if the incidental comparison of the Servant of God to a lamb in the complex poem of Isa. 53 should provide the illuminating significance of John's *Lamb of God*.

With great probability, therefore, it refers to (iv) the Passover lamb, for the Gospel makes frequent and systematic references to Passover, gives a chronology of the final days such that Jesus was crucified at the time when the Passover animals were killed, and comments (19.36) that the soldiers' decision not to break the legs of Jesus fulfilled the rule for the Passover sacrifice in Exod. 12.46, Num. 9.12 (see p. 164). It is indeed true that the Passover sacrifice was protective, not expiatory: it prevented the dangers of their desperate situation from destroying them. Somewhat in the same way is the work of Jesus to be understood: the *kosmos* is protected by Jesus as the *Lamb of God* from the dangers inherent in its failure or refusal to recognise the *logos*.

This tentative, perplexing search in the OT is not wasted effort: it is the main purpose of John's designation for Jesus. Through his disciples the OT imagery of salvation entered the Christian community, thus enriching the possibilities for understanding the work of Jesus.

Rather more perplexing is the dove (as regards any symbolic meaning) which comes from the traditional account of the baptism of Jesus. The Evangelist may assume that his readers know the story; or he may have refrained from telling it to avoid any impression that the person baptised is inferior to the baptiser. To John the descent of the dove is a divine signal that on this person the Spirit has *come to rest* (in the manner perhaps of Isa. 11.2 'On him the Spirit of the Lord will rest'). John, who previously *did not know who he was*, may now be recognising what was always true of the Logos-become-flesh (whereas the synoptic story suggests that Jesus first received the

Spirit at his baptism). John now knows that this is *the one who is to baptise in Holy Spirit: ho baptizōn*, lit. 'who baptises' from the viewpoint of the later community, since according to 7.39 and 20.22 the outpouring of the Spirit comes only after the resurrection. Even more important for the later community is the statement that the Spirit had *come to rest* on Jesus (using a verb that is exceedingly common in the Gospel and the Epistle): for him the Spirit was not a temporary gift for *ad hoc* inspiration but a permanent endowment, and the rest of us could not obtain the Spirit except from him. And finally, John caps his initial designation of Jesus by saying: *this is God's Chosen One* (perhaps in the manner of Isa. 42.1 'My chosen . . . I have put my Spirit upon him' – referring to 'my servant' in the Hebrew OT, to 'Israel' in the Greek). Hence John sees the Lamb (repeated in v. 36) as God's special agent, chosen to do his work. That may preserve a sound memory that 'Son of God' was first said by one of John's *disciples*; but there is equally ancient and more widespread evidence that John *himself* said 'Son of God'. The true text cannot be decided: early copyists may have changed *Chosen* to give Jesus his more eminent designation, or may have changed 'Son' to permit the instructive reference to Isa. 42.

The First Disciples

1.35–51   Two of John's disciples, prompted by his testimony, turn to Jesus. The brief exchange of question and answer provides a model enquiry: *What are you looking for?* (or 'What do you want?') – *Rabbi, where are you staying? – Come and see*. The Evangelist explains that *rabbi means teacher*: so it did in his day, after 70 CE; but earlier it was more widely used in respectful address to persons of eminence (hence its use in 1.49, and of John Baptist in 3.26). In the disciples' question, the word *staying* translates the 'remaining' verb (already used in 1.33 *come to rest*) which has such important overtones in the Gospel. So here: is it 'Where are you living?' or 'Where do you live?' When they ask about his temporary lodging, are they committed to learning about his permanent home (cf. 14.2)?

Before long there are three from Bethsaida: Andrew, Simon and Philip – no doubt representing the earliest group of disciples within the community. We do not know, and are not required to know, what they discussed with Jesus. They simply testify to their conviction that by leaving John and joining *Jesus son of Joseph, from Nazareth* they had *found the Messiah*, the *man* promised by *Moses* and *foretold by the prophets*. So the community can be assured that Jesus is greater than John. More than that, there is a man from central Galilee, Nathanael, who knows Nazareth and despises it: he is brought to confess that Jesus is *the Son of God, the king of Israel*. Nathanael speaks as *an Israelite worthy of the name*. Indeed such a man (remembering Ps. 2.7 where God says to the Israelite king 'You are my son . . . this day I become your father') could indeed address Messiah as Son of God. But it was seldom done, since Son of God was an accepted term of *Hellenistic* religion. Thus an irreproachable Israelite witness with *nothing false in him*, addresses Jesus in Hellenistic fashion and thus establishes the credentials of the main title for Jesus throughout the Gospel.

Thus there is a chain of testimony from John, via his disciples, leading to Jesus. But we must not suppose that the disciples alone were responsible for their decision to acknowledge and follow Jesus – for it was Jesus who recognised *them* and gave them a name. He recognised *Simon son of John* and said that he would be *called Cephas*; he recognised Nathanael under the figtree and marked him as a *worthy Israelite*. Commentators usually say that Jesus exercised supernatural knowledge of the men's characters and indeed startled Nathanael by his prescience. For two reasons that suggestion will not do. (i) Whenever did Jesus use 'character' as a test of discipleship? 'Have I not chosen the twelve of you? Yet one of you is a devil' (6.70). Jesus is a saviour, not a management consultant. (ii) Nor is Jesus behaving like the fortune-teller in an oriental bazaar, enticing people by knowing what he cannot know. Jesus was not discerning character but assigning roles. He chose the people God had given him (cf. 17.6) – with a vivid picture in v. 51 of how the giving was done.

Simon will be called *Cephas*. That is old tradition: it comes from Aramaic-speaking disciples and is known to Paul (I Corinthians; Galatians); the naming appears in the synoptic gospels in the Greek form *Petros*, where only Matt. 16.18 suggests a meaning for the new name Rock. ('Peter' was not previously a personal name.) In this Gospel, Peter is less prominent (only in John 6, 13, 18, 20–21) though he displays his synoptic reputation for over-confidence and poor judgment. Not until 21.15–17 is he given responsibility as leader, and then he is changed from fisherman to shepherd and placed somewhat behind the Beloved Disciple. If we ask 'What is it about Peter's function in the community that corresponds to "my rock" (the enheartening description of God throughout Ps. 18)?' – the answer must surely be Peter's lapidary statement in 6.68f., 'Lord, to whom shall we go? Your words are words of eternal life. We believe and know that you are God's Holy One.'

Andrew, having brought his brother to Jesus, has thereafter only a small, helper's part (6.8; 12.22). Jesus himself recruited *Philip* who, to judge by 6.5, 7; 12.21–22; and 14.8–9, is useful but rather a simpleton. *Nathanael* (again in 21.2) all the more stands out as the typically devout old-time Israelite (cf. Ps. 24.4), at peace with God and the world (*under the fig tree*, Micah 4.4) who is pulled out of his contentment to acknowledge Jesus and to carry the weight of addressing him with both Hellenistic and Jewish terms. To him Jesus is indeed *Son of God*, but understood in the sense *King of Israel*. That understanding is repeated when he rides into Jerusalem (12.13), but thereafter it is changed into the hostile form 'king of the Jews' (18.33, 39; 19.3, 19, 21) – and on that charge he is put to death.

Hence Nathanael, and the whole company, must *see greater things than that* – namely, *Son of God* must be understood in terms of *the Son of Man* (for the former, see Awareness of God, p. 15; Father and Son, p. 52; for the latter, p. 136). The first indication of what that means is provided by the symbol of Jacob's ladder (Gen. 28.12). The *angels ascending and descending* are an introduction to the ascending and descending Son of Man in 3.13 and to the departure and return language of the final discourses. A number of phrases suggest synoptic links: *heaven wide open* recalls Mark's story of Jesus' baptismal vision (Mark 1.10); and the combination of *you will see, heaven, angels, Son of Man* recalls the eschatological sayings in Mark 14.62; 13.26–27; 8.38b. In this Gospel, however, the Son of Man is not the figure who ends one age and reveals the new; he is the permanent revealer of what is necessary between God and mankind. The symbolic angels mean that Jesus sends a request to God, and God tells him whom to choose.

AMEN

The promise of v. 51 begins *In very truth I tell you* – a phrase which is used twenty-five times in the Gospel (you being sometimes singular, mostly plural). It is a rendering of *amēn amēn legō hymin*, an emphatic form (*amēn* double in this Gospel, single in the others) of a manner of speech peculiar to Jesus.[3] *Amēn*, meaning 'certainly',

[3] See J. Jeremias, *New Testament Theology*, London and New York 1971, pp. 35ff.

is familiar at the end of prayers, remarkable at the beginning of statements. In the Gospel it gives powerful support to four kinds of assertion:

(i) promises and predictions: 1.51; 5.25; 8.51; 13.21, 38; 14.12; 16.20, 23.

(ii) conditions for receiving God's benefits: 3.3, 5; 5.19; 6.53; 12.24.

(iii) the self-knowledge of Jesus: 3.11; 5.24; 6.26, 32, 47; 8.58; 10.7; 13.20.

(iv) general maxims: 8.34; 10.1; 13.16; 21.18.

Every time Jesus says 'In very truth I tell you', it can be regarded as an invitation for readers to add their own Amen (sometimes a shamefaced Amen). When three Amens have been spoken, the matter is agreed and certain. 'Amen, amen' is a disclosure formula which invites our believing response.

CHRIST/MESSIAH

The Gospel was written to encourage belief in Jesus as Christ, the Son of God (20.31) even though the result might be exclusion from the synagogue (9.22). The community itself followed early Christian custom and spoke of 'Jesus Christ' (1.17; 17.3) as a matter of course; and some disciples explicitly identified him as Messiah (1.41; 4.25, 29; 11.27). But the majority of Jews were uncertain and divided in opinion (7.25–27, 31, 40–43): they asked him to tell them plainly whether he was the Messiah (10.24) and could not reconcile their expectation with his teaching about the Son of Man (12.34). Perhaps the Jews themselves were not entirely clear about the kind of deliverer they expected – so in 1.20–21: Christ, Elijah, the prophet; and in 7.40–41: the prophet, the Christ. What then did they mean by 'the Christ'?

Christ is a Greek adjective (corresponding to Hebrew māshîah, *messiah*) meaning anointed, smeared with oil. In normal Greek use it is applied to things, never to people. So its application to people is Hellenistic Jewish. It began its important career in Israelite religion when popular demand was dissatisfied with Yahweh as King and asked for a tribal king instead (I Sam. 8). Since a messiah is someone (whether king, or priest, or prophet) who acts in Yahweh's name and by his authority, Saul became the Lord's anointed. This new beginning was marked by the special designation, and it was passed on to David and some of his successors (at least in Judah). In eight psalms concerned with the ruling king he is called his, or my, or thy anointed who is protected, and granted victory, and sometimes even repudiated by God. Never is he *the* (expected) messiah – nor anywhere else in the OT.

In the prophetic writings, it is true, there are numerous proposals for a genuine revival of Davidic rule. The writers look forward to a king who would be endowed with the necessary qualities in superlative measure, e.g. Isa. 9.6–7; 11.1–5 (possibly reflected in John 1.32 and 7.24); Jer. 23.5 (possibly influencing John 7.42); Ezek. 34.23 (John 10.11, 16); Micah 5.2–4 (behind John 7.42); Zech. 9.9 (quoted at John 12.15). In Zech. 4.14; 6.9–11 there is the prospect of a twofold king-and-priest deliverer foreshadowing the two messiahs of Qumran. But nowhere in the prophets is the expected deliverer called *messiah*.

The word came back into use during the hundred years before Jesus, but with more than one meaning. Indeed its meaning was still not settled in the second century of our era when the influential Rabbi Akiba welcomed the insurgent leader Simon bar Kochba as messiah, and was opposed by fellow rabbis. Indeed there is nothing about *messiah* in the writings of Philo of Alexandria (first half of the first century), or of the historian Josephus (end of the first century), and only a single passing mention in the Mishnah, the coding of religious law that was complete by the end of the second century. Yet 'king messiah' is common in the Targumim, the popular Aramaic paraphrases of scripture for the sake of most ordinary Jews who understood little Hebrew. Such evidence as we have suggests that *messiah* was first introduced by marginal groups (in the so-called Psalms of Solomon and the Qumran writings) and then given a more popular appeal in two rather similar writings that were circulating at the end of the first century of our era. One is the Fourth Book of Ezra (confusingly entitled II Esdras in the Apocrypha of English Bibles) and the other the Second (Syriac Apocalypse of) Baruch. Messiah brings relief from present troubles and promotes visionary blessings: every vine shall be unbelievably fruitful and every grape shall produce 120 gallons of wine; the treasury of manna shall come down again from on high, and all who sleep in hope of messiah shall rise (II Baruch 29.5–30.1). Is it therefore surprising that the Gospel shows Jesus producing enormous quantities of wine, and allows him to say: 'I am the vine, the bread of life, the resurrection and the life'? Even the crowd's puzzled conviction: 'Our law teaches us that the Messiah remains for ever' (John 12.34), may be justified by Ps. 89.35–36, but it is encouraged by II Baruch 40.3 where 'the dominion of my messiah will last forever until the world of corruption has ended'. The reader can well understand why Jesus shows considerable reserve about popular expectations of messiah. The messiah with warlike functions (in the Psalms of Solomon and the Qumran writings) does not appear in the Gospel.

This note keeps strictly to *messiah, christos* – a Hellenistic Jewish designation. Other designations were in use for a general saviour bearing God's authority, but understanding is not promoted by assuming that other designations were the equivalent of *messiah* or interchangeable with it. The adjective 'messianic' (a nineteenth-century invention) introduces the maximum confusion into this complex subject.[4]

The Marriage Sign

2.1–12   This episode takes place in Nathanael's home town. The story is told very concisely, and there is no point in asking idle questions of fact when so much is implied by its main features. A week-long wedding feast is in progress when (to the social humiliation of the family) the wine runs out. Jesus solves the problem by causing purificatory water to become excellent wine in enormous quantity (some 120 gallons). That at once recalls the bread miracle in John 6 when, out of very little, so much bread is produced that 5,000 people cannot consume it all. Here we have two signs of the divine superabundance, one relating to the Jewish manna tradition, the other to the Hellenistic wine tradition. There were popular stories about Greek villages where the wine-god Dionysus on his festival day caused the local stream to run wine instead of water.[5] As an

[4] The Introduction to *OTP* I, pp. xxxi–xxxiii, keeps *messiah* distinct; so does the article on *christos* in *TDNT* IX, pp. 501ff. Schürer, II, pp. 514–47, provides a rich stew of all possible ingredients. For new directions in this subject, consult *Judaisms and their Messiahs at the Turn of the Christian Era*, ed. J. Neusner, W. S. Green and E. S. Frederichs, Cambridge and New York 1987.

[5] For the possibility (at some period) of Dionysus worship in Galilee, see S. Freyne, *Galilee, Jesus and the Gospels: Literary Approaches and Historical Investigations*, Dublin and Philadelphia 1988, p. 185.

image of the divine generosity and happiness this thought appeared among the Hebrew prophets, e.g. Amos 9.13 when God restores the fortunes of his people and causes the mountains to run with fresh wine. The philosopher Philo allegorised the Genesis story of Melchizedek, and said 'Let Melchizedek instead of water offer wine, and give to souls strong drink, that they may be seized by a divine intoxication, more sober than sobriety itself. For he is a priest, namely Logos, having as his portion him that is, and all his thoughts of God are high, and vast and sublime.'[6] So both Jews and Greeks could read the lesson of abundant wine, but because Jesus' gift was made at a wedding Jews would understand more completely. Hosea had shown them the image of a divine wedding when the Lord would renew the marriage with his formerly faithless, now repentant wife Israel. Hence the wine miracle at Cana symbolizes the transformation from repentance to joyful communion. This is not a story about the contemptuous replacement of *Jewish rites of purification* by a superior Christian equivalent; it is about a miraculous possibility that Jewish purification and Christian baptism could be converted into the joy of the divine wedding feast.

There is another striking feature: *the mother of Jesus was there* (see also 19.25–27). At her prompting, he performed his first sign. She simply stated the need: *They have no wine*, in words apparently simple but deeply resonant. Jesus' immediate response is a kind of refusal. (i) *That is no concern of mine* is a rather desperate attempt to render the Greek here (where all translators are in despair, since English fails to provide the necessary equivalents). The Greek words respond to a threat or an intrusion. Hence: 'what [common intention could there be] for me and for you?', followed by 'woman' which, in Greek, is an address of formal courtesy (almost 'my lady' – see 4.21; 20.13, 15 – impossible in English, and so omitted from REB). It is common enough in ordinary speech but most surprising from a son addressing his mother. (ii) Jesus explains this negative response by *My hour has not yet come*. At various points in the Gospel his hour is said to be coming: the hour for his arrest, departure from the world to the Father, death and glorification. In the words of Jesus himself, it has come (12.23, 27; 16.32; 17.1) and there will be a similar crisis for his disciples (16.2, 4, 25). But on two occasions Jesus says, '*the time is coming, indeed it is already here*': the hour for true worship (4.21, 23) and for the dead to hear the voice of the Son of God (5.25, 28).

[6] Philo, *Allegories of the Law* III.82.

These are not only promises for the future, but a genuine present anticipation. Thus Jesus tells his mother that the time for him to show his glory (which is the glory of his Father) has not yet come. But behind the NO, she hears a YES. She tells the servants to obey him, and then Jesus performs an anticipatory sign of the divine glory. Jesus addresses his mother with studied courtesy and is led to the necessary paradox of 'is coming and is already here'. It is not by chance that, in doing the will of his Father, he is prompted by his mother; nor is it by chance that the Jewish component of the later community is validated by a mother in Israel who says '*Do whatever he tells you.*' The story is rounded off by the departure of Jesus with his mother, his brothers (who reappear in fractious mood at 7.2–10 and cause further discussion of 'the right time'), and his disciples (who are called his brothers at 20.17) to Capernaum which is named again at 4.46; 6.17, 24, 59.

If it is agreed (as suggested above) that idle questions of fact are pointless, it is still possible to ask; was water really changed into wine? Two things may be suggested. (*a*) It will not do to say: 'Jesus is God, and God can do anything he pleases.' That charges God with frivolity and undermines the reliability of the world. A miracle is not something that God can throw off if he feels inclined; if done at all, it is done at enormous cost. The whole point of a miracle is that, by everything we know, it is impossible – and yet it happens. Just as it is impossible that water should become wine, so it is impossible that even repentant people should share the divine glory – yet it happens. And a water-miracle is less significant than a people-miracle. (*b*) If, however, we want to fix attention on the water-miracle as an actual event, two ways seem open. *Either* the physical qualities of water were not changed but the wedding guests were given appropriate mental stimulus to *perceive* the water *as* wine (which, however improbable, is a perfectly acceptable miracle); *or* water – a compound of hydrogen and oxygen – was transformed into an aqueous solution of ethyl alcohol (plus various complex esters) – a compound of carbon, hydrogen and oxygen. The atomic transformation required would be very remarkable.

SIGNS

Sign is the Evangelist's word: twice only on the lips of Jesus (rather disapprovingly), elsewhere used to describe the miracles of wine (2.11), recovery (4.54), healing (6.2), bread (6.14), sight (9.16) and recall to life (12.18) – with the implication that these are selected from a larger number, perhaps already known to the readers (2.23; 12.37; 20.30). The Evangelist uses the word to express the response of others: Nicodemus says in effect 'Even if you attack the temple, you perform *signs*' (3.2); many of the crowd ask whether messiah would do more *signs* than this man had done (7.31); many said that John performed no *sign* but everything he said about this man was true (10.41); the chief priests and Pharisees admitted that this man was performing many *signs* (11.47). The Jews ask for a *sign* to justify his attack on the temple, i.e. evidence that he had prophetic authority and was not an impostor (2.18). The Galileans ask what *sign* he would perform to show that he was a true prophet and not a deceiver (6.30).

The Greek word is *sēmeion* (related to semantics, the fashionable term of language sciences). There is another word, *ergon* (see Work, p. 49), used by Jesus himself to describe his 'work(s)', but that suggests another aspect of his miracles. What does the Evangelist imply by using *sign*? He agrees with Jesus that a miracle is unsatisfactory if it is no more than a sign and portent (4.48) – a mind-boggling prodigy, unsatisfactory also if it goes no further than the mere satisfaction of physical need (6.26). For the Evangelist, when Jesus *performed . . . the first of the signs he revealed his glory and led his disciples to believe in him* (2.11). It sometimes happened again (4.53; 6.14) though in summarising the ministry it has to be admitted that 'in spite of the many signs which Jesus had performed in their presence they would not believe in him' (12.37).

Signs have a long history in Jewish prophetic tradition. Some prophets perform striking symbolic actions which both prefigure the future and cause it to happen. The signs of Jesus both prefigure what is promised and also reveal what is already present in him. 'They are not an attempt to read the future but . . . to extract the future from the present.'[7] Or, to put it more simply, a sign is a parable that hints at a miracle. The great aim is to move from repentance to rejoicing in the divine marriage (John 2). But are not God's people, like the officer's son, at death's door (John 4)? Is not a whole generation crippled and immobile (John 5)? Are they not desperate for food in the wilderness (John 6)? Are not the most devout and godly blind to the truth (John 9)? Is there any hope of recovery? Surely Israel must be allowed to die (like Lazarus, 11.6)

---

[7]   K. H. Rengstorf, '*semeion*/sign', *TDNT* VII, p. 217.

and then receive new life. The glory of God is shown not in preventing what ought to die from dying, but in giving new life to what has inevitably died. In Lazarus, Judaism is not rescued but reborn.

The Temple Protest

2.13–22   For the next phase of his work, Jesus goes to Jerusalem just before *the Jewish Passover* (note how the phrase dissociates the Christian community from the Jewish celebration). He turns his attention to the Judaean area, and begins a programme that will be associated with various festivals (5.1; 7.14; 10.22; 12.12), using the occasions as opportunities of teaching (5.14; 7.14, 28; 8.20; 10.23; 11.56 (the people expected him); 18.20).

On this occasion, however, he did more than teach: he enacted a prophetic protest against the temple. He interrupted the arrangements that were customarily made, a few days before Passover in an outer court of the temple, to satisfy the needs of any worshippers who wanted to buy suitable animals or obtain the approved Tyrian coinage for their temple dues. Imagine some 5,000 people in and around the temple courts, and 250 animals. How could one man upset the tables of the money changers, rebuke the dealers in pigeons, and (even with a whip of cords) drive out people and cattle?[8] Where would they go? and what would happen when his intervention ended? It would be more understandable if Jesus made a token protest involving a few people and cattle, thus performing an enacted prophecy – with the implication that what he had done in miniature would be repeated on a large scale until sacrificial animals were totally removed and temple revenues were finished. Jesus thus rejected the temple system as too much like a market, buying God's protection with sacrifices and hierarchy. For him *my Father's house* had a different meaning (14.2): for the first time in the Gospel Jesus speaks of God and calls him Father – thus disclosing a relationship

[8] For pilgrim numbers, see J. Jeremias, *Jerusalem in the Time of Jesus*, London and Philadelphia 1969, pp. 77–84; modified in S. Safrai, *The Pilgrimage at the Time of the Second Temple*, Tel Aviv 1965 (in Hebrew), pp. 71–74. For a good defence of the Jewish practices see I. Abrahams, *Studies in Pharisaism and the Gospels*, 1st series, Cambridge and New York 1917, pp. 82–89.

that will dominate the rest of his teaching. And he was moved not by indifference but by costly zeal for the manner of God's presence, as foreseen in Ps. 69.10.

If Jesus was indeed sent by God, his prophetic act would have dangerous consequences. Hence the administration must ask for a sign of his authority. His answer was faithful to Moses' instruction ('when the word spoken by the prophet is not fulfilled . . . it is not a word spoken by the Lord'): *'Destroy this temple* [as you are indeed doing], *and in three days I will raise it up again.'* By building the temple which had already taken forty-six years, and would require thirty-six more for completion, they were in fact inhibiting the divine presence. If the massive buildings of the temple complex (on which the economic prosperity of Jerusalem greatly depended) were destroyed, together with the inmost sanctuary, it would be possible in three days to prepare a place where the word of God could be heard. That sign, of course, could be verified only when its promise had succeeded or failed. The Christian community read its success in the resurrection of Jesus (not in the ruin of the temple in 70 CE), and thus justified its conviction that the place of God's dwelling was the body of Jesus.

The Pharisee Nicodemus

2.23–3.21   Despite that attack on the temple many put their trust in Jesus – with the implication that many Jews were dissatisfied with the temple (cf. Stephen, Acts 7.47–51) and rallied to his support. But Jesus had reservations about their adherence, and made his reasons plain in the dialogue with Nicodemus, *a member of the Jewish Council*, a Pharisee and in some ways a representative *teacher of Israel*. Nicodemus regarded Jesus as a *teacher sent by God* and later in the Gospel made an ineffective plea for Jesus to be heard before being condemned (7.50–52). After the crucifixion he joined Joseph in taking burial spices for the dead body (19.39). He visited Jesus by night – and was always somewhat in the dark. He represents reflective Jewish teachers of good repute who are drawn to Jesus but cannot take in certain necessary consequences of his teaching. Hence he can stand for a section of the later community, or at least for sympathetic Jews with whom they were in contact; but he is certainly not to be regarded as a bemused hearer who asks silly questions.

Jesus himself introduces *the kingdom of God*, only to dismiss it from further consideration (rather as he dismissed the temple in the previous episode). No one can experience (*see* and *enter* are equivalent in meaning) the divine kingship unless then are *born again* or (using a possible and, in view of v. 31, more probable meaning of the Greek word) 'from above'. In effect Jesus is telling Nicodemus that he must abandon the Jewish hope of the kingdom and adopt the Greek hope of rebirth. Nicodemus shrewdly replies: '*How can* a [Jewish] man *be born when he is old?*' Born of a Jewish mother he belongs to the elect people, and already knows the divine kingship. '*Can he enter his mother's womb a second time and be born* with any greater privilege?' But Jesus insists that he must be *born from water and spirit* – presumably from cleansing and the uninhibited power of God. To a Jew that may suggest the promise in Ezek. 36.25–27 that God will wash his people with clean water and put a new spirit within them; though Christians will also think of baptism and the gift of the Spirit. But Jesus goes much further in justifying rebirth or birth from above: '*Flesh can give birth only to flesh; it is spirit that gives birth to spirit.*' And *spirit* like the *wind* (the same word can have both meanings), is not predictable or within human control. Hence the Jewish confidence in birth, and the gnostic conviction that some are spiritual by nature, are both rejected. Yet Nicodemus seizes on the difficulty: if flesh and spirit are totally separate, *how is* birth from above *possible*? Indeed this does appear to be very uncompromising teaching, and the community includes it within its accepted expressions of belief. Jesus does not explain *how* it is possible, but (speaking on behalf of the Christian community, addressing the Jewish community) firmly insists *that* it happens. The dialogue is broken off with the enigmatic comment of v. 12 which perhaps implies: if Jewish teachers were not persuaded by the earthly Jesus, were they likely to be convinced by the heavenly Jesus speaking through the testimony of the community?

In the statement to Nicodemus much was left unsaid. Now it is said in a notably formal manner: Jesus speaks of himself in the third person. He is speaking (shall we say?) rather like the academic head of a university when he says: 'The Vice-Chancellor under the Charter has the power to confer degrees' – referring to himself acting in his official capacity. There are three fundamental statements, with an extensive development of the third.

(i) The first explains by what means birth from above is possible

(v. 13). No one belonging to the world can go up to heaven. Only *the Son of Man who is* (i.e. exists) *in heaven,* and has come down from heaven to earth can return there. But by virtue of his office he has the power to confer birth from above on those who entrust themselves to him. For those born from the flesh there is no access to birth from the Spirit except by the descending and ascending Son of Man, whose existence is in heaven. Many versions of the Gospel (following ancient manuscripts) omit these last three words, but unwisely. They are necessary to the Gospel's view of salvation. The point is this: those who find life on earth unsatisfactory – unhappy, worrying, terrifying, frustrating – may hope for one of two things: *either* that God will reach down from heaven, relieve their distress, and make a happy life possible on earth; *or* that the way will be disclosed to them whereby they can live the life of heaven where their human representative, the Son of Man, always exists. The Gospel exploits the second hope.

SON OF MAN

Jesus uses this self-designation some dozen times in the first thirteen chapters. Although the Gospel does not reproduce any synoptic Son of Man saying, it preserves the same general profile of submission and honour. At the same time it introduces its own special features. We already know from 1.51 (the ascending and descending angels) that the Son of Man is the centre of communication between earth and heaven. We now know that only he has gone up into heaven, and will ascend to where he was before (3.13; 6.62). Indeed the Son of Man must be lifted up (3.14) – only so will people know who he is (8.28; 12.34); and lifting up has the double meaning of crucifixion and glory (12.23; 13.31). As the Man (cf. 19.5) he is shamefully killed, as the Man from Heaven he is gloriously triumphant. As humanity's representative in heaven he gives us the food of eternal life (6.27), but we have no inward life unless we eat the flesh of the Son of Man and drink his blood (6.53). As the Man from heaven he naturally gives sight to the blind; but precisely because he is the Man he has authority to pass judgment (5.27).

(ii) What is now required for access to the world above? The lifting up of the Son of Man *in order that everyone who has faith may in him have eternal life* (vv. 14–15). For a Jew like Nicodemus, lifting up the Son of Man might seem like honouring a teacher bent on the destruction of Israel (and in the end he was lifted up on a cross because of that fear). So appeal is made to Num. 21.8–9 when the Israelites, as they were approaching the promised land, were in serious danger from poisonous snakes. 'The Lord told Moses to make a bronze serpent and erect it as a standard, so that anyone who had been bitten could look at it and recover.' The threat to their life was not greater than the providence of God (cf. Wisd. 16.5–7); and Jesus was a threat to Israel only in order that *everyone who has faith may have eternal life.*

ETERNAL LIFE

We know from the Prologue that *life* is a leading theme of the Gospel, often called *eternal life.* The addition of 'eternal' does not change the meaning, though in English (where the word means 'that which has always existed and always will exist') the reader may be misled. In Greek *aiōn* means a long period of time, and *aiōnios* (translated as 'eternal') what is appropriate to such a period. Hence 'eternal life' means the kind of life appropriate to the period (or indeed the phase of experience) in which you are or will be living. In Mark 10.30 Jesus promises his disciples various rewards in this age and 'in the age to come eternal life'. In this Gospel, however, eternal life is already available to those living in awareness of God and his emissary Jesus Christ (17.3).

Eternal life is the opposite of walking in darkness, coming to judgment, experiencing God's wrath, perishing, and death (8.12; 5.24, 29; 3.36; 3.16). It is compared to a spring of running water, a harvest of grain, and imperishable food (4.14, 36; 6.27, 33). It is explicated by the words 'way' and 'truth' (14.6). It implies being securely in the hands of Jesus (10.28), who speaks the life-giving commands of his Father (12.50) and prompts the spirit that gives life (6.63). One may have eternal life by hearing his word and believing him who sent him (3.15, 16, 36; 5.24, 40; 6.35, 40, 47, 53, 54).

BELIEVING, HAVING FAITH

In the Gospel these expressions render the various uses of the same Greek verb (not the noun). Because they have a variety of associations in English, care is needed in grasping the Evangelist's meaning: (i) To believe someone, to accept what he says or does, as a reliable indication of the truth (e.g. 5.46–47), usually in arguments. (ii) To believe that Jesus is what he says he is or shows himself to be (e.g. 6.69). (iii) To believe in Jesus as the challenging and effective Agent of God (so that believing in him *is* believing in God, 12.44), who makes striking promises and sets some against him, some for him. To those who put their faith in him he promises eternal life, becoming sons of God and sons of light (1.12; 12.36), doing God's work (6.29), doing even greater things than Jesus showed (14.12), and causing others to believe through their words (17.20). Throughout John 2–12 there are occasions when many believed on him (2.11, 23; 4.39; 7.31; 8.30; 10.42; 11.45; 12.11); but not his brothers (7.5), nor the Pharisees (7.47–48) who deterred some in authority from acknowledging him (12.42–43). The final assessment is scripturally pessimistic (12.37, 39). (iv) To believe, to have faith is to become a believer – a member of the believing community which has seen the glory of God (11.40).

(iii) If Jesus is a threat to Israel it is not because of God's hostility to them, but because of God's love for the world. In the word 'love' it is not affection that stands in the forefront but a generous activity to support, protect, and save. God is not content to let the world perish, but instead offers life and illumination. Elsewhere it is said that God loves the Son (3.35; 5.20; 10.17; 15.9; 17.24, 26) and his disciples (14.21, 23; 16.27; 17.23). Thus what is said here is very striking, that *God so loved the world that he gave his only Son* (v. 16) – *gave* (past tense) implying 'gave to be his Agent and our introduction to *eternal life*'. In the Gospel, Son of God focuses on the relation of Jesus to deity (Son of Man suggests his relation to humanity) and is more fully expressed in ch. 5. What is notable here is that *God sent his Son* to do his will and show his glory, to do his work and speak his words, to save and not to condemn. In itself 'sending' is a prophetic formula (e.g. John Baptist, 1.6, 33; 3.28), but in the case of Jesus it goes much further and is persistently expressed in his words (some forty times). Jesus acted under the constraint and with the immense authority of being his Father's Agent. (See also Sent by God, pp. 59–60.)

Verses 17–19 are better understood if *judgment* is replaced by 'condemnation' (as in NIV). The essence of judgment is separation, distinguishing good from bad. It is never denied that Jesus came to do that; indeed, it is specifically asserted that he did (9.39). But the condemnation is self-administered. *The light has come into the world*: either we choose the light by trusting *God's only Son* and living *by the truth* or, for fear of exposure, we prefer darkness. If the latter, we shut ourselves off from God's love. A gnostic writing would imply that Jesus came only to search out those capable of welcoming the light, thus discarding the rest; but the words *everyone who has faith* indicate a different intention. He came not only to show but also to open up the possibility of preferring the light to the dark.

Baptising
3.22–4.3

3.22–36   A further paragraph is needed, in addressing Jewish hearers, to stress the seriousness of the choice that must be made, to balance insistence on God's love by reference to his wrath (vv. 31–36). For that the setting is provided by returning to John Baptist who gives the least unsatisfactory Jewish testimony to Jesus. Both are presented as baptising at a time before John's imprisonment. Aenon near Salim, with its plentiful supply of water, cannot be identified with confidence; but the very mention of a fixed place and its resources indicates the solid earth to which the heavenly visitor comes, utters the words of God, and offers eternal life (vv. 31–36). Nor can we discover why *John's disciples were engaged in a debate with some Jews* (some manuscripts say 'a Jew') *about purification*. But we are reminded that the water-jars at Cana were intended for Jewish rites of purification, and that marriage symbolism both illuminates that story (2.1–10) and reconciles John to his diminishing role. According to the community's tradition, Christian baptism is rooted in the baptism that Jesus performed, and that in turn derived from John's baptism. In that case, was not John the true founder of the community and the true prophetic source of its benefits? No, for even in John's day everyone was flocking to Jesus' baptism. After all *one can have* (as one's appointed task) *only what is given one from heaven*; Jesus *must grow greater*, John *must become less* (v. 30).

Why? Because adherence to John means joining another devout Jewish group on earth. But, whether anyone believes it or not, Jesus bears witness to the life of heaven. To accept that witness is to make an affirmation about God: to say that God has sent Jesus, that God's words are spoken by him with no restriction but with the full force of divine Spirit; to assert that the Father loves the Son and has entrusted him with full authority as his proper Agent. That affirmation secures eternal life. Refusal to make it is a self-inflicted wound – turning one's back on life and choosing God's wrath. That which could be read as love is perforce read as hostility (v. 36).

4.1–3 At this point there comes a hint that the *Pharisees* could be hostile (as they indeed were later: 7.32–52; 9.13–16; 11.46–57; 18.3), because *Jesus was winning and baptising more disciples than John*. If Jesus himself baptised we cannot know what he intended; but v. 2 at once issues a correction: not Jesus himself but his disciples. That sounds like a comment from the later community: what they did, Jesus did. The principle of agency applies ('whoever receives any messenger of mine receives me', 13.20) and may perhaps be given content by 20.22–23.

The Samaritan Woman
4.4–42

4.4–30 Jesus therefore decided to go north to Galilee, and *he had to pass through Samaria* (because God so instructed him?) instead of using the avoiding route. His meeting with the Samaritan woman is, at the simplest, a story about moving from ignorance to disturbing self-knowledge. But more than that, it brings into view some consequences of social and religious conflict between Jews and Samaritans, between men and women. It is not to be ignored that Jesus talks theologically with a woman, that in response to her question he makes one of his most radical statements (vv. 21–23), and for her benefit alone explicitly admits that he is Messiah (contrast 10.24–25). In studying their conversation – one of the so-called Johannine 'misunderstandings' – it is unwise to assume that the woman was stupid, or indeed that Jesus spoke so obscurely that no one could understand. Jesus was indeed talking about heavenly realities, but in an earthly context of tiredness, thirst, hunger, fetching water, and harvesting; and the episode may have been recorded, in part at least, to provide an origin-story for Samaritan members of the community.

Jews and Samaritans had long felt mutual resentment, not without justification on both sides. All Palestinian history is about who has a right to the Land, and religion is used to add bitterness to the conflict. Obviously there were some relations between the two groups (see v. 8) but they kept themselves to themselves when they could, even to the extent of not using common cups and dishes. So why does a Jewish man *ask for a drink from a Samaritan woman*? According to a pre-Christian tradition, the Sages of Israel said: 'He that talks much with womankind brings evil upon himself and neglects the study of the Law and at the last will inherit Gehenna.'[9] The Samaritan woman, with her history, would guess why a man who broke the rules should speak to her. Could she, however, read the riddle of his reply? *If only you knew what God gives, and who it is that is asking you for a drink, you would have asked him and he would have given you living water*. In the Gospel *God gives* many things: the Torah through Moses (1.17; 7.19), bread from heaven, the Spirit, his only Son (to whom he gave authority, judgment, work to do, people to recruit, and glory to show), and the right to become children of God. In this conversation the first is meant: God's commandments and promises through Moses – which Samaritan religion firmly accepted. Jesus asks her for a drink of water and in return promises her *living* (i.e. running) *water*. Since Eastern (and African) people wash by pouring water over themselves, this aspect of water symbolism brings together the maintenance and the cleansing of life. *Living* (i.e. running) *water* was a powerful symbol to Jews and Greeks: in Jer. 2.13 for God himself: 'My people . . . have rejected me, a source of living water.' At Qumran: for the divine instruction of Torah or the cleansing Spirit of God. A similar combination in the Odes of Solomon: 'I drank and became intoxicated, from the living water that does not die . . . I abandoned vanity, and turned towards the Most High, my God, and was enriched by his favours.'[10] Thus the symbolism suggests both cleansing and refreshment. The woman quite properly chooses to continue with the refreshment theme. With skill and tact she tells the man that he seems unable to give even a simple drink of water, let alone a cleansing supply of running water. Jesus accepts her choice, and re-defines his offer: not an external source of the life-giving water, but a permanent internal supply. That is a symbol of *eternal life*, less obliquely expressed than the promise of the divine Wisdom that 'whoever drinks from me will thirst for more' (Ecclus. 24.1).

[9] Aboth 1.5 (Danby, p. 446).
[10] Odes of Solomon 11.6–11 (*OTP* II, p. 744); Damascus Rule iii.16, vi.4–11: the Law; Community Rule iv.20–22: the Spirit (*DSSE* pp. 85, 87, 66).

It is a high-minded offer, but is it practical? Considering what a woman has to do, she would accept the offer it it would relieve her of the burden of fetching water. Whereupon Jesus drops symbolic language and refers to the burden of her relations with men. Who cares whether a Babylonian rabbi sixty years later ruled that a barren woman should not remarry more than two or three times (as all the commentaries say)? This is a case of a woman's socio-sexual dependence on or manipulation of men. She is not free to accept eternal life. The woman admits his prophetic insight into her condition, but she still has a reply. If *she* is not free to accept eternal life, *he* is not free to offer it; for Samaritans are bound to this mountain, he is bound to Jerusalem by the obligations of worship. Jews and Samaritans were locked into permanent hostility by (non-creative responses to) their past. So Jesus, addressing the woman with the same formal courtesy that he used towards his mother (though that is not evident in REB), says *the time is coming when you will worship the Father neither on this mountain nor in Jerusalem* (v. 21). Not that Samaritan or Jewish convictions are a matter of indifference. For whereas Samaritan religion accepted the Five Books of Moses and stopped there, Jewish religion added the histories, the prophets, the writings and, under some Greek influence, the Wisdom books – to which the Gospel is closely related. That way lies knowledge of God and of the kind of worshippers he desires. *It is from the Jews that salvation comes*; and *salvation* in the Gospel means the opposite of condemnation, the possibility of coming to the light, of having knowledge of the *truth*, i.e. the real state of things. So *the time is coming, indeed it is already here*, for a worship not constricted by the past but responsive to the future. *God is spirit* (i.e. transforming energy), *and those who worship him must worship in spirit and in truth*. This is not a demand that external, cultic worship should be replaced by internal, reflective worship. That contrast was very familiar to Jews and Greeks, but both those forms of worship belong to the lower world. Jesus indicates a worship that belongs to the upper world, where transforming energy gives access to reality. 'But', says the woman in effect, 'that is reserved for *Messiah when he comes*' (using the Hebrew name instead of the Samaritan *Taheb*, the expected restorer of all things). *Jesus said to her, 'I am he, I who am speaking to you'* (v. 26). The woman half-believes and, when the disciples return, goes to tell her townspeople: she may still be wondering who he is, but realises that he has opened up for her a thorough awareness of herself, as she is and as she may be.

4.31–42 The end of the Samaritan story is now postponed until the disciples have been educated in its meaning (hence providing a lesson for readers of the Gospel). Jesus makes a statement (vv. 31–34) and presses it home against two objections (vv. 35–36 and 37–38). In view of ch. 6 he cannot be supposed indifferent to physical hunger, but doing the will of him who sent him and finishing his work takes first place. The first objection: 'the time is not ripe', he answers by saying: *The reaper is* now *harvesting a crop* (of people who are ready) *for eternal life*. The second objection: *'we* have the trouble, *others* get the benefit', he answers by saying: *Others laboured and you have come in for the harvest of their labour*. It is not necessary to spend time discussing who the *others* were, for this is a revelatory signal: Jesus is proclaiming 'the year of the Lord's favour' (Luke 4.19; II Cor. 6.2). In effect he says: 'You go to buy food from the Samaritans, but otherwise will have nothing to do with them. I find them ready for eternal life.'

So it proved. The Samaritans, having heard for themselves, went beyond the woman's hesitating thought (v. 29) and acknowledged him *Saviour of the world* (cf. 3.16 and I John 4.14). In the NT *saviour* is uncommon and mostly confined to the later writings; in Jewish writings it is sometimes applied to God, e.g. 'God of Israel, the Saviour' (Isa. 45.15) and 'the Saviour of all' (Wisd. 16.7, with reference to the danger from snakes already in mind at John 3.14). But the title was commonly applied to the gods, e.g. to the healer Asclepius and the deities of private religion such as Isis and Osiris; as well as to persons active in the world's affairs. Soon after the Gospel was written the full title saviour of the world appeared on inscriptions dealing with the Emperor Hadrian. The Samaritans, aware that Jesus has breached the barrier between them and the Jews, recognise him as active in the world's affairs.

The Sign of Life

4.43–54 Now he continues to Galilee, his own country (1.45; 6.42; 7.41; 18.5; 19.19) where he does not expect to have the same prophetic recognition that he received in Samaria. Although *the Galileans made him welcome*, having *seen all he did at the festival in Jerusalem*, Jesus by no means approves their response to him (so 4.48, and throughout ch. 6). But he performs his *second* Galilean *sign* in the very place where the first was performed (2.1–11) – and the reader is obviously invited to compare them. Jesus answers the pleading of *an officer in the royal service*, probably a Jew (possibly a Gentile, but nothing suggests it) attached to the court of Herod who had the courtesy title of 'king'. Whereas the first sign was done for a large family party and village celebration of a wedding, the second sign touches on the political scene in Capernaum and relieves the distress of one administrator. In itself the sign is not exceptional: the request, the answer, the exact coincidence of Jesus' words and the time when the fever left the child. Almost exactly the same story is told in the Talmud of Rabbi Hanina ben Dosa (active between 80 and 120 CE), and in the earlier Mishnah[11] it is reported that the rabbi used to pray over the sick and say 'This one will live' or 'This one will die'. When asked how he knew, he replied: 'If my prayer is fluent in my mouth I know that he is accepted; if it is not I know that he is rejected.' (The biblical model is Elijah, I Kings 17.23.)

But there are some remarkable features in the story. Jesus at first makes a testy reply: *'Will none of you* (political officials) *ever believe without seeing signs and portents?'* The implications of *signs and portents* (here only in the Gospel) demand reflection. In the Lukan tradition, Jesus and the apostles did signs and wonders in confirmation of the gospel, and Jesus himself in this Gospel is not averse to that idea (14.11). But signs and portents are ambiguous: they may be misleading trickery (Mark 13.22; II Thess. 2.9) or terrifying warnings such as Moses showed to Pharaoh (Acts 7.36, cf. 2.19). The true test (according to Deut. 13.1–3) is whether such experiences lead to the Lord or to a false god. All that the royal officer at this moment can see is the portent of death, and Jesus gives him the sign of life. First he took Jesus at his word, then he saw what that word had done; *and he and all his household became believers* – of course they did, because this was a gift of life to the household. So in what sense was this a sign – a second sign, undiscussed like the first (so that the reader has to work it out)? The first sign suggested the change from repentance to rejoicing in the divine marriage. This sign suggests that Jewish political life – the household of Israel – is near to death but can be brought to life if Jesus is taken at his word. The *kosmos* can be saved. And just as in the Samaritan story there was no waiting between

---

[11] Berakoth 5.5 (Danby, p. 6).

sowing and reaping, so here: if Jesus is taken at his word, he speaks and it is done.

Jesus and the Jewish People
5.1–12.50

The character of the story now changes: remarkable signs are again performed and they give rise to discussion, perplexity, and opposition. After the Bethesda healing in ch. 5, Jesus is charged with sabbath-breaking and blasphemy, and he defends himself. In ch. 6 the feeding of the people is related to God's manna in the wilderness, the crowd's response is ambiguous, hostile voices raise objections, and the loyalty of disciples is tested. There is a prolonged dialogue with hostile Jews and Pharisees in chs. 7–8, and the crowd is divided. Disciples do not appear until the giving of sight in ch. 9, when Jews are incredulous and Pharisees are hostile – and they remain hostile in ch. 10 when they hear Jesus' shepherd parables. In ch. 11 the disciples are important witnesses of the Lazarus story and many Jews are led to faith by the miracle; but chief priests and Pharisees make plans to kill Jesus. Despite the welcoming festival crowds in ch. 12, and the adherence of believers even from the authorities, Jesus knows that his appeal has not succeeded. Greeks appear, wishing to see him, and to that end he prepares himself for death.

THE JEWS

The Jews, according to the Evangelist, are the source of this persistent hostility. Sometimes opposition comes more specifically from the Pharisees and chief priests, but many passages can be read as if the Jewish people as a whole are hostile, guilty, and to be rejected. That is distressing for Jewish readers and dangerous for Christians. Therefore attention must be paid to certain distinctions in the use of 'the Jews'. (i) The expression is never on the lips of Jesus, but always part of the author's story-telling. It may be (as has been suggested) that the author was influenced by the hostility in his own day between church and synagogue: in those who oppose Jesus he sees the hostile Jews of a later time. (ii) But that cannot be the whole story, for the main disputes between Jesus and 'the Jews' take place in the absence of disciples. (iii) Nor are 'the Jews' invariably hostile. In 8.30–31 and 12.9–11 many of them believed (in) him: elsewhere they were divided, some in favour, some against (10.19–21; 11.36–37, 45–46). (iv) But in most references 'the Jews' means 'the Jewish religious authorities', headed by the Pharisees. They suspect sabbath-breaking and blasphemy (ch. 5) and raise objections to the bread discourse (ch. 6) in Galilee. In Judaea they seek to kill Jesus, intimidate people from talking openly about him and giving support (7.13; 9.22); they are puzzled and disturbed by what he says, judge that he is possessed, and try to stone him (7.15, 35; 8.22, 48, 52, 59; 10.31–33). Perhaps unorganised hostility becomes official, because in the middle of ch. 7 the chief priests and Pharisees try unsuccessfully to arrest Jesus (7.32, 45–52). The Pharisees object to self-testimony and to sabbath healing (8.13; 9.13–16, 40), and then Caiaphas gives his famous advice to chief priests and Pharisees at a meeting of his council (11.47–53). In the passion narrative the Pharisees are named in 18.3, but thereafter 'the Jews', often identified as the chief priests, provide officers for the arrest of Jesus, denounce Jesus and negotiate with Pilate, and demand crucifixion. When he *is* crucified, the inscription reads 'Jesus of Nazareth, King of the Jews', despite protest from the Jewish chief priests (19.19–22).

The Jewish refusal to accept that title is the condemnation they pass upon themselves, but that does not require Jesus to repudiate his people, to reject Jews as Jews. The saying to the Samaritan woman that salvation comes from the Jews (4.22) is confirmed by his dying word to his Jewish mother: 'There is your son', and by his risen word to his Jewish disciples: 'Receive the Holy Spirit' (19.26; 20.22). Nevertheless, it may be suspected that the Evangelist, writing long after the event, was influenced in describing the opposition to Jesus by the emotions of a later day, not untouched by Galilean suspicion of Jerusalem and not helped by an imperfect memory of the early Pharisees.

The Sign of Mobility

5.1–18   The festival is not identified, and the exact location in Jerusalem is obscured by odd grammar and textual variations, though modern excavations have discovered a suitable pool with colonnades, whether its name was Bethesda or (as in RSV, GNB) Bethzatha. After thirty-eight years (the time for a whole generation to pass away, according to Deut. 2.14) the cripple was healed instantly – so the motif 'no waiting for salvation', already evident in Samaria and Galilee, is forcefully repeated. But does the cripple *want to get well?* (v. 6), and what are the *sinful ways* which he must give up for fear of *something worse* (remembering that in 9.3 Jesus does not accept sinning as a direct cause of blindness)? The cripple's self-defence was his helplessness: '*I have no one to put me in the pool when the water is disturbed*'; but he is not aware of his real difficulty. The pool was presumably served by an intermittent spring, and the periodic bubbling of water, in popular superstition, was given a supernatural cause. According to the not-original words of v. 4, *from time to time an angel stirred up the water* and the first in could be cured. In other words, the healing power of God was spasmodic and only one sufferer, with energy and friends, could profit from it. What an appalling doctrine of God! When Jesus later says: '*Give up your sinful ways,*' that is what he means. In response to Jewish objections he says 'My Father has never yet ceased his work' (NEB), and that conviction is common to Greeks and Jews. In the Letter of Aristeas, written by a Hellenistic Jew about a century and a half before Christ, the question is asked 'What is the essence of godliness?' The Jewish answer is: 'The realisation that God is continually at work and that man cannot hide from him an unjust deed or an evil action.'[1] The pool of Bethesda was crowded with people who knew they were *blind, lame and paralysed*, but less certain of the unceasing work of God. They could therefore be a parable of the whole generation of Jewish people; and if anyone is puzzled by the supernatural knowledge possessed by Jesus (v. 6), the explanation is that he knew his contemporaries. The question *Do you want to get well?* is for the Jews to answer; but what right has Jesus to put it to them?

That begins to appear when we learn that the cripple was healed on sabbath. (It is characteristic of the Evangelist that he gives

---

[1]   Aristeas 210 (*OTP* II, p. 26).

information, not when the reader expects it, but when the writer thinks he should have it.) When Jesus said: *Stand up, take your bed and walk*, he did two things: he showed the immediacy of the cure, and he encouraged the man to break the sabbath rule against carrying burdens (Jer. 17.21).[2] He did so deliberately – not so much to devalue sabbath (for he surely knew that an attack on sabbath would impair Jewish self-definition) but to move into an area where God alone had the right to act. Every Jew knew that God had rested from his creative work on the seventh day (Exod. 20.8–11) though not from his work of ruling the world, i.e. in Jewish style 'judging' it (hence the reference to judgment in vv. 22–29). Hence Jesus defends himself by saying *My Father continues to work, and I must work too*. His sabbath work is to be understood like God's sabbath work. His questioners draw the correct conclusion that Jesus claims to be exercising God's judgment. His defence increases the offence. Jesus calls God his own Father (instead of the Father of Israel) and makes himself equal with God – not of course in the sense that he is what God is, but that he does what only God can do. The Jews 'can only conceive equality with God as independence from God, whereas for Jesus it means the very opposite'.[3]

The questions thus raised, about God's work and sabbath, are partly dealt with in the speech that follows but they also appear again elsewhere in the Gospel. Jesus performed another sabbath healing in giving sight to the man born blind, and that caused great perplexity (9.14–16), even though the possibility had already been debated in 7.22–24. That should be set alongside the Jewish anxiety about the sabbath of great solemnity when Jesus was dead (19.31).

WORK

The *work* of God has a special status in the Gospel, often displayed in *deeds* (as the plural is usually translated in REB, instead of 'works' which is now archaic in this usage). In a Jewish setting, a good deed is an action done in obedience to Torah and prompted by love for God and compassion for our neighbours. The work of God is to give sight to the blind (9.3–4). The Father lovingly shows the Son all that he is doing (5.20) and so commissions him to carry out that work and bring it to completion (4.34; 5.36; 10.25; 17.4). The

---

[2] The later rabbinic rules in Shabbath 7.2 (Danby, p. 446).
[3] Bultmann, *John*, p. 245.

Father dwelling in him does his own work (14.10). The deeds themselves show that the Son is in the Father, and the Father in the Son (10.38; 14.11), yet despite many good deeds performed by the Father's power, the Jews want to stone Jesus for blasphemy (10.31–37). Nevertheless, these deeds are critical: anyone who has faith in him will do what he does, and indeed greater things (14.12); anyone who sees his deeds and hates him is guilty of sin (15.24).

Jesus' Relation to God

5.19–30   Here Jesus makes his defence, and begins a counter-attack, in words that are of the greatest importance for understanding the theology of the Gospel. The speech uses several images (the son learning a trade from his father, the resurrection of the dead, the great judgment, the envoy being received as a prince) which sometimes seem to point in different directions. Yet they are held together by an arrangement of corresponding statements: vv. 19–20 correspond to v. 30; 21 to 28–29; 22 to 27; 23 to 26; and 24 to 25, in this case both beginning *in very truth*. The line of thought is set out in vv. 19–24, then repeated in reverse order.

It begins with *In very truth* (see Amen, p. 26) and is phrased in the third person, thus indicating an important, formal statement: Jesus is wholly dependent on God (hence 'the Father is greater than I am', 14.28) and therefore does and says what God says and does (hence 'The Father and I are one', 10.30). By asserting no independence, he makes the highest possible claim. The relation of Jesus to God uses this Gospel's favourite Father and Son imagery: it is as if a son were watching his father at work, and practising accordingly; as if the father, out of love for his son, shows him everything he does. Thus the activity of God finds expression in the masterpieces of Jesus (to use, for a moment, the old language of apprentice and craftsmanship). It is not as if Jesus first formed his own intention and then made submission to God's intention. From the beginning *I seek to do not my own will, but the will of him who sent me*. Thus he is God's envoy or Agent: the deeds he performs (such as the healing at Bethesda) are signs of God's activity and intention, and everything proceeds from love. (So 3.35: the Father loves the Son and entrusts him with complete authority; and 14.31: the Son loves the Father and does all that he commands.)

This carries the promise of *even greater deeds* – not more astonishing miracles (though that would be true) but the extension of God's healing power from one crippled man to a whole generation of Jews. That is indicated in v. 21 where *the Father raises the dead and gives them life*. For Jews, death was not simply the end of physical life (nor is it to us). Remember the Prodigal Son: 'This son of mine was dead and has come back to life' (Luke 15.24); and the converts at Ephesus, brought to life with Christ when dead because of their sins (Eph. 2.5). Death is separation from God, whether self-inflicted or not. The Bethesda cripple, paralysed for thirty-eight years, represents the living dead. The accepted Pharisaic answer was the double resurrection (modelled on Dan. 12.2–3) at the end of the present age: *those who have done right will rise to life; those who have done wrong will rise to judgment*, i.e. condemnation (vv. 28–29). The rights and wrongs of a social community are clearly in view and, in the end, they must be dealt with. But before that final judgment the Son, acting for the Father, *gives life as he chooses*. He sets his own choice, not against the Father's choice (which would contradict v. 30), but against the demand for reward and punishment. God does not stand behind Jesus as an implacable judge, for the Father *has given full jurisdiction to the Son* (v. 22) for as the *Son of Man* he represents our humanity in the heavenly world (v. 27). That sudden shift from Son to Son of Man betrays the influence of Dan. 7.13, 22. It reminds us that Jesus is not only God's Agent for dealing with his people but also the people's representative before God; and leads us to interpret *jurisdiction* and *authority to pass judgment* as referring to the government of the world (cf. 'the Lord is our judge, the Lord is our ruler, the Lord is our King; he will save us', Isa. 33.22). It then follows (v. 23) that God's Agent is to be honoured as God is honoured. To refuse honour to the Son is to dishonour the Father. Thus the Son is not a second deity alongside the Father (to think so would be to adopt a gnostic view of deity); indeed (v. 26) the Son *has life in himself* only as the gift of the Father who is the one self-existent being, drawing no life from outside but possessing it in himself. It is with such a God that we have to do; it is of his life that we partake. Whatever kind of death describes our existence, we may *hear the voice of the Son of God and . . . come to life*. If we put our trust in God who sent his Son, we already have eternal life; we are not bound for judgment (i.e. condemnation), not even self-condemnation, for we have *already passed from death to life* (vv. 24–25).

To speak of passing from the world of death to the world of life sounds at first like the promise of gnostic religion. The gnostic *knew* that he had an undeniable claim to move out of this world of illusion and return to the world of reality from which he came. The Christian *knows* that this world is not illusory, for it is the place where the Son and Agent of God gives his signs and performs his deeds. There is no inherent right to a place in the heavenly world: only the certainty that the Son of Man is our representative. We therefore learn to live in the world without succumbing to it.[4]

FATHER AND SON

The passage just considered is the only extended speech by Jesus about the Son of God. References are almost always in the third person, here and in the more scattered references in chs. 6, 8, 11, 14 and 17 (an exception in 10.36). Jesus is acknowledged as Son by John (1.34, but see p. 24), Nathanael (1.49), and Martha (11.27), and rejected by the Jews (19.7). The title appears in statements by the author in 1.18; 3.16–18, 35–36; and 20.31. The synoptic gospels produce more but different acknowledgements: by the divine voice (Mark 1.11; 9.7), by demons (Mark 3.11; 5.7), by the centurion (Mark 15.39), and by disciples (Matthew, Luke). There is little in sayings of Jesus: in Mark 14.61f. the High Priest asks Jesus whether he is Son of the Blessed One, and he says 'I am' (though not in Matt. or Luke). In Matt. 11.27/Luke 10.22 Jesus utters a sentence about the Father and the Son in thoroughly Johannine fashion.

In this Gospel the sonship is even more impressively shown by the very numerous references (especially in chs. 5, 6, 8, 10, 12, 14–17) by Jesus to 'the Father' and 'my Father' and by his prayers which begin by saying 'Father'. A comparison with the synoptic gospels is again instructive:[5]

	Mark	Matt./Luke	Luke	Matt.	John
The Father	1	1	2	1	70
My Father	0	1	3	13	25
Father (prayer)	1	3	2	1	9

[4] Haenchen, *John*, vol. I, p. 252.
[5] See J. Jeremias, *The Prayers of Jesus*, London and Naperville 1967, reproduced in J. G. D. Dunn, *Christology in the Making*, London and Philadelphia 1980, ch. 2.

The great frequency of Father and the lesser frequency of Son prompts two comments. (i) Jesus talked more about God and less about himself, and even then only that his hearers might reach God through him. (ii) 'In the first century AD "son of God" and "god" were used much more widely in reference to particular individuals than is the case today.'[6] When this Gospel, therefore, wished to present Jesus to the Hellenistic world, it was sparing in its reporting of Son-language in comparison with its insistence on the priority and character of the Father. See the note on Awareness of God, p. 15.

Three Witnesses

5.31–47 Jesus has stated his defence against the charge that he claims equality with God and defies God's law. But self-testimony by itself is not valid. In ancient trial procedure, witnesses are required who will give support to the accused and will attack the accusers; and the business of the judges (who are also the jury) is to question the witnesses, assess their reliability, and decide what should be done for the general good. To bear witness or testify is to put your knowledge, experience and reputation behind a statement or at the service of a friend in need. Jesus, however, follows the principle stated in I John 5.9, 'We accept human testimony, but surely the testimony of God is stronger' and therefore calls God as his witness (v. 32), following the model of Job: 'My witness is in heaven; there is One on high ready to answer for me' (Job 16.19). How will God's testimony be presented? (i) By the word of his most recent prophet (vv. 33–35); (ii) by the evidence of the work that Jesus does for the Father (vv. 36–38); or (iii) by the understanding of scripture (vv. 39–47)?

(i) We have already heard John's testimony to himself as the wilderness voice (1.19–23; 3.28) and to Jesus as the light, the possessor of the Spirit, God's Chosen One (1.7, 8, 15, 32, 34). The accusers of Jesus once saw John as *a brightly burning lamp* but plainly the prophet's voice was for them not a divine but a human testimony. Therefore Jesus puts it aside in favour of *a testimony higher than John's*. In

[6] Dunn, p. 18.

consequence, neither in Jerusalem nor in the later Christian community does Jesus stand on the shoulders of John or of any prophetic figure.

(ii) *The work my Father has given me to do and to finish* should be satisfactory evidence that *the Father has sent me*. In this case, his appointed work was to restore mobility to a long-time cripple. Finishing the work would require extending that mobility to a whole generation of Jews. When the Jews reject this testimony they are failing to hear the voice of God, to discern the form of his presence. When Jesus puts forward his deeds and signs as witnesses on his behalf, he is not expecting them to be accepted as compelling marvels (remember what he said to the officer at 4.48). Like all witnesses they must be questioned, and their implications assessed, their consequences discerned. But that is impossible if *his word has found no home in you, because you do not believe the one whom he sent*. It is impossible to begin in distrust and then, by means of the 'miracles', be persuaded to trust: first believe on him, and then the testimony of the 'miracles' will be cogent and their consequences pressing.

(iii) For all Jews, however, the decisive appeal must be to the testimony of *the scriptures* (not only the five books of Moses, but also the prophets and psalms). In them they diligently sought for *eternal life* (v. 39). But how was the witness of Torah presented? Among the Pharisees, according to 'ancient tradition' or (as Jesus puts it in Mark 7.1–8) 'the tradition of men'. Interpretations of Torah were memorised, and cited by a particular teacher's name. Jesus complains that his accusers welcome some self-accredited interpreter, but give no welcome to him who is *accredited by his Father* (v. 43). Torah indeed offers eternal life, not however by following tradition but by approaching him to whom Torah bears witness (vv. 39–40). The teachers of tradition *accept honour from one another, and care nothing for the honour that comes from him who alone is God* (v. 44). It is a severe accusation, but not unknown to the ancient teachers. Rabbi Hillel (teaching at the time when Jesus was born) used to say: 'He who has gained a good name has gained (something) for himself. He who has gained words of Torah for himself has gained for himself life in the world to come.'[7] Jesus is concerned not with the rival reputations of teachers and their exegetical skills (v. 41 – a temptation as much Christian as Jewish: see I Cor. 1.12), but with the presence or absence of the love of God. Does that mean human love for God or God's

---

[7] Aboth 2.7 (Danby, p. 448).

love for humanity? Since love for God is shown in obedience to him, no one can doubt that the Pharisaic teachers intended everything to show love for God – as well as God's love for humanity. But *self-accredited* might have become self-deceived. Nevertheless it is not Jesus who is their accuser but Moses on whom they set their hope (v. 45). In ancient days Moses had been Israel's champion (or paraclete) before Pharaoh, and indeed before God (e.g. Exod. 33.12–23; Deut. 9.25–29); but now another had taken the place of Moses as their champion (according to his own prediction, Deut. 18.18). What Moses had said was not discarded; its full meaning was disclosed in Jesus (vv. 46–47).

What Jesus said about Moses and the Jews is obviously open to dispute. That dispute begins when Jesus teaches in the temple at Tabernacles (7.19–24). Before then, however, the scene is changed to Galilee which provides a detailed example of reinterpreting what Moses wrote. The narrative begins with the feeding of the five thousand (6.1–13) which is called a sign (2.14, 26), continues with the walking on the water (6.16–21) which is not called a sign, and then moves to the Capernaum synagogue for scriptural exegesis about the bread of life. It would be a superficial judgment to assume that only the feeding sign was developed in the bread-sermon, and that the walking on water was mechanically included simply because it followed the feeding in old tradition (as in Mark). Both episodes are present as scriptural illustrations – one for the benefit of the Jews, one for the disciples.

The Sign of Feeding

6.1–15   Whereas the sign at Bethesda was performed on a single person, this sign is done for *a large crowd of people*. Thus its symbolic significance for the Jews as a people is evident; though Jesus himself, by evading one form of political pressure (v. 15), takes his own independent line. Disciples are present but, apart from gathering *the pieces left over* at the end (perhaps a symbolic suggestion that there will be ample resources for their own later mission), they have a rather feeble role (on Philip and Andrew see p. 26). It is Jesus who takes the initiative, sees that the crowd needs food, and knows what to do. This is not only a feeding but also a test of faith (v. 6; see also

vv. 60–71). In these matters the Gospel differs from the synoptic tradition, as also in placing the episode at Passover (see p. 23). It is possible that the synagogue already had a cycle of scriptural readings in which the lections for the last sabbath of Passover were the crossing of the Reed Sea (Exod. 15) and the gift of manna (Exod. 16, Num. 11).[8] The loaves and fishes are provided by a boy (*paidarion*), and the loaves are barley bread. This recalls the famine in Elijah's time when a man brought him twenty barley loaves and a sack of grain (II Kings 4.42–44). He told his servant (called a *paidarion* in the Greek of II Kings 4.38, 41, though a *leitourgos* in v. 43) to distribute the food. When he objected: 'I cannot set this before a hundred men', Elijah insisted: 'They will eat and there will be some left over.' And so there was. It can scarcely be doubted that this manner of telling the traditional story was intended to imply that Jesus was no less a prophet than Elijah. And the crowd took the point: '*Surely this must be the Prophet who was to come into the world*' (v. 14). Moses had made the prophecy (Deut. 18.18), the people of Qumran expected it to be fulfilled,[9] and Jesus had indeed fulfilled it in true prophetic style – though he did not go further with the Qumran expectation of a king messiah and a priest messiah. Did the story also imply that Jesus was doing in public what (according to the synoptic gospels) he would later do in private at the Last Supper? When *Jesus took the loaves, gave thanks, and distributed them* was he performing a symbolic action which he would explain as eating his flesh and drinking his blood (vv. 52–56)? At this point Jesus was doing something much simpler, namely beginning a meal in the proper Jewish manner by blessing God for his gifts (or offering the thanksgiving, the *eucharistia*, as Greeks would more naturally say). That he did the same with the fish removes any direct eucharistic reference. That he said nothing, during the final meal with his disciples (ch. 13), about eating his body and drinking his blood makes it necessary to examine the synagogue sermon without assumptions derived from the synoptic and Pauline accounts.

So far the meaning of the sign is reasonably clear: Jesus is to be regarded as the great Mosaic prophet who can amply supply the needs of Israel in its time of difficulty. Later in the chapter, Jesus himself explains the symbolic meaning more fully. What then of the sign as 'miracle'? – if we are bold enough to ignore Jesus' disapproval

[8] A. Guilding, *The Fourth Gospel and Jewish Worship*, London and New York 1960, pp. 61–62.
[9] A Messianic Anthology 4Q175 (*DSSE*, p. 295).

of that enquiry (v. 26). This is not the place to develop a justification of miracles, but a few comments are in order. (i) The use of five loaves and two fish to feed so many people, with much to spare, is meant to be 'impossible' (on the principle that only God can do the 'impossible'). Any attempt to explain the feeding – the crowd were persuaded to share the food they had meanly concealed, or each person received a token crumb in a bare ritual – is a destructive expedient, and should be rejected. (ii) The older view of 'miracle' was dominant, by and large, when people accepted *that* a marvel had happened without asking *what* exactly had happened. They did not ask 'what?' because they had few means of raising the question, let alone answering it. We, however, ask it when we encounter some astonishing event, and can reasonably expect an answer – sooner or later. So we ask *what* happened when Jesus distributed bread and fish. But we cannot watch the hands of Jesus or get an answer from the Evangelist. So we have no way of assessing the sign as 'miracle'. (iii) The multiplication of bread and fish on a large scale is now commonplace, e.g. by modern agriculture and fish farming. But instantaneous multiplication has never formed part of the church's programme for feeding the hungry. Nevertheless, the teasing imagery of the feeding miracle is still powerful. It would be as unwise to reject it as to take it literally.

Danger at Sea

6.16–24   This section describes journeys across the sea of Galilee. The description is not quite satisfactory (though REB makes plausible sense of it) because the wording is sometimes perplexing. Ancient copyists found it so, and made changes in the text; so that it is no longer possible to be confident about what was written. Nevertheless it probably implies that Jesus fed the crowd on the eastern shore of the sea, opposite Tiberias; and that he, the disciples, and (some of) the crowd returned to Capernaum, north of Tiberias on the western shore, for the explanation of the feeding (v. 59). More important than topographical uncertainties is the realisation that 'the sea is no longer a threatening barrier, but a bridge between two hitherto opposing ways of life'.[10] Jesus shows that Jews may be fed in heathen territory

[10] Freyne, *Galilee, Jesus and the Gospels* (see p. 29 n. 5), p. 55.

by God's word, in a way that can be defended in the Jewish synagogue.

Because *darkness had fallen* (darkness often has symbolic force in the Gospel), the disciples began the return by themselves. They encountered contrary winds and rough seas (which also may be symbolic, though nothing is made of them here) and rowed for *three or four miles* (the direct distance to Capernaum is about eight miles). *They saw Jesus walking on the sea* and *were terrified*; but when they knew him and *were ready to take him on board, immediately the boat reached the land they were making for*. There seems to have been a double marvel: Jesus walking on the sea and the immediate conclusion of their crossing. (For the immediacy, see pp. 48–49.) It will scarcely do to suggest a comical confusion: that the disciples had lost their bearings in the dark and were in fact near the shore, where they came across Jesus walking *beside* the sea (as the same Greek is translated in 21.1). An attentive reader will hear an echo of Job 9.8, which (in the Greek version) speaks of God who 'by himself spread out the heavens, and walks upon the sea as on solid ground' (cf. Job 38.16). That in turn may lead to the divine Wisdom who says: 'Alone I made a circuit of the sky and I walked in the depth of the abyss. The waves of the sea, the whole earth, every people and nation were under my sway' (Ecclus. 24.5–6). Thus on the further shore the crowd has recognised Jesus as the great Mosaic prophet; on this nearer shore the disciples can learn that he is the divine Wisdom. In fact Jesus used an encouraging identification formula (v. 20), primly translated by REB *It is I; do not be afraid* – literally 'I am', implying 'I am Jesus whom you were expecting to join you' (cf. his similar reply in 18.5, 6, 8; and the blind man's answer in 9.9; see 'I AM', p. 61).

But *was* he the Jesus they were expecting? Presumably they expected him to join the boat in the ordinary way and to endure the whole journey with them. But this was a magical Jesus and a legendary journey. Is there anything, earlier in the Gospel or later, which suggests that the physical body of Jesus need not behave like our bodies? In all the other marvels that he performed he brought the power of God to bear, not on himself, but on people in danger. In this instance it is *not* called a sign (which points to *God's* activity and intention to help); it is a disclosure of the true nature of Jesus which in fact became plain to the community *after* the resurrection. Unlike the feeding marvel, which has a long explanation of its meaning as a sign, there is no direct discussion about the walking on the water. Instead, Jesus patiently explains its significance by the 'I am' sayings. The simple implication of the story is that the Christian community can expect Jesus to spring a surprise on them when, in the dark and the storm, they think he has abandoned them. That rather indefinite conviction is given definition by the 'I am' sayings, of which the first soon follows.

It comes in the course of a dialogue sermon for which the congregation provides the text and moves the exposition along by means of questions, requests, and complaints. Jesus follows customary synagogue practice in his manner of exposition, though he reserves a startling surprise for the end. The total effect is to give the commonplaces of existence – food, work, hunger and thirst, life and death, flesh and blood, heaven and earth – an inner significance, without diminishing their normal observable meaning. There are many possibilities of dividing the sermon. It seems sensible to make the divisions where the congregation intervenes with some strength: thus vv. 25–29; 30–40; 41–51; 52–59.

The Synagogue Sermon
6.25–59

6.25–29 Jesus rebukes his congregation for thinking only 'our hunger is satisfied'. Not that hunger is unimportant either to people or God: the feeding of the crowd is a sign of God's intention. But human beings do not simply live to eat. Ordinary food sustains a life that will end in death. A special food is needed for *eternal life*, and that will be given by *the Son of Man, for on him God the Father has set the seal of his authority* (see 5.27, and the note on p. 36). The congregation of course realises that the preacher is using food as a symbol for teaching or instruction. If Jesus is indeed the Mosaic prophet (v. 14), then he will surely give authoritative and binding Torah as Moses had done. *'What must we do', they asked him, 'if our work is to be the work required by God?'* His reply: God requires only that you believe in his Agent, *the one whom he has sent*.

SENT BY GOD

Jesus knows himself primarily as *sent by God*. The living Father sent him, and he lives because of the Father (v. 57; cf. 5.38; 7.29;

8.42; 10.36). He who sent him has not left him on his own, but is present with him (8.29), he is his witness (5.37; 8.18), and to him he will return (7.33; 16.5). In due course he will send out disciples as he himself was sent (17.18; 20.21), and from the Father he will send the Spirit (14.26; 15.26; 16.7). It is important to know that God sent him (11.42; 17.3, 8, 21, 23, 25), so that they should honour the Son as they honour the Father who sent him (5.23). Believing in him and seeing him, they believe in him who sent him, and see him (12.44–45).

The basic rule is that 'whoever receives me receives the One who sent me', and 'a messenger is not greater than the one who sent him' (13.16, 20). Jesus is sent to do what is pleasing to God (8.29); to seek his glory and do his will, not his own (4.34; 5.30; 6.38; 7.18). He gives the teaching of him who sent him (3.34; 7.16; 8.26; 12.49; 14.24; 17.8) and does his work (5.36; 9.4). In judgment he acts with God, though rather to save the world than to condemn it (3.17; 8.16). It is God's will that he should not lose those given him, though none can come to him unless drawn by the Father (6.39, 44).

6.30–40   On what grounds should they believe in Jesus as God's Agent? They need a sign; not, it would seem, a more astonishing marvel – for prophetic signs and wonders in themselves are possibly a betrayal of God, and thus merit death (Deut. 13.1–5). So a sign from scripture is needed (cf. Matt. 12.39/Luke 11.29 where Jesus is asked for a sign and produces the scriptural example of Jonah); and the congregation itself suggests the proper passage: *He gave them bread from heaven to eat.* Theirs was a composite memory: the words quoted are somewhat like Exod. 16.4 and 15, more like Ps. 78.24 with a touch perhaps of Neh. 9.15. Be that as it may, Jesus took them at their word and at once began to expound the four points of the text: (i) the word *He* means *not Moses* but *my Father*; (ii) change *gave* into *gives*, and the truth will be found not in what Moses once did but in what the Father now does; (iii) what Moses obtained, the manna, was *perishable food; the true bread from heaven* is now provided by God, and it *brings life to the world.* Thus vv. 32–35 are the response of Jesus to his hearers' text in v. 31. Then he takes up their remark in v. 30 about seeing and believing, and replies in vv. 36–40. But that is only the beginning, for he develops the theme of the *true bread* in vv. 41–48, and finally turns to (iv) the last words of the text, *to eat*, in vv. 49–58.

For the sake of the story-telling, it is assumed that the Capernaum congregation, like the later readers of the Gospel, were familiar with the homiletic use of bread as a symbol of divine Wisdom. According to Deut. 8.3, 'He afflicted you with hunger and then he fed you on manna which neither you nor your fathers had known before, to teach you that people cannot live on bread alone but that they live on every word that comes from the mouth of the Lord.' 'Word' can mean commandment or instruction (e.g. Exod. 34.28): therefore God's people live by his instructions, and it is possible that he may have instructions previously unknown, or new interpretations of old instructions. In Hellenistic Judaism, Philo comments on Exod. 16.4: 'Of what food can he rightly say that it is rained from heaven, save of heavenly wisdom which is sent from above on souls which yearn for virtue?'[11] When therefore the congregation says *Give us this bread now and always* (v. 34) they are expecting new instructions, or high-minded moral and mystical utterances. Instead, Jesus says *I am the bread of life*, and puts himself in the place of the divine Wisdom by adding: *Whoever comes to me will never be hungry, and whoever believes on me will never be thirsty* (v. 35). The reference to both eating and drinking suggests the Lady Wisdom who will give the godly man 'the bread of understanding and for drink the water of wisdom', so that 'whoever feeds on me will hunger for more; whoever drinks from me will thirst for more' (Ecclus. 15.3; 24.21). When Jesus identifies himself as the bread of life – i.e. the food which makes (eternal) life possible, and nourishes it, and allows it to grow – this is to be regarded as a self-disclosure of God who gives inner life to mankind.

I AM

The *I am* formula has already appeared (see p. 58) as a simple method of *self-identification*. To those instances can be added 4.26 where Jesus says 'I am (the Messiah you expect)' and the corresponding denials of 1.20; 3.28. It can also be used for *identification by origin*: 'I am from the world above . . . I am not from this world' (8.23) which carries with it 'unless you believe that I am (from the world above)' (8.24), and 'then you will know that I am (from the world above)' (8.28 – all this is disguised in REB). So also for *identification by association*: 'I am a witness in my own cause, and my other witness is the Father who sent me' (8.18) which has

---

[11]   Philo, *On the Change of Names* 260.

echoes of Isa. 43.10 in Greek: 'Become my witnesses, and I am witness, says the Lord God, and the servant whom I have chosen, that you may know and believe and understand that I AM.' Other passages in (Deutero-)Isaiah use the same words for the self-assertion of the deity: 41.4; 46.4; 48.12; as also Deut. 32.39. None of those passages bears close resemblance to the seven sayings of Jesus when he identifies himself by the analogies of bread, light, door, shepherd, resurrection, way and vine (6.35, 41, 48, 51; 8.12; 10.7, 9; 10.11, 14; 11.25; 14.6; 15.1, 5). The meaning of these sayings cannot be separated from the divine I AM, but their form seems to belong to a type of divine speech familiar in Hellenistic religion. In Prov. 8.1–31 the divine Wisdom announces her qualities and gifts: 'I have force, I also have ability; understanding and power are mine' (8.14). Outside Judaism the parallel is rather closer. An inscription beginning 'I am Isis the sovereign ruler of every region' records a lengthy hymn to this enormously popular deity of Egyptian origin. It includes such lines as 'I am in the beams of the sun,' and 'I am she who is called lawgiver.' In Poimandres, the first of the Hermetic writings, there is a vision of light and darkness. Poimandres explains 'I am that light, Mind, thy God.' Such examples from popular religion suggest that the Hellenistic world was familiar with I AM sayings whereby the deity disclosed his or her presence and effect. Nothing, however, approaches the seven sayings of Jesus in clarity, or in their consistent use to mark out what matters we are concerned with when we have to do with God. The I AM sayings are not so much attempts to work out a persuasive christology, as a sketch of what we can expect from God when we believe in his Agent – namely: nourishment, illumination, protection, recovery from disaster, direction, and community. Jesus takes the expectation of popular religion, joins it to the Jewish awareness of the sole majesty of deity, expresses it in images which he himself guarantees, and calls for faith.

But they *have seen and yet do not believe* (v. 36). So Jesus puts the case for faith with increasing rhetorical force: the Father gives, they come, and I accept them (v. 37). Not my own will but God's will; and it is God's will that I should lose not one of those he gives, but *raise them all up on the last day* (vv. 38–39). It is the *Father's will that everyone who sees the Son and has faith in him should have eternal life; and I will raise them up on the last day* (v. 40). Thus it was the will of God that prompted those who came, and prompted Jesus to accept them, that promised eternal life to those who saw and believed him, and backed the promise of Jesus that he would not lose them but would raise them up on the last day. But why raise them up if they already *have* eternal life? Because the double thought is present: that believers may indeed experience in this present age the life of the heavenly world, and also may have their share in the new age when this present age has ended. It is true that this Gospel insistently presents the *present* possibility of eternal life, and makes few direct references to the conviction (which scholars conceal in the world 'eschatology') that our present social condition must be brought to an end and replaced by something marvellously better. Lest it should seem to endorse the gnostic plan of abandoning the world and claiming our fulfilment in heaven, the Gospel introduces here (vv. 30–40; also in vv. 44, 54, and 12.48) the old imagery of *the last day*, meaning the day when this age is condemned and replaced. But another gnostic conviction is not so clearly avoided. *All that the Father gives me* (v. 37) might imply that God had given *some* to be believers, but not others. Gnostics knew that only some properly belonged to the higher world. It would have been a convenient way of explaining why Jesus provoked much unbelief, and finally reported that he had made the divine name known to those God had given him out of the world (17.6). The answer must lie in what is meant by *my Father's will* – namely his settled intention, the purpose to which his power is directed. It is his intention that *everyone should have eternal life*. That is what human beings are made for; that is why the Son of Man is their representative. So it depends on the will of God, and on faith. And since faith is not certainty, Jesus repeatedly makes the promise to raise believers on the last day.

6.41–51　Just as the Israelites in the wilderness complained to Moses (e.g. Exod. 15.24; Num. 11.1) so the hearers of Jesus *began to grumble* (the same Greek verb in both places). How could he be *the bread which came down from heaven* – both the provider and the provision? How can someone whose *father and mother* they know claim to have come down from heaven (taking up v. 38 which in turn took up v. 33)? These are serious and necessary questions, given the position from which the Galileans start. In relations between earth and heaven, there is the divine being on one side and human beings on the other: therefore a human being cannot have come down from heaven (i.e. they have not understood the meaning of Son of Man, p. 36). Further, what God provides for human sustenance (i.e. his Torah) is distinct both from God and the messenger who brings it. There was God who gave Torah on Sinai, and Moses who brought it down to earth, struck the rock and gave the manna. But Jesus is saying something else: that God *is* what he says, and that the messenger not only speaks the Word of God but *is* the Word of God.

In reply to the complaints Jesus reasserts v. 37 (when they come to him it is already the Father himself who draws them) and v. 39b (Jesus promises to exercise the life-giving prerogative of God). In their engagement with Jesus it is already God at work. Then (following the custom of synagogue homiletics) he supports that by introducing the subsidiary text from Isa. 54.13 *'They will all be taught by God'* (v. 45). This comes from an oracle which compares salvation to the rebuilding of a ruined city when 'your children will all be instructed by the Lord, and they will enjoy great prosperity'. It is God himself who makes his intentions known, says Jesus, and *everyone who has . . . learned from him comes to me*. It is true that no one has *seen* the Father (reverting to v. 36) except him who comes from God. Our approach to God is through hearing and believing, and by that means we possess *eternal life* (v. 47). But it is God himself who has worked on us to make this possible.

When Jesus now repeats the announcement *I am the bread of life* (v. 49, picking up v. 35) he returns to the *ancestors* who *had manna to eat in the desert* (v. 31) – and pointedly contrasts life with death. Manna was emergency food for starving people – *yet they are dead*. Better than manna is the bread from heaven that prevents death. He himself is the living bread from heaven; *if anyone eats this bread, he will live for ever* (v. 51) – and (he will surely say) I will raise him up on the last day. But no! Here is the startling surprise: *The bread which I shall give is my own flesh, given for the life of the world.* Using the symbol bread, Jesus has identified the message from God as life-giving food. He has said that he himself, not just the words he speaks, *is* that food. Further, that anyone nourished by that food will live for ever, for it is food of immortality. With an effort, that can be understood and welcomed: speaking in symbolic fashion, it says that eternal life is the result of God's disclosure of his intentions and our trust in Jesus. But *now* he says that he is concerned with the world (see pp. 17–19) and, to ensure its life, he will give – not his teaching or his intercessions – but his flesh (cf. 3.16).

6.52–59   Not surprisingly, this produces conflict among the Jews: *How can this man give us his flesh to eat?* We need not suppose them misled by the symbolic language. They mean: how can the giving of his flesh (presumably in death) promote eternal life? How can any action of the flesh promote the life of the spirit (for 'flesh can give birth only to flesh; it is spirit that gives birth to spirit', 3.6)? By implying such questions the Jews would be anticipating the views of some members of the later community who were eager for the spirit but wanted nothing to do with Jesus in the flesh (I John 4.2–3).[12] It would be easy to develop a gnostic self-confidence if eating the bread of life is exclusively commitment to Jesus as the divine Wisdom which alone makes genuine life possible. The surprising references to the death of Jesus are intended to correct such a tendency by asserting that the believer who possesses eternal life is unmistakably committed to sharing that death. *Unless you eat the flesh of the Son of Man and drink his blood you can have no life in you.* This no longer sounds like the divine Wisdom but a person of flesh and blood (the familiar Hebraic expression for genuine human existence). In v. 27 the Son of Man gives the food of eternal life; in v. 53 he gives himself – otherwise they are lifeless. But if they consume him they have *eternal life and* – here comes the safeguard against the demise of all this-worldly experience – *I will raise them up on the last day* (v. 54).

We cannot know whether the first readers of this Gospel were already familiar with one or more of the synoptic gospels, or with ancient tradition that lies behind all of them. No present reader can ignore the similarity between the words of Jesus in vv. 51, 53–55 and his words at the synoptic account of the Last Supper. Here he speaks of eating his flesh and drinking his blood; there he gave them bread to eat and said: 'This is my body' ('body' and *flesh* being possible alternatives for the Aramaic word he used). He gave them also a cup of wine and said (according to Mark): 'This is my blood'. And *my own flesh, given for (hyper) the life of the world* is similar to the longer text of Luke 22.19, 'my body which is given for (hyper) you'. Given our knowledge of the synoptic words, it is natural to suppose that the Evangelist knew them as part of the Last Supper but deliberately transferred them to the present setting. If so, why? (i) Perhaps because he needed to be specific about what believing required, namely consuming the real food and drink of the community meal (v. 55). The eucharist would then be, not a substitute for faith, but an expression of it. Yet that can scarcely be intended in a Gospel which omits these words from the final supper with the disciples,

[12] Grayston, pp. 120f., 18f.

and transfers them to an open synagogue service. (ii) Perhaps the words are really alien to a Wisdom sermon: the sudden change from bread and flesh in v. 51 to flesh and blood in vv. 53–56 is surprising. Could an editor be responsible for introducing sacramental tradition into a Gospel whose way of thought is non-sacramental? Something rather unusual is indeed happening, but it depends on what 'sacramental' implies. If by 'sacrament' is meant an action of Jesus which he designated with appropriate words as a means whereby faith first recognises and then grasps the benefits of God's goodness, the Gospel is rich in them.

But (iii) a reason can be suggested which is closer to the main thrust of the Gospel. Consuming human flesh and blood was repulsive to the people of antiquity. It is used here as a symbolic expression for the universally loathed act of crucifixion.[13] Believers in Jesus gain eternal life because he endured so shocking a death. They are not invited to eat him literally or even metaphorically, but they must stomach the thought that their experience of new life arises from his humiliating death. The aim of these verses is resurrection and life (v. 57), life defined by the promise that *whoever eats my flesh and drinks my blood dwells in me and I in him* (v. 56). But the way thereto is not only (as with the gnostic) by religious knowing and self-awareness, not only (as with the devout Jew) by Torah-obedience and Wisdom-instruction; but by sharing the death of Christ in whatever way is presented to us. If that is our meat and drink we shall live for ever.

The Testing of Disciples

6.60–7.1 If the quest of eternal life required believers to share the dreadful death of Jesus, it is not surprising that many disciples came to think the demand objectionable. The departure of many of them on that issue foreshadows the defection from the later community when (according to I John 2.19) 'they left our ranks' because – among other things – they believed that 'he came by water alone, not by water and blood' (I John 5.6). *Then what*, Jesus says to the objectors, *if you see the Son of Man* (who descended as nourishing heavenly food, 6.35–51) *ascending to where he was before?* Would you still object? For

---

[13] Proof in M. Hengel, *Crucifixion*, London and Philadelphia 1977.

the crucifixion of the heavenly Son of Man is not a descent into final humiliation but the beginning of a return to God. When his human opponents lift up his *flesh* on the cross (3.14; 8.28; 12.32, 34) *the Spirit that gives life* takes charge – in fact the Spirit which had come to rest on him (1.32) and was effectively present in *the words I have spoken to you*. Not other human words, not even charismatic words, but the words of Jesus are both *spirit and life*.

This is no longer a matter of unbelieving Galileans or hostile Jews, but of *disciples* who *drew back and no longer went about with him* (v. 66). Sometimes his (spirit-filled) words could not promote faith; sometimes they drew followers who fell away once they understood the requirement of being disciples. How could the divine Agent be so poorly served by the Spirit? The answer is twofold: *Jesus knew from the outset* (of each person's approach to him?) *who were without faith and who was to betray him* (betray, as in v. 71, is a key-word of the passion story); and *no one can come to me unless it has been granted to him by the Father* (vv. 64–65). Thus the work of Jesus is not marred by illusory hopes: he is working out the intention of his Father. It would be rash to draw the conclusion that God intended only a limited number to receive eternal life – other indications are decisive against that thought – but it may well be right that the Father required only a limited number to become agents of the Agent of God. That number included *the Twelve*; presumably known to readers of the Gospel, for they are nowhere else mentioned or explained. *Simon Peter*, as their spokesman, voices their agreement that '*your words are words of eternal life*' (cf. v. 63), and makes the formal confession: *We believe and know that you are God's Holy One*. That unusual designation marks Jesus 'as the one who comes from the other world and belongs to God, and indeed is the sole one to do so'.[14] The Twelve, chosen by Jesus, have true faith and right judgment – yet their support is not guaranteed. One of them, *Judas son of Simon Iscariot, is a devil* and later will betray him. That full form of his name probably records ancient memory when (of the several people named Judas) he was identified by his father and village (man of Kerioth). To say that he *is a devil* does not mean that he is possessed by a demon. This Gospel and the Epistles lack all interest in demon possession. The devil (*diabolos*) is a symbolic name for that which probes the weaknesses of God's people and perverts the undeserved generosity of God. Satan in Job 1–2 is the prototype. Both Satan and *diabolos* in origin mean 'accuser, slanderer'.

[14] Bultmann, *John*, p. 449.

It was a familiar practice to use them in denouncing opponents who seemed to threaten the community. This reference to Judas anticipates 13.2, 27; in this Gospel he is not the uniquely guilty disciple but the representative of all disciples who mar the work of Jesus. In any event, the betrayal and crucifixion were not unforeseen, unforeseeable accidents in the life of Jesus, especially as *the Jews* in Judaea *were looking for a chance to kill him* (7.1).

The Great Controversy
7.2–52

7.2–13   But remaining in Galilee was made difficult by the brothers of Jesus. They suppose that he hopes for recognition, that as yet he has made no impression in Judaea, that he should emerge from obscurity, and show himself to the world (see pp. 17–19). He should take advantage of Tabernacles, considered especially sacred and important by the Hebrews (according to Josephus[15]), and show his disciples the great things he was doing. It is clear that Jesus has no credibility with his natural family. So he is exposed as one of the many Galilean drop-outs, detached from the family network: like so many he must try his fortune in the great city. Family support is withdrawn – how serious for a Jew! Jesus, in his turn, rejects his brothers – first by insisting that he is working to a time-table: *'The right time for me has not yet come, but any time is right for you'* (v. 6). A typical riddling saying: not yet *the right time for me to* do my decisive action; *any time is right for you* to make the decision of believing. Second, by telling his brothers that they are part of the world (since the world loves its own) whose wickedness he must expose (cf. 3.19–21) and whose hatred he must bear. Third, by not accepting their cynical advice to make a demonstration at the festival. They themselves should go up to it, for this joyful harvest festival is also a reminder of separation from the world when the Lord brought his people out of Egypt (Lev. 23.23–36, 39–43). So they went and he stayed. *'I am not going up to this festival* in response to your challenge' . . . though *he went up too, not openly but secretly* when the time was ripe. Ancient copyists (like modern interpreters) thought

[15] Josephus, *Antiquities* 8.100.

that Jesus had been economical with the truth, and so changed '*I am not going*' in v. 8 to 'I am not yet going'. But that enfeebles the refusal, and the perplexing wording must be right. By this means Jesus devises a noticeable absence. Before he arrives he is under discussion: is he *a good man* or is he *leading the people astray*? (for which the penalty in Deut. 13.1–5 and in Qumran was death[16]). So he went up to Jerusalem, not to perform new signs, but to continue his defence begun in ch. 5. Anyone who thinks the gap between chs. 5 and 7 intolerable cannot be remembering how long disputes last in the Middle East (and not only there). He goes in fact to confront the settled hostility of 'the Jews' (see pp. 46–47).

From this point to the end of ch. 10 Jesus is in Jerusalem, in conflict with the Jewish authorities. The rather disorganised controversies at Tabernacles occupy chs. 7–8 (with a surprising intrusion in 7.53–8.11). The giving of sight to a man born blind (ch. 9) defines the main question, and Jesus offers the Jews a way of responding, in his use of biblical shepherd-imagery; but they remain divided (10.1–21) . At the festival of the Dedication there is open hostility, and Jesus withdraws (10.22–42).

7.14–52   At mid-festival Jesus began teaching in the temple. The Jews were astonished not so much *at* his teaching but *that* he taught at all. *How is it that this untrained man has such learning*? That was an entirely proper question, for a trained teacher carries the assent of the community; an untrained teacher may, from ignorance or malice, teach what is destructive of the community. All Jewish instruction was related to the teaching of scripture. It was necessary to ask: does the teaching come from a recognised, well-tried tradition? or does scripture contain within itself what this teaching recognises and develops? or does this teaching adjust the tradition to practices now approved by the community? It was all the more necessary to ask these questions because, at times, Jesus was given to arguing in the manner of traditional teachers (examples in vv. 22–24; 8.17–18; 10.34–36), and ought therefore to abide by their rule: that truth is agreed when it is in line with tradition and expresses a consensus of opinions. But what if tradition imprisons the truth, if consensus misreads it? Jesus disclaims all responsibility for what he teaches: *My teaching is not my own but his who sent me* (v. 16). What God requires of his people is sought not in tradition nor in consensus but in God

---

[16] Damascus Rule xii.3 (*DSSE*, p. 76).

himself. Only someone who says: 'Not my own will, but the will of God' will know whether *Jesus* truly says 'Not my own will, but the will of God' (v. 17). A self-instructed teacher seeks influence for himself; an Agent seeks to increase the influence of the one who sent him – and so can be trusted to do precisely that (v. 18).

Jesus now carries the attack to his critics, for the sake of argument adopting a stance of separation from them. *Did not Moses give you* (not 'us') *the law? Yet* (by your treatment of conflicting demands) *not one of you keeps it* (literally and totally). In that case, *why are you trying to kill me* (because I allowed the law's larger obligation to override one commandment)? The argument is straightforward if the necessary supplements are made (and anyone who reads the Mishnah learns to do that). It need not be denied that passages such as this reflect later debate between Jews and Christians; but surely they were intended to make sense in this narrative as it stands. And so they do. The crowd think that Jesus is obsessed by the threat of death (v. 20 – though they begin to realise his danger in v. 25); but he defends himself against the charge of sabbath-breaking and thereby opens out the purpose of his mission. The argument can be put like this: keeping the sabbath, which is the distinctive social practice of Jews, is of absolute obligation in Mosaic Torah. So is circumcision, the distinctive mark of male Jews. Since circumcision originated *with the patriarchs*, it takes precedence if the eighth day after birth falls on sabbath. Hence, if in special circumstances work can be done on sabbath to deal with one part of the body, how much more is it possible to do work on sabbath if the whole body needs attention. It can be replied that the Bethesda healing could have been postponed for a day, but that had been said for thirty-eight years. If the cripple and his treatment is symbolic of the whole generation of Jews, then the sooner the better – and especially on the Lord's day (cf. 9.14). *'Stop judging by appearances*; judge the situation as it really is' (v. 24).

Some of the people of Jerusalem begin to feel that this teaching is indeed risky. Why is he allowed to speak publicly? *'Can our rulers have decided that this is the Messiah?'* (vv. 25–26). Yet according to one expectation, Messiah's origin would be wholly mysterious. Two writings from the end of the first century perhaps encourage that view: 'No one on earth can set eyes on my son and those who accompany him until the appointed day' (II Esdras 13.52); and the Chosen One 'was concealed in the presence of the Lord of the Spirits' (I Enoch 48.6). Once again, the perplexity of the people raises the right question: where does Jesus come from? At one level the answer is easy: he comes from Nazareth in Galilee, and such an origin makes no claim upon their attention (see vv. 41, 52). On another level he is mysteriously *sent by one who is true* as his Agent, *'and him you do not know'* (v. 28), i.e. they do not know God as the hidden origin of Jesus. If his hearers were touched by gnostic religion, they would speculate about their own true origin. The Christian answer was to concentrate on the true origin of Jesus and to believe in him.

Among the people many believed in him: whatever the theoretical expectations, might not a person who did such signs be Messiah (v. 31)? But others were hostile, and Jesus knew that his time was short. Until the moment came he was divinely protected against arrest (vv. 30, 32). The short span of his Agency will come to an end: *'then I am going away to him who sent me'*. Then *'where I am, you cannot come'*. Is that a threat that Jerusalem Jews will be denied eternal life? Is he turning his attention to Jews dispersed in the great cities of the Roman world? Or is he abandoning his own people and offering his teaching to Gentiles? (vv. 34–35). Must the Jews defend the traditions of their fathers and reject Jesus, or accept Jesus and embrace Hellenistic religion with its tainted origin in Galilee? The chief priests and the Pharisees were not wholly wrong in thus defining their predicament; and with Jesus gaining support, they were under great pressure.

On the last and greatest day of the festival Jesus gave them his answer: in the manner of Moses who produced water in the wilderness for desperate Israelites, so Jesus offers life-giving water to his own wilderness generation. Two ways of reading his words are possible:

> *'If anyone is thirsty, let him come to me and drink.*
> *Whoever believes in me – as scripture says,*
> *"Streams of living water will flow from within him." '* (REB)

That probably implies that the believer will drink from Jesus and then himself become a source of water for others (cf. 4.14). Otherwise:

> *'If anyone is thirsty, let him come to me;*
> *Whoever believes on me, let him drink.*
> *As scripture says,*
> *"Streams of living water shall flow from within him." '*
> (REB mg and NEB)

That probably implies that Jesus is the sole source of living water. It is not easy to be sure which reading was intended and expositors disagree. There is no single passage of scripture that fits the quotation, but of course water imagery is common. The *believer* could be suggested by Prov. 18.4: 'The words of the mouth are a gushing torrent, but deep is the water in the well of wisdom' (perhaps also Isa. 58.11). *Jesus* would be suggested by Ps. 78.15–16, 'He split the rock in the wilderness and gave them water to drink . . . ' (perhaps also the water flowing from the temple, Ezek. 47.1–12). In view of v. 39, either interpretation could claim support from Isa. 44.3: 'I shall pour down rain on thirsty land, showers on dry ground. I shall pour out my spirit on your offspring and my blessing on your children.' Both interpretations must be in any reader's mind; but here the stress falls on the offer that Jesus makes, not on the subsequent endowment of believers. That is reserved for the farewell to disciples, and even there it is insistently said that Jesus (not the disciples' enthusiasm) is the source of the Spirit. And here too the Spirit, as a communal experience, is not available until Jesus has *been glorified* (v. 39), i.e. until he has returned to him who sent him. But here and now, if there are hearers who have a thirst for God, he (like the divine Wisdom) offers them satisfaction.

Tabernacles was a cheerful festival which, if anything went wrong, could become a riot. According to Lev. 23.40 there were seven daily processions of people carrying 'the fruit of citrus-trees, palm fronds, and leafy branches, and willows from the riverside'. About eighty years before the birth of Jesus, the festival crowd quarrelled with the high priest and pelted him with lemons as he stood to sacrifice.[17] According to the Mishnah, there were other, non-scriptural ceremonies: the seven-days water-pouring on the right of the altar, and the illumination of the Court of the Women by enormous candelabra. It is often suggested that Jesus' promise of running water was prompted by the festival custom (an old rain-making ceremony), even though the water was poured away and not drunk. It seems improbable that at least Gentile readers of the Gospel would possess such cultic information, or that any readers would find it necessary for understanding what Jesus meant. If he did take notice of the water-pouring, what he said must have been by way of protest.

The offer of water reminds some hearers of Moses; they therefore identify Jesus as *the Prophet* (see Deut. 18.18). Others speculate about Messiah but are promptly told (in contradiction of v. 27) that Messiah will come from *David's village of Bethlehem*, according to Micah 5.2–4. Since that was only six miles south of Jerusalem, the prophecy was convenient to the Judaean authorities for keeping control of messianic

[17] Josephus, *Antiquities* 13.372–3. Sukkah 4.9 and 5.2 (Danby, p. 179).

pretenders (cf. Matt. 2.3–8) though at the moment *no one laid hands on him* (v. 44). Indeed the *temple police* had been ineffective and the Pharisees (who in this Gospel seem to have more official power than otherwise they are known to possess) give way to panic. They abuse the officers for having been impressed by Jesus, the *rabble which cares nothing for the law*, and one of their own number (*Nicodemus, the man who once visited Jesus*) for suggesting that they *first* give him *a hearing*. They are gripped by deep passion for the law and suspicion of Galilee – even to saying that *the Prophet* (v. 40) does not *come from Galilee*. In fact, almost all witnesses to the text say 'the prophets' (REB mg): in which case the Pharisees would have ignored Jonah (II Kings 14.25).

The Charge of Adultery

7.53–8.11   At this point (in the canonical text) the confrontation is interrupted by the episode of the woman accused of adultery. It was not originally part of the Gospel, and may not have been added until the third century. It is generally regarded as a reliable item of oral tradition, specially treasured among Western Christians. Although known, it may not have been written down earlier because its attitude to adultery was suspect.[18]

The scribes and the Pharisees allege that the *woman was caught in the very act of adultery* (v. 4). Doubtless the charge was admitted, and the family had already made the usual arrangements for the wife to be divorced and for the man (who is absent from this scene) to pay heavy compensation. But some religious men would like to enforce – at least against the wife – the old Mosaic command that both parties to the adultery should be put to death by stoning (Lev. 20.10; Deut. 22.22–24). They hope to entrap Jesus who is known to have rigid views on adultery (Matt. 5.28). If he accepts the family arrangement, he will discredit his interpretation of the commandment; if he agrees

[18] John 7.53–8.11 is placed after 7.52 by one early Greek manuscript and by the majority of later ones (in some between asterisks), by the earliest Latin version, and by some other versions. No Church Father gives evidence for the story before the fourth century. In manuscripts from the eleventh to the fifteenth centuries, one places it after 7.36, a group place it after 21.25, and another group after Luke 21.38. In wording and style the passage resembles Luke rather than John. The story was perhaps known to Bishop Papias of Hierapolis at the beginning of the second century.

with stoning he will provoke hostility from the family (and perhaps, if Jews could no longer apply the death penalty, from the Romans). But are they asking Jesus to give a serious ruling? Then where are the witnesses? In a Jewish trial you do not *believe* witnesses, but *question* them – separately. (The trial of a bogus charge of adultery in Daniel and Susanna 50–59 is essential reading for understanding this story.) What had they really seen? Had they warned the wife and tried to rescue her from her danger? When *Jesus bent down and wrote with his finger on the ground*, he clearly meant: 'Your accusation can be inscribed in dust'. *When they continued to press their question, he . . . said: 'Let whichever of you is free from sin* (in bearing witness against this woman, take the responsibility of an honest witness (Deut. 17.7) and) *throw the first stone at her'* (v. 7). They departed, and no one condemned her to die. Jesus said: '*Neither do I condemn you* to die. *Go; do not sin again.'*

This contrived episode has nothing to say directly about modern attitudes to adultery, but it may prompt reflections about a definition of adultery which bears chiefly on the wife. Tannaitic Judaism (the rabbis close in time to Jesus) was aware of the injustice; and it should be noted that the Greek text of v. 10 has Jesus address the woman with the same courtesy as he used to the Samaritan woman, to Mary Magdalene and to his mother (4.21; 20.13, 15; 2.4 and 19.26). But why was the episode included in the Gospel at this point? When the controversy continues in ch. 8, Jesus will speak very harshly to the Jews, even to those who believed in him. If it is right to regard the signs as parables of God's people, may it not be possible to regard this woman and her treatment in a similar way? If so, the story was so placed that we might hear Jesus saying to the Jews: 'Neither do I condemn you to die.'

The Controversy Renewed

8.12–59 The narrative resumes with an I AM saying and reaches a climax with 'Before Abraham was born, I AM.' The controversy is marked by cross-purposes and sudden variations. The arguments sometimes seem weak and evasive; the cross-accusations are often offensive. This may be explained, in part, if the narrative has been written to take account of the community's later disputes with the synagogue; but the reader is obliged to ask why the opponents of Jesus opposed him, and why Jesus exercised patience with such severity. A simple interpretation of this section would be a misinterpretation. The opening offer of illumination (v. 12) leads to a dispute (conventionally divided into vv. 13–20, 21–29, and 30–59) which is dramatically transformed by the sign of ch. 11.

Jesus presents himself as *the light* needed to save people in this dark *world*. This theme was announced in the Prologue (1.4, 5, 9) and is now extended by the promise that *no follower of mine shall walk in darkness; he shall have the light of life*, i.e. the illumination which describes what life is and also makes it possible. This is different from a light to help us find our way in the dark (much as that is needed); it is a light to banish the dark: 'The darkness is passing and the true light already shining' (I John 2.8). 'I have come into the world as light, so that no one who has faith in me should remain in darkness' (12.46). This imagery was widespread in the ancient world. 'The righteous ones shall be in the light of the sun and the elect ones in the light of eternal life which has no end . . . They shall seek light and find righteousness with the Lord of the Spirits' (I Enoch 58.2f.). The members of the Qumran sect were 'sons of light', receiving this blessing from their priests: 'May He lighten your heart with life-giving wisdom and grant you eternal knowledge! May He raise His merciful face towards you for everlasting bliss!'[19] For these devout Jews, the illumination was Torah properly understood. Somewhat the same were Jews known to Paul who were confident that they could enlighten the benighted because in the law they saw the embodiment of knowledge and truth (Rom. 2.20). There were Christians in Matthew's community who thought themselves a 'light for all the world' (Matt. 5.14) when they knew the Beatitudes and the Sermon on the Mount. But this I AM saying belongs to a different kind of self-knowledge, closer to the Odes of Solomon. 'The Lord has directed my mouth by his Word, and has opened my heart by his light. And he has caused to dwell in me his immortal life, and permitted me to proclaim the fruit of his peace . . . (*Christ speaks*) . . . And the traces of light were set upon their heart, and they walked according to my life and were saved, and they became my people for ever and ever . . . ' 'A lamp you set for me both on my right hand and on my left, so that there might not be in me

---

[19] Community Rule ii.3f. (*DSSE* p. 63).

anything that is not light.'[20] Nothing suggests that knowledge of festival illuminations would help us to understand what Jesus said.

Not without reason, the Pharisees are sceptical. It was well known that 'Your word is a lamp to my feet, a light on my path', and that God's word comprises precepts, statutes and commandments (Ps. 119.105, and *passim*). Jesus ought to be speaking in a tradition and with an authority behind him, but *'you are witness in your own cause'* (v. 13). In this utterance he does not even call on the testimony of John, the signs and scripture (see on 5.31). Why not? To bring out what is required by a decision to believe in him. How can he bring forward witnesses, supporters and authorities if he is offering the life of the heavenly world? He alone is in a position to know what he is offering and whether his offer is genuine. He alone knows *where I come from*, and *where I am going* (v. 14; cf. 9.29–30). He knows his origin and destiny. That knowledge is indeed the aim of gnostic enlightenment; and the language is adopted in the Gospel to claim for Jesus the exclusive right, as Son of Man, to deal validly with the comprehensive need of mankind. While his critics are operating in the Pharisaic world of sanctification rules, Jesus takes no part in *passing judgment* (v. 15). If his saving activity leads to judgment (as indeed it must) it is the necessary consequence of accepting his knowledge of origin and destiny. He speaks as the Agent of the person who sent him (v. 16). This confrontation is not the case of an accused person who acts freely and must produce witnesses in his favour, but of a Son who appears as Agent of his Father (vv. 17–18). This brings the debate back to the Father and Son theme of 5.19–30, and to the suspicion that 'by calling God his own Father, he was claiming equality with God' (5.18). The Pharisees cautiously ask *'Where is your father?'* If later, Philip can say: 'Show us the Father' (14.8) his questioners can be excused for this probing enquiry which allows Jesus to withdraw to a safe position. A father is someone whom one acknowledges and respects, whose will one carries out. Was the father of Jesus associated with temple, or Torah, or tradition (like father Abraham in the parable of the rich man and Lazarus, Luke 16.19–31)? Jesus, however, is uncompromising: *'If you knew me you would know my Father too'* (v. 19). He cannot of course deny that, in a way, they know both him and God – but they do not know him as sent by God, or God as the Father who sends him.

Jesus begins the next phase with a threat: he will go away and

[20]   Odes of Solomon 10.1, 2, 6; 25.7 (*OTP* II, pp. 743f., 758).

leave them to their fate. *'You will die in your sin'* (v. 21) or *sins* (v. 24), i.e. you will die because your condition cannot grasp life and sustain it. In this setting, *sin* has a special meaning. In common speech, *sin* is the neglect or defiance of a commandment (so frequently in ch. 9; and in matters of community discipline in 20.23). But here *sin* is the condition of those to whom Jesus says: *'Your home is in this world, mine is not'* (v. 23). The Pharisees are by no means without perception: *'Perhaps he will kill himself'*, they say. This going away where they cannot come may be some extravagant action to induce God to act (cf. 'I may give my body to be burnt', I Cor. 13.3). As Christian readers know, they were not far from the truth; but the point that Jesus makes is different. They belong to the world below, he belongs to the world above; and the only way from this world to that is by believing that *'I AM what I am'* (i.e. from above, v. 24). So the Pharisees ask *And who are you?* The answer in Greek is puzzling: it can yield the evasive words *'What I have told you all along'*, or the petulant reply *'Why should I speak to you at all?'* (REB mg.). It is better rendered: 'Precisely what I am saying to you.' That is, Jesus is not to be explained as a familiar type of leader from the world of religion or politics, nor as a strange figure from the turbulent world of apocalyptic. He is simply someone who comes from above as God's Agent, speaks truth and judgment and then returns. All he asks is that they should lift up the Son of Man (v. 28) – if they will, by honouring him as the Agent of the Father (5.23); if they dishonour him (v. 49), then by lifting him up on the cross. Whatever happens *'he who sent me is present with me, and has not left me on my own; for I always do what is pleasing to him.'* That statement already prepares our mind for reading about the crucifixion.

Many put their faith in him (v. 30) including some of the Jews, i.e. the religious authorities (see pp. 46–47). Jesus sets before them the condition and benefits of being his genuine disciples: *If you stand by my teaching* (and do not abandon it for other inspirations), *you will know the truth, and the truth will set you free* (to follow the proper way to God). If Jesus had been a visitor from Qumran his words might have been more welcome; for a member of the sect 'shall undertake by a binding oath to return with all his heart and soul to every commandment of the Law of Moses in accordance with all that has been revealed of it to the sons of Zadok . . . and to the multitude of the men of their Covenant who together have freely pledged themselves to His truth and to walking in the way of His delight.'[21] But Jesus was far from saying that, and the Jews objected vigorously: 'We are Abraham's descendants (argued out in vv. 37–40); we have never been in slavery to anyone' (taken up in vv. 34–36).

The true descendants of Abraham claimed Sarah as their mother, not the Egyptian slave Hagar. As Paul said: 'We are no slave's children; our mother is the free woman' (Gal. 4.31). Even when Jews used 'slave' as a self-description it was a proud courtesy, not a humiliation (as Abraham did when receiving the three divine visitants, Gen. 18.1–5). As much as the Greeks, the Jews were proud of their freedom – and Jesus expected it of his friends (15.15). One judgment that flowed from being the Agent of the Father was the perception that the Jews were in fact not free, but slaves of sin. They had *no permanent standing in the household*. Unlike the Son they were not aware of God's intention, and only the Son could set them really free (v. 36).

TRUTH

The words for *truth* in the Gospel are sometimes used in a special way. The adjective '*true*' means 'reliable, authentic': when applied to bread, food and drink, and the vine (6.32, 55; 15.1) it suggests that Jesus provides the reality of which these things are symbolic. The adverb '*truly*' implies that something really is what it seems to be. One would expect the noun '*truth*' to be associated mostly with statements (e.g. 'this is the truth, that is a lie'), or with speculative systems of thought (e.g. 'the truth of the incarnation'); and indeed the Gospel speaks of knowing and telling the truth (8.32, 40, 45, 46). But truth which sets you free (8.32) is to be understood from its opposite, namely sin which enslaves (8.34, 46). In a characteristically Hebrew phrase you perform the truth (3.21 'live by the truth'). Simply to believe or accept the truth leaves it external to your life; to perform it means that you can be rooted in the truth, the truth can be in you (8.44). In the Qumran writings *truth* means the Mosaic Torah as interpreted by the sect in preparation for the last days. The Master instructs members 'so that they may practise *truth*, righteousness and justice on earth and no longer stubbornly follow a sinful heart and lustful eyes committing all manner of evil'.[22] For Jesus, however, *truth* is not a reinterpretation of Torah

[21] Community Rule v. 7f. (*DSSE* p. 67).
[22] Community Rule i.5 (*DSSE* p. 62).

but a newly available way to God by belief in his Agent ('I am the way, the *truth* and the life', 14.6). And sin, the opposite of truth, is not simply wicked behaviour but being on a path that leads yourself and others away from God – and being unable to leave it. Sinners are not on that fateful path because seeing God truly they wilfully disobey him; but because they perceive God wrongly, and dreadfully worship the false image. That is why the question of *truth* is so important and so contentious.

The last phase of the controversy debates, in a rather involved manner, the contrasting claims between 'my father' and 'your father'. The Jews say: '*We are not illegitimate* (like perhaps the Samaritans, if that is how they regard them); *God is our father, and God alone*' (v. 41) (i.e. not God *and* his Agent, 'claiming equality with God'). Jesus retorts that they are not God's children because they do not listen *to the words of God* (v. 47) or indeed understand what he himself is saying (v. 43). '*I tell you what I have seen in my Father's presence*' (v. 38). '*I have told you the truth, which I heard from God*' (v. 40), '*but you do not believe me*, even though you cannot *convict me of sin*' (vv. 45–46). '*God is the source of my being, and from him I come – not of my own accord* but because *he sent me* – but you do not love me' (v. 42). Far from being a Samaritan (sympathiser) or possessed (with delusions of power), Jesus cares nothing for his own glory, only for the honour of God – and they dishonour him (vv. 48–50). He knows God and obeys his word, so God glorifies him. They do not: therefore '*you do not know him*' – a judgment that Jesus must make because God is judge (v. 50) and Jesus must *obey his word* (vv. 54–55). The Jews withdraw behind Abraham: '*Abraham is our father*' (v. 39), i.e. 'we rely on the promise to Abraham that God would abundantly bless him, and multiply his descendants, and cause the nations to envy his blessing' (Gen. 22.17–18). 'If that were so', says Jesus, '*you would do as Abraham did. He* welcomed God's agents, but *you are bent on killing me . . . because I have told you the truth, which I heard from God*' (vv. 37, 40). '*In very truth I tell you, if anyone obeys my teaching he will never see death*' (v. 51). Thus the teaching of Jesus goes beyond the ordinary calculations of life and death to the origin and destiny of all things – though, in the way he phrases it, it sounds ridiculous. What can Pharisees (who no doubt believe in resurrection) make of that claim, when Abraham and the prophets are dead? (vv. 52–53).

The answer seems to rely on the first part of an episodic scheme for relating God's dealings with Israel: the original creation by the

Logos; the second disclosure through Abraham and the patriarchs (7.22); the third through Moses and our fathers; the fourth through the prophets (Isaiah in John 12.37–41, as well as Ezekiel and Zechariah in John 10); and the final disclosure through Jesus. What Jesus brings, however, is not novelty but originality. *'Before Abraham was born I AM'* (v. 58), i.e. my existence expresses what has always been the intention of the Logos. *'Your father Abraham was overjoyed to see my day'* means that the patriarch was a whole-hearted witness to the promised blessing (in his laughter at the expected birth of Isaac).[23] Thus Jesus takes his message back to first principles, as he also does with the Pharisees' response: *'Your father is the devil and you choose to carry out your father's desire. He was a murderer from the beginning, and is not rooted in the truth; there is no truth in him. When he tells a lie he is speaking his own language, for he is a liar and the father of lies'* (v. 44). This most severe statement reintroduces *the devil* (see on 6.70 where *diabolos* is applied to Judas), a standard name for opponents who persistently resist the work of God, from fear, blindness or malice. The devil can be given a legendary image, e.g. 'It was the devil's spite that brought death into the world' (Wisd. 2.24); and he can be associated with the serpent who misled Eve (II Cor. 11.3). But it must be remembered that the Gospel contains no demon possession (except the accusations against Jesus in 7.20; 8.48, 49, 52; 10.20, 21) and records no exorcisms. Hence the devil-language is powerful emotionally but not to be interpreted literally. It is similar to the (now old-fashioned) Communist habit of calling their enemies 'fascist hyenas'.[24] Despite strength of language, Jesus in effect says no more than Stephen in Acts 7.51: 'How stubborn you are, heathen still at heart and deaf to the truth! You always resist the Holy Spirit. You are just like your fathers.' It was enough to infuriate his listeners and prompt them to take up *stones to throw at him* (v. 59).

---

[23] So interpreted in Jub. 15.17: 'Abraham fell on his face and he rejoiced and pondered in his heart whether a son would be born to one who was a hundred years old' (*OTP* II, p. 86).
[24] The Qumran Scrolls are full of Belial and other devil language, none of it to be taken literally.

The Sign of Restored Sight

9.1–41   The conflict is restated and brought into focus by the giving of sight to a man born blind. Jesus himself takes no part in the debate, except at the end to issue a judgment. The healing (vv. 1–7) is typical of folk-religion. It is taken for granted that any defect to a new-born child comes from the careless neglect of a religious taboo; and the disciples put the stock superstitious question to Jesus. He rejected their assumption, but followed the practice of a village healer by using spittle and dust to make a paste, smearing it on the man's eyes, and sending him to *wash in the pool of Siloam*, namely 'Sent', i.e. the blindness was to be sent away. And it was. It should be clear that this is nothing to do with baptism: there is no liturgy, no prayer, no repentance or response of faith. Not every mention of water implies the sacrament. But it is clear from vv. 4–5 that this sign is a parable of something greater. Jesus is the *light of the world: while daylight lasts we* (i.e. I and my Father) *must carry on the work of him who sent me*. In this naive and extraordinary healing we hear the questioning of Jews who say: 'Why were we born blind? Did we sin, or our parents?' And Jesus, in effect, replies: 'You are what you are that God's power may be displayed in curing you.'

The cure does not take place at once. The man is able to see, and knows himself as the formerly blind beggar (despite the doubts of his neighbours). '*All I know is this: I was blind and now I can see*' (v. 25). He begins with '*the man called Jesus*' (v. 11); under pressure says: '*He is a prophet*' (v. 17); stubbornly insists that he must be *from God* (v. 33); and finally, asked by Jesus: '*Have you faith in the Son of Man?*', says, '*Lord, I believe.*' Now he really sees that the person speaking to him is the one who communicates between earth and heaven (see p. 36).

The cure produces not only astonishment and uncertainty, but also disbelief. These consequences are displayed with dramatic skill. First the beggar is seen with his neighbours (vv. 8–12), then the neighbours involve the Pharisees because the healing had been done on sabbath. It need not be supposed that later Mishnaic rules were already in force, e.g. the prohibition of kneading anything on sabbath, or the carrying of enough water to rub off an eye-plaster.[25] It need not be supposed that the neighbours were sticklers for sabbath rules; but it may be that the Pharisees were, and were vigorously pressing

---

[25] Shabbath 7.1; 8.1 (Danby, pp. 106–107).

for them. When therefore the formerly blind man was taken to the Pharisees, the implied question would be: 'When a man can be healed like this on sabbath, why are your sabbath rules so negative?' There is the dilemma that divides them: *this man does not keep the sabbath* and so *cannot be from God*, but *how could such signs come from a sinful man?* The story must be false – as questioning of the beggars' parents will surely prove. But no! – when the surly and anxious parents give their testimony, it is not welcome to the Pharisees (vv. 18–23), for they know that *this man is a sinner* and see themselves as *disciples of Moses* defending the word of God (vv. 28–29). So doing they hand victory to this deplorable beggar *born and bred in sin* (v. 34). His argument – popular, but persuasive – runs thus: God grants benefits to the devout, not to sinners; it is an unheard-of benefit that the eyes of a man born blind should be opened; to do that Jesus must be from God. And so, without actually being present, Jesus dominates the scene throughout.

The disconcerted opponents are Pharisees, on whom Jesus pronounces a severe judgment (v. 40). Who they are is not entirely clear. In the Gospel the chief priests are the ruling group in Judaea. The Pharisees seem to be their ears and eyes: they make enquiries about John (1.24) and are interested when Jesus wins more disciples than John (4.1); they take note when people begin to compare Jesus with Messiah (7.31–32); they complain that his self-testimony is not valid (8.13); they are informed about his sabbath healing (9.13) and about the raising of Lazarus (11.46). The chief priests and the Pharisees send temple police to arrest Jesus and the Pharisees reprimand the officers when they return unsuccessful (7.32, 45–48). The chief priests and the Pharisees convene a meeting to consider the danger from Jesus, and give the order for his arrest (11.47, 57; cf. 18.3). In 9.15–16 it is the Pharisees who investigate the sabbath healing, though in vv. 18, 22 they are called *the Jews* (it was 'the Jews' in 5.16 who took action against him for sabbath-breaking). Thus the Pharisees often seem to be the most determined part of the religious authorities (see pp. 46–47 for this meaning of 'the Jews'), causing fear by their agreement *that anyone who acknowledged Jesus as Messiah should be banned from the synagogue* (v. 22). That Pharisees could be intimidating is known from Paul's example (Phil. 3.5–6 – much developed in Acts). That the elders of the congregation could exclude members permanently or for a period is known for Qumran and is probable for other Jewish societies. But 'there was no sin in making the error . . . of believing someone to be the Messiah',[26] and no ban was in operation if the opening chapters of Acts give a reliable picture. It is in any case surprising that the Pharisees should have been hand-in-glove with the Sadducean priestly families when it is realised that a famous paragraph in the Mishnah (composed before the destruction of the temple), excluding certain people from a portion in the world to come, is Pharisaic in origin and directed against the Sadducees and certain Hellenised Jews.[27]

It may well be that the Gospel narrative has been framed in terms that seemed appropriate after the destruction of the temple, when the Sadducees had disappeared and the Pharisees had become dominant. We lack sufficient information to verify the historical bearing of the account. But there can be no doubt about the theological conviction: that both priests and Pharisees are equally a hindrance to the truth, and that neither can give house room to those *who acknowledge Jesus as Messiah* (v. 22). Not that Pharisees are wholly condemned: Nicodemus pleads for Jesus to have a fair trial (7.50–52) and helps to give him proper burial (19.39–42). At the end of this story Jesus explains the judgment for which he came into the world, namely *to give sight to the sightless* (to illuminate those who know their need) *and to make blind those who see* (to remove the confidence of those who falsely think that everything is clear). When some Pharisees ask (anxiously or angrily?) *'Do you mean that we are blind?'* he replies: *'If you were blind* (and knew you were) *you would not be guilty, but because you* (confidently) *claim to see, your guilt remains'* (vv. 39–41). The Pharisees were truly devoted to sanctification; Jesus to salvation which is enlightenment.

Sheep and Shepherd

10.1–21   The opening of blind eyes is again mentioned at the end of the section, a brief renewal of the dispute whether Jesus is demented or not. Whereas Jesus, though absent, dominated the dispute in ch. 9, now he dominates by exploiting the shepherd imagery. No one

---

[26] L. H. Schiffman, 'At the Crossroads: Tannaitic Perspectives on the Jewish-Christian Schism', in *Jewish and Christian Self-Definition*, Vol. 2, ed. E. P. Sanders, London and Philadelphia 1981, p. 147.
[27] Schiffman, pp. 140–143.

should approach 10.1–18 without first reading – preferably aloud, and with passion – Ezek. 34. Jesus was not the first to denounce the Jewish leaders: the pre-exilic complaint of Jer. 23.1–4 was intensified by the exilic words of Ezekiel, and recast in the savage irony of the post-exilic oracles of Zech. 10.2–3; 11.4–17; 13.7–9. It is as if the Jewish people in Jesus' day were suffering 'internal exile' in conditions no more tolerable than their forefathers had known. Whose interests are served by the walls of the sheepfold: the safety of the sheep or the profit of the shepherds?

The imagery in 10.1–5 provides more a riddle (*paroimia*) than a *parable* (v. 6), a teasing suggestion that must be turned over and reflected upon. (In 16.25, 29 a *paroimia* is veiled language, the opposite of plain speech.) A flock of sheep is penned inside a yard, protected by a wall and adjoining a village house. It has a door and a guardian. The shepherd is admitted by the doorkeeper; he calls the sheep, of which he is the owner, by name and leads them out when they recognise his voice. The words *calls his own sheep* do not imply that there are other sheep in the fold *not* belonging to the shepherd (which would be an elitist gnostic thought), but simply that the sheep *belong* to the shepherd (a common meaning of 'own', *idios* as at 1.41). The sheep indeed are threatened by thieves and robbers, but *they do not recognise the voice of strangers*, and so *run away*. Thus far the riddle. It is not an allegory like *Animal Farm*, where every animal in the fable disguises a real actor on the political scene. It is a riddle which says: 'Look at your problem somewhat like this, and you should see the answer.' The problem is that Jesus has been accused of sheep-stealing. He is removing Jews from their true allegiance to Moses and demanding allegiance to himself. The riddle says: 'It is the chief priests and Pharisees who are the thieves and robbers.' The sheepfold image is controversial and defensive. There follow three explorations of the image: (i) vv. 7–10, (ii) vv. 11–13, (iii) vv. 14–16, and a theological comment vv. 17–18.

(i) The first exploration in 10.7–10 is the most difficult to understand. Surprisingly it explores the function of *the door of the sheepfold*: it does so in two stages, and makes it impossible to grasp the first stage before the second stage has yielded its meaning (a stylistic device not uncommon in this Gospel). Properly the door should ensure the safety of the sheep in the fold, should allow them to enter and leave and *find pasture* (v. 9). But in fact the door has confined the sheep in the fold where they are at the mercy of shepherds who *steal, kill and destroy* (v. 10). *Any who came* (to shepherd the sheep) *before me* (i.e. before I was in place as the door) *were all thieves and robbers*. (That is not a wholesale condemnation of previous Jewish teachers – remember Jesus' respect for the patriarchs, Moses, and the prophets (p. 80) – but an attacking reply to his present opponents.) But it is not God's intention that his people should be the prey of their shepherds; therefore *I have come that they may have life, and may have it in all its fullness*. It is therefore not specially odd that Jesus should say: '*I AM* (from the world above and therefore) *the door*' (in 14.6, 'I AM the way') – a tolerable Logos symbol of two-way traffic: cf. 1.51 and Jacob's verdict: 'This is the gateway to heaven' (Gen. 28.17).

(ii) In the second exploration (10.11–13) the sheep are no longer in the fold and in danger from sheep-stealers, but are in open pasture where a wolf may attack. *The hired man* (like the worthless shepherds of Zech. 11.15–17) may run away and leave the sheep to their fate, but not the *good shepherd* who owns the sheep. Any determined shepherd can drive off a wolf (in Palestine they came singly, not in packs), but he risks his life to do so. *Lays down his life* can scarcely be right (if he did the wolves would indeed grow fat): the odd Greek (*tēn psychēn autou tithēsin*) means 'he lays his life on the line'. Jesus is fully aware that his attacks on the Jewish leaders are dangerous; but God's people are in good hands and Jesus is willing to die in protecting them. The designation 'shepherd' was widely applied to great men in the ancient world, and is common in scripture. It is specially associated with David whom God 'chose to be his servant and took him from the sheepfold . . . to be the shepherd of his people . . . ; and he shepherded them in singleness of heart and guided them with skilful hand' (Ps. 78.70–72). Much later it was promised that 'My servant David shall become king over them; they will all have one shepherd. They will conform to my laws and my statutes and observe them faithfully' (Ezek. 37.24). Clearly that is remote from the intention of Jesus which looks more to Ps. 23, 'The Lord is my shepherd' and Isa. 40.11, 'Like a shepherd he will tend his flock and with his arm keep them together; he will carry the lambs in his bosom and lead the ewes to water.' When Jesus says '*I AM* (from above and therefore) *the good shepherd*' he is acting wholly in the character of the Lord.

(iii) The third exploration, 10.14–16, is about knowledge and enlightenment, a very common theme in Hellenistic religion. It is characteristic of *the good shepherd* that *I know my own and my own know me*. This mutual knowing does not derive from scriptural shepherd imagery; it cannot be deduced by meditating on the riddle. It is a revelation, which Jesus himself makes, of how he and his disciples are related. Two components of it are given in v. 15. (*a*) *As the Father knows me and I know the Father*: Jesus knows what the Father intends and is doing; and the Father knows (i.e. acknowledges) and honours the Son. Such is the model of our relation to Jesus (which theme is developed in ch. 17). (*b*) This knowing is not simply contemplative inwardness but also self-giving for the benefit of others: *I lay down my life for the sheep*. It is more than risking life (as in v. 11), for here the Hellenistic religion of enlightenment is being remodelled by taking account of the crucifixion. The death of Jesus was necessary for the enlightenment of the Jews and for the spread of light to the Gentiles. The shepherd lays down his life, not now to protect the sheep, but to make mediation possible and to give a special context to enlightenment. The extension of the one flock from a purely Jewish to a partly Jewish, partly Gentile community provokes Pharisaic hostility to the one shepherd.

The first theological comment in v. 17 is a defence against seeing the crucifixion as proof of God's displeasure. It is surprisingly evidence of the Father's love, i.e. his confidence in what the Son is doing and his confidence that he lays down his life *to receive it back again*. This establishes the principle: resurrection is not the meritorious reward for heroism or the compassionate dealing with tragedy, but the proof that eternal life arises only from surrendered life. The second theological comment in v. 18 defends Jesus against the thought that he died unwillingly. Jesus lays down his life to initiate the power of resurrection. In surrendering his life he acts in freedom within the possibilities genuinely open to him, not making the best of a bad thing but acting in the conviction that what is done in freedom creates freedom.

It is contentious stuff (vv. 19–21). It caused a division among the Jews. Was he demented – or opening blind eyes?

The Climax of Controversy
10.22–42

10.22–39   The running fight between Jesus and the Jews again breaks out in this passage. Questions and answers from earlier chapters are repeated and some features of later conversations with the disciples are anticipated.[28] This section sums up the basic conflict between Jesus and his disbelieving critics, records their verdict (in place of the Jewish trial in the other Gospels), and drops hints about his real defence which is disclosed to believers. The scene is Solomon's Portico (according to Acts 3.11; 5.12 a favoured meeting place for the earliest Jerusalem Christians), the time was winter (when storms could be expected), and the occasion was the Dedication (celebrating the reconsecration of the altar after its pollution by Antiochus some two hundred years earlier). Indications of time and place in the Gospel can often be read as giving the mood of a situation, as well as defining it. The encounter is provoked by an irritated demand from the Jews (who are tantalised, not 'kept in suspense'): *'Tell us plainly: are you the Messiah?'* (v. 24). But explicit statements of messiahship are rare. At the beginning of the ministry Andrew so acclaims him (1.41); towards the end so does Martha (11.27). Jesus so identifies himself to the Samaritan woman when she describes Messiah as 'he who will make everything clear to us' (4.25–26). Christians of course know that he is the Christos, the Son of God anointed with Holy Spirit (though even that is a matter of dispute within the community, cf. I John 2.20–22).[29] But what do the Jews mean by Messiah? Jesus had put shepherd imagery into their minds: were they thinking of Ezekiel's promise (see p. 85)? How could Jesus say yes to that? Was he to be the Shepherd Messiah or the Agent of the Divine Shepherd? Until the Jews had decided what they wanted the Lord's anointed to do, they could not have a plain answer. 'They demand an answer which would relieve them of the decision.'[30] They must simply judge whether the actions of Jesus are the actions of God (vv. 25, 37–38). In this matter he is quite explicit: what he does in gathering and protecting his flock and giving them eternal life is God's action, and it cannot be undone. Behind it stands the universal superiority of the Father (vv. 27–29). *'The Father and I are one* – not 'one and the same' but 'at one' (since one in Greek is the neuter *hen* – as in 17.11, 21–23): the Father is wholly committed by the actions of the Son, and the Son is wholly dependent on the decisions of the Father (v. 30). If they cannot or will not believe that, then they exclude themselves from

---

[28] Namely the evidential value of the actions of Jesus: vv. 25, 37, 38 (from 5.36); Jewish disbelief: v. 26 (from 6.36; 8.45); those who hear: v. 27 (from 8.47; 10.3); the ability of Jesus to protect his own: v. 28 (from 6.39); the attempt to stone Jesus: v. 31 (from 8.59); the charge of blasphemy: v. 33 (from 5.18). Also v. 28 is a preview of 17.2, 12; v. 30 of 17.21; v. 38 of 14.10–11; 17.21.

[29] See Grayston on the passage.

[30] Bultmann, *John*, p. 362.

the flock or show that they do not belong to it: *'because you are not sheep of my flock you do not believe'* (v. 26).

Does that imply that some Jews, by their very nature, are excluded from the saved people of God? It could be heard in that manner, and *the Jews picked up stones to stone him* (v. 31). But that cannot be the real intention, for Jesus urges upon them the good deeds done before their eyes, and says *'even if you do not believe me, believe the deeds'* (v. 38). Belief is still possible; but the Jews feel that their community is seriously threatened, and charge him with blasphemy: *'you, a man, are claiming to be God'* (v. 33). Strictly speaking, *blasphemy* is ridicule or contempt deliberately addressed to God in such a way as to make people fear for the safety of their community. But since the charge always arises from shocked emotions, even unintentional words which may be careless, stupid or arrogant can be judged blasphemous. And so it is here. Behind the accusation and the replies we can detect the friction between two cultures, the Jewish and the Hellenistic, as they misconstrue each other's language about God. According to 9.22 the Jewish authorities excommunicated anyone who confessed Jesus as Messiah – not because a human teacher and healer could not be so identified but because the Christian way of using 'Christ' seemed to imply a kind of divine being. The Gospel was written to persuade readers that 'Jesus is the Christ, the Son of God', and what could be closer to a Hellenistic divine man than that? Indeed, Jesus was prepared to defend such an idea from scripture itself (vv. 34–35). In Ps. 82.6–7 God can be thought of as addressing the judges of Israel to whom he has entrusted his own prerogative of justice. In that case they stand in the place of God and so can be called gods. But they judge unjustly and show favour to the wicked. So God says to them: 'Though you are gods, all sons of the Most High, yet you shall die as mortals die.' If, therefore (the argument runs), such language is sanctioned by *scripture* which *cannot be set aside*, if *those to whom God's word came* (instituting them as judges) can be *called 'gods'*, why is Jesus – *whom the Father consecrated and sent into the world* – charged with blasphemy for saying *'I am God's son'*? (vv. 34–36).[31] The argument is more ingenious than persuasive for it does not reach the underlying convictions of either side. The real question is about God: what is God's work? *If my deeds are not the deeds of my*

---

[31] For OT references to blasphemy: II Kings 19.4; Lev. 24.11–16 (penalty death); Num. 15.30 (penalty exclusion); Isa. 52.5. The requirement of Sanhedrin 7.5 (Danby, p. 392) that 'the blasphemer is not culpable unless he pronounces the NAME itself' is a moderation of earlier savagery.

Father, do not believe me (v. 37). Only by making that fundamental decision can anyone *recognise and know that the Father is in me, and I in the Father* (v. 38, see v. 30).

In 10.40–42 Jesus withdraws to the place where he began. As far as 'the Jews' are concerned he is no further forward than when John bore testimony to him. Outside Judaea, across Jordan, people can still say '*All that* John *told us about this man was true,* even though *John gave us no miraculous sign*' – presumably implying: 'How much more true must this man be, who performs such marvellous signs.' In that case attention must be paid to the paragraph that ends the association of John with Jesus, and its concluding words: 'Whoever disobeys the Son will not see life; God's wrath rests upon him' (3.36).

Thus far Jesus has offered signs, sometimes defending and explaining them, which point to the great wedding celebration, to rescue from imminent death, to the restoration of movement in a paralysed body, to nourishment, and to illumination. In definitive I AM sayings he has presented himself as God's Agent from the heavenly world to bring nourishment, illumination, access to freedom, and protective leadership. The shepherd image should make it plain that he is not concerned with human beings in their separateness, but with human beings in their relatedness as God's people. Jesus now moves towards answering Ezekiel's question: 'Man, can these bones live?' (Ezek. 37.3). Yes, but only by death and resurrection. Lazarus is indeed a beloved brother, but he is chiefly important as a symbolic figure who speaks to no one and no one speaks to him. He is desperately sick and must be allowed to die; that is cause for both anger and sorrow. His death shows the inadequacy of stock reproach, consolation and religious hope. His resurrection and the command 'Loose him, let him go' is symbolic of the judgment that Judaism must die to be born again – as the chief priests and Pharisees rightly see.

The Sign of Restored Life

11.1–44   The story begins with Jesus at Bethany on the east bank of Jordan (see 10.40 and 1.28) and Lazarus with his sisters at *Bethany* in Judaea, *just under two miles from Jerusalem* (v. 18). Lazarus is wholly passive and silent, even when he is an object of great interest in ch. 12. It is not he but his sisters who contribute to 'the furtherance of the gospel' (as Paul would have said). In this narrative Martha has the leading role and makes the confession of faith (v. 27); in the preparation for Passover, it is Mary's turn when she *anointed the Lord with ointment* (v. 2, which deliberately binds the two stories together). It is not a matter of chance that Jesus works out the theological and spiritual consequences of death and resurrection with two women. His male disciples are too cautious, too easily reassured, and too heroic (vv. 7, 12, 16).

When Jesus learns that his friend is ill, he declares: *'This illness is not to end in death; through it God's glory is to be revealed and the Son of God glorified'* (v. 4). He does not mean (though he may be taken to mean) that death will be prevented. Death must take place – but death is not to be seen as the final indignity that deprives people of the love and presence of God. It is the means by which his glory is displayed – and 'the glory of God is not his praise but his activity'[32]. So out of love for his friends, Jesus *stayed where he was for two days after hearing of Lazarus' illness* (v. 6) – until he had *fallen asleep*. This is not the invalid's healthy sleep when his sickness has abated (vv. 12–14): however great a relief that might be, mere recovery would simply restore the *status quo*. This is falling asleep in the old life and awaking in the new life (as far, that is, as the imagery of the story permits). When Lazarus fell asleep, Jesus was not there (v. 15); when he was called forth from the tomb, he encountered Jesus and was given freedom. But to give that freedom, Jesus had to risk his life in Judaea. He knew quite clearly what he was doing: he was walking in the daylight, not in the dark (vv. 9–10). Neither for himself nor for Lazarus was death a forlorn expedient or a hopeless surrender – though for Thomas no doubt it was a shot in the dark (v. 16). When Thomas says *'Let us also go and die with him'* it sounds like a brave offer (which Jesus will later take up, e.g. 15.13) and a protest at what Jesus is about to do. In 14.5 and 20.24–29 Thomas is a model of stolid perplexity.

Martha is altogether more forthcoming. She begins with a statement of faith in Jesus which is also a reproach: *'Lord, if you had been here my brother would not have died'* (v. 21). In v. 32 Mary says the same: these are two witnesses agreeing in a complaint against Jesus, and from v. 37 it appears that opinion is not with him: *'Could not this man, who opened the blind man's eyes* (note the memory of ch. 9), *have done something to keep Lazarus from dying?'* In other words, what is the value

[32] Barrett, *John*, p. 390.

of illumination if it is extinguished by death? So the question that Jesus must answer affects his own reputation, the sorrow of his friends, and the hopes of the community. Martha presses him relentlessly: *'Even now I know that God will grant you whatever you ask of him.'* Her implied demand makes two assumptions: that death can be temporally set aside and ignored, and that Jesus can use his standing with God to obtain any concession he pleases. She does not yet know that 'the Father and I are one' (10.30), and that death cannot be ignored but is necessary to the purpose of God (v. 4). But Jesus makes her a direct promise: *'Your brother will rise again'* (v. 23), which Martha understands not as a promise but as a consoling statement of stock Pharisaic belief: *'I know that he will rise again at the resurrection on the last day'* (v. 24). That belief is indeed agreeable to the teaching of Jesus that 'the Father raises the dead and gives them life' (5.21) and his promise that he would 'raise them all up on the last day' (6.39, 40, 44, 54). So his reply to Martha (vv. 25–26), emphatic and carefully structured, must be set out in full:

> *I am the resurrection and the life.*
> *Whoever has faith in me*
> *shall live,*
> *even though he dies;*
> *and no one who lives*
> *and has faith in me*
> *shall ever die.*

The statement is compressed and needs expansion. Thus: *'I AM* (he who comes from above, and therefore brings) *the* (expected) *resurrection and* (hence) *the* (offer of) *life* (from beyond the last day)'. Anyone who possesses that life is fully aware that human existence is precarious and is moving towards its extinction. Yet even death is only of relative, not final, importance. Anyone who has faith in Jesus is not preserved from dying in this world below, but he is promised unfailing life in the world above. *Not* the promise of a substitute life when we depart this one, but a promise that the life of faith continues when we die. Nor is life-in-the-world-above promised as a reward for faith in Jesus; for the life of faith already *is* that other life. Jesus asks: *'Do you believe this?'* and Martha answers with a confession of faith, a composite acknowledgement of Jesus: *'I believe that you are the Messiah, the Son of God who was to come into the world.'* Possible meanings of those three descriptions have already been indicated (Messiah, pp. 27–29; Son of God, pp. 52–53; and see 6.14 for 'the Prophet who was to come into the world'); but Martha's confession does imply that Jesus is now seen to conform to three configurations existing in the minds of expectant Jews and Greeks. It implies that when Christians use these three terms as the shorthand of their christology, they are referring to the bringer of resurrection and life. And the Christian community, according as they make discoveries about Jesus, can develop the implications of the three designations in terms of anointing, sonship, and the heavenly world. Not that Martha understood all this, but that is the benefit of a robust confession of faith: it leaves so much to be discovered.

Jesus had responded to Martha when *she went to meet him, and left Mary sitting at home* (v. 20). Pointedly he waits for Mary outside the village, and when she answers his call (*'The Master is here and is asking for you'*, v. 28) others follow her. They expected to see people mourning, as indeed they did; but they also saw an extraordinary outbreak of emotion by Jesus – tears which could be read as signs of love, deep inward distress, and even indignation (v. 33, and v. 38 where it is hidden behind *deeply moved*). Is it possible that Jesus was following the practice of magicians in antiquity and working up his restorative power before attempting a miracle? That would certainly be in the popular vein, but it would divert interest from the point of this economically told story. Was Jesus irritated by the weeping and wailing as showing unbelief (if so, how insensitive to be angry!)? Or, though accepting his friend's death, was he not resigned to it? If God intends death and resurrection (and not simply restoration of the *status quo*), death is still upsetting. What if Lazarus is a symbolic representation of Jewish religion (see p. 89) which Jesus deeply loves and openly mourns? There are situations where love and sorrow combine with protest and indignation. Think of a doctor, doing what can be done for a young child with the AIDS virus, knowing that the drug-dependent parents have used contaminated hypodermic needles – with compassion for the helpless child-victim, and indignation at the consequences that (for whatever cause) we bring upon ourselves. When people said *'Could not this man have done something to keep Lazarus from dying?'*, the questioning did not go far enough.

There are more surprises. When Jesus orders the stone to be removed from the tomb, Martha protests: *'Sir, by now there will be a stench; he has been there four days'* (v. 39). When it comes to the point (despite her boldness in v. 22) death must be faced, and it is unbearable. And then, to that protest, Jesus says: *'If you have faith you will see the glory of God'* (v. 40 – rephrasing the promise of v. 26, *'no one who . . . has faith in me shall ever die'* in the words of promise made to his disciples in v. 4). They would see God's glory in the death-and-raising of Lazarus; would they equally see it in the forthcoming death of Jesus himself? To secure for them that possibility, he allows them for a moment to overhear his communion with the Father. In saying *'I know that you always hear me'* he carefully safeguards the primacy of the Father without disturbing the truth of 'the Father and I are one' (10.30); and the people standing around are to believe that *'it was you who sent me* (to do what I must now do)'. Thus the thanksgiving prayer of v. 41 may (to those with keen hearing) be understood thus: *'Father, I thank you for hearing me* (when I offer my death in place of Lazarus, and my life for the renewal of Judaism).' Whereupon *he raised his voice in a great cry* (contrast the great cry from the cross in Mark 15.34 and 37): *'Lazarus, come out.'* And he came out, unable to see, bound hand and foot (how like ordinary Jews, bound by temple taxation and Pharisaic rules of purity!). Jesus said, *'Loose him; let him go.'*

The Decision of Caiaphas

11.45–54   The raising of Lazarus caused many Jews to put their faith in Jesus, and others felt that the Pharisees should be told (see p. 82). *Thereupon the chief priests and the Pharisees convened a meeting* (not *of the Council*; all action by Jewish officials in this Gospel is informal and *ad hoc*).[33] They are alarmed by the growing influence of Jesus which may cause the Romans to think that the high priest is losing control of the situation. If this goes on *then the Romans will come and sweep away our temple and our nation* (v. 48). They had reason for anxiety since Pilate (appointed in 26 CE) was a difficult man and insensitive to Jewish feelings, though they too readily assume that their own loss of power would ruin everything. More confidence is shown by Caiaphas, a shrewd and successful operator, who remained high priest for eighteen years until 36 CE, and ceased only when both he and Pilate

---

[33] The Greek word *synedrion* (sanhedrin), which occurs only here in the Gospel, means a group of people assembled in council; in this case, people chosen by the high priest to advise him, including members of the high priestly family and some disturbed Pharisees. There is no question of a formal meeting of 'The Sanhedrin', even assuming that such a formal body existed.

were removed by the proconsul of Syria.[34] This powerful figure *was high priest that year*, i.e. that fateful year (repeated in v. 51, and in 18.13 where the high priestly junta again appear). An unwary reader might get the impression that high priesthood was an annual appointment. In principle it was for life (Num. 35.25), but the Romans appointed and deposed at will. Caiaphas, however, gained his influence because he was a stayer, and the repeated reference to *high priest that year* gains its significance precisely because of his long-term power – of which the Gospel is oddly respectful. He speaks not only as a shrewd politician but also as God's high priest when he says that *it is more to your interest that one man should die for the people, than that the whole nation should be destroyed*. The famous precedent (in King David's day) was the handing over to death of the rebel Sheba to save the town of Abel from destruction (II Sam. 20.18–22). Reluctant as they might be to follow that precedent (because Jesus though troublesome had supporters, and handing over a Jew to the Romans was detestable) Caiaphas spoke prophetically as high priest. It was said of the famous John Hyrcanus of a former age that 'he was accounted by God worthy of three of the greatest privileges, the rule of the nation, the office of high priest, and the gift of prophecy; for the Deity . . . enabled him . . . to foretell the future.'[35] But that was a Greek view of prophecy, not the ancient Hebrew view that God's word was spoken by the prophet and, once uttered, it caused things to happen. So here: once Caiaphas has spoken, the necessary process begins whereby *Jesus would die for the nation* (v. 51). Thus Caiaphas unwittingly or cynically gives voice to a Christian judgment about the death of Jesus. But although the sentiment is noble, it is rather difficult to discover (in Christian terms) what process of salvation is in mind. The nearest parallel is the plea of the Maccabean martyrs (almost two hundred years earlier) as it was expressed in a Hellenistic Jewish writing of the first century CE:[36] 'Be merciful to your people and let our punishment be a satisfaction on their behalf. Make my blood their purification and take my life as a ransom for theirs.' The basic presumption is that God's people have indeed sinned and doubtless deserve some punishment, but that their brutal and godless oppressors are far, far worse and deserve extermination.[37] Any attempt to adopt such emotions for Christian doctrine is blocked by

---

[34] Information from Josephus, *Antiquities* 18.35, 95.

[35] Josephus, *Antiquities* 13.299.

[36] IV Maccabees 6.28–29 (*OTP* II, p. 552).

[37] II Maccabees 7.37–38.

v. 52. The death of Jesus is not an inducement for God to re-establish Jewish religion at its best, but a new initiative to overthrow Jewish religion as it was and to re-establish it in a new fashion. The newness consists in extending *children of God* to those who are scattered abroad, the other sheep of 10.16. 'Jesus collects those who belong to him within and without Judaism and lays down his life for them.'[38] The death of Jesus breaks the familiar Jewish mould and makes possible a new unified gathering of God's people. This prepares us for the moment when the Greeks who have come to the feast ask to see Jesus (12.20–26).

Jesus now withdraws *to a town called Ephraim* (not to be identified with certainty, but possibly a dozen miles north-east of Jerusalem) *bordering on the desert* (v. 54). This totally unimpressive piece of information is a good example of how the Gospel is rooted in early memories and impressions of the land even when the author makes no pretence of writing a consecutive historical account.

The Passover in Jerusalem

11.55–12.19   Now it is time to prepare for Passover by beginning the necessary purifications (familiar to all Jews in the rigorous search for leaven – a symbol of decay and putrefaction – and its prohibition through the eight-day celebration). This festival, remembering God's protective power in Egypt and hoping for it to be renewed, is to be carried out in the purity of home and heart. The Gospel's solitary reference to purity is intentionally ironical (cf. the solitary reference to defilement at 18.28). For Jesus this was to be his last Passover. The authorities had ordered his arrest and were waiting for him to be caught; the assembling festival crowds knew his danger (vv. 55–57). He comes out of retreat and openly appears at a supper in his honour at the house in Bethany. The reader is again reminded of the raising of Lazarus and the two sisters, but now it is Mary who claims attention, and provokes comment, by an extraordinary action. She produces half a pint of *pure oil of nard* (an immensely expensive perfume, imported from India, in this quantity worth a year's earnings of a farm labourer) and with it first anoints the feet of Jesus,

---

[38] Barrett, *John*, pp. 407–8.

then wipes them with her hair. *The house was filled with the fragrance* (v. 3). Nobody could ignore what had been done. In every sense the action was extravagant, but that was its intention: those present had to applaud it or rebuke it. Judas rebukes it, and the Gospel's description of him makes him the patron saint of politicians who announce crying needs in the hope of profiting from them. But Jesus applauds the action: *'Leave her alone . . . let her keep* (the credit of) *it for the day of my burial'* (v. 7). Like many remarks of Jesus, these words need some expansion to draw out their meaning. What is she to keep? Clearly not the remainder of the oil (for that had all been used, according to Judas' protest), and in any case it was not needed (for the dead body of Jesus was handsomely anointed by Joseph and Nicodemus, 19.38–40). She was to keep the credit with God of her total giving and her total involvement. Why did she anoint the feet of Jesus? This is clearly not the commonplace courtesy done to a guest tired with walking, though performed on a grotesquely embarrassing scale. Nor is it an attempt to push Jesus into claiming rebel kingship (as it may be in Mark 14.3–9 where an unnamed woman anoints his head). Anointing of *feet* is simply not an expected or traditional practice: therefore it is to be understood as Mary's own inspiration, prompted perhaps by two Jewish memories. One is the story of Elisha and the Shunnamite woman (II Kings 4.18–37): when her son died, she went to the prophet and caught hold of his feet in entreaty (v. 27); when her child was brought to life, she fell at his feet in thanksgiving (v. 37). The second is Isa. 52.7: 'How beautiful . . . are the feet of the herald, the bringer of good news.' Mary's act is a passionate thanksgiving for her brother's resurrection, and an anointing of Jesus' feet for the work he now must do. One sister showed anticipatory faith, the other grateful love – with which support Jesus was content to approach the day of his burial. The permanent duty, never to be evaded, of relieving the poor must now make its demands on the other side of a decision about the death of Jesus.

The entry of Jesus into Jerusalem (vv. 12–16) is framed by two similar paragraphs which sketch the situation in which the Jews and the pilgrim crowds are showing excited interest in anything to do with the raising of Lazarus, whereas *the chief priests resolved to do away with Lazarus as well* as Jesus, and the Pharisees are more or less in despair (vv. 9–11, 17–19). A plausible understanding of the official reaction can be produced: the authorities perhaps supposed that the public were wickedly led astray by a bogus miracle and could be disabused if Lazarus were put to death. No one knows what Near Eastern religion is capable of doing when under great emotional stress; but the suggestion is rather implausible. It is more likely that, in the literary structure of the Gospel, the raising of Lazarus is a code symbol for the conviction that Judaism must die to be reborn. In that case, what Jesus was doing, and the interest he was arousing, were severe threats to Judaism. Hence the significance of his entry into Jerusalem, which provoked a spontaneous demonstration. People *went out to meet him with palm branches in their hands* (which to a Jew would revive the memory of Tabernacles in chs. 7–8, or more remotely the triumphant entry of Simon Maccabee in I Macc. 13.51), shouting *'Hosanna! Blessed is he who comes in the name of the Lord! Blessed is the King of Israel!'* (v. 13). The shouted words come from the processional Psalm 118.25–26 beginning with 'Hosanna' (originally a liturgical prayer for God's help) and continuing with a welcome to the bringer of that help, identified by words from Zeph. 3.15, 'The King of Israel, the Lord, is among you'. Plainly this is a dangerous popular demonstration welcoming Jesus as Messiah (see pp. 27–29), very alarming to the authorities whether he is Messiah or not. But then *Jesus found a donkey and mounted it* (v. 14) and so continued his entry. *At the time* (the author explains) *the disciples did not understand this;* only later did they remember this strange response to the acclamation, and realise that it was prompted by scripture. The illuminating prophetic words come mostly but not entirely from Zech. 9.9:

> *Daughter of Zion*, rejoice with all your heart . . .
> *See, your king is coming* to you . . .
> humble and *mounted on a donkey*, on a *colt* . . .

Yet the opening words are not 'rejoice greatly' but 'Fear no more'. What the disciples did not grasp at the time – and perhaps no one else did – was that Jesus tried to show himself not as a threat but as the peaceable king of Zech. 9.

The Hour Has Come

12.20–36   The Pharisees' gloomy cry that *'all the world has gone after him'* is aptly followed by the arrival of Gentiles (a common meaning of 'Greeks' in Jewish writings) *among those who went up to worship at the festival*. It is the business of Philip and Andrew to respond (both now and after the resurrection) to their request: *'We should like to see Jesus.'* That enquiry was sufficient indication for Jesus to make the decisive announcement that *'the hour has come for the Son of Man to be glorified'* (v. 23). What follows provides something more about *the hour* (vv. 27, 31), the glory (v. 28) and *the Son of Man* (v. 34).

The *Gentiles* were presumably non-Jews attracted by Jewish religion but not necessarily converted to it. The historian Josephus mentions that worshippers at Passover in Jerusalem must all be pure and holy: defiled persons 'were not permitted to partake of this sacrifice, nor yet any foreigners present for worship, and a large number of these assemble from abroad'.[39] So here are these foreigners, who do not belong by birth to the elect people of God and so do not deeply experience Jewish religion and morals; but they ask to see the Agent of God. Can they be given anything less than an outward sign of God's power and presence, i.e. his glory (see on 1.14)? *The hour has* therefore *come for the Son of Man* (who keeps communication open between earth and heaven – see on 1.51 – and who is the representative in the heavenly world not only of Jews but of all humanity – see p. 36) *to be glorified*, i.e. to display God's glory as he returns to the heavenly world by crucifixion. The representative character of the Son of Man is at once evident in three sayings that generalise what is true of Jesus and apply it to his followers. (*a*) There is a general analogy: *'unless a grain of wheat falls into the ground and dies, it remains that and nothing more; but if it dies, it bears a rich harvest'* (v. 24). For modern readers the analogy needs adjustment, for if indeed the *seed* dies it fails to germinate and that is the end of it. Hence: just as the life of a plant cannot continue except by the plant's death and the renewal of life in a buried seed, so the life of the Christian *community* (since the analogy is not obviously true of the *individual* believer) cannot continue except by the death and resurrection of the Son of Man (who is the seed of humanity), and then of his servants. Even with such an interpretation, however, the analogy is not without difficulty: it may suggest that death and resurrection belong to the normal cycle of nature and are nothing extraordinary. Perhaps it implies that while the Son of Man's exaltation in death and resurrection is indeed extraordinary, it is by no means contradictory to natural existence. (*b*) Then there is a general rule of life (used with proverbial generality in Luke 17.33): *'Whoever loves himself is lost, but he who hates*

---

[39] Josephus, *Jewish War* 6.426f.; cf. 7.45.

himself in this world will be kept safe for eternal life' (v. 25). 'Love-hate' is a proverbial Hebraic contrast: to say 'I love coffee and hate tea' means 'I greatly prefer coffee to tea'. (Why the emotional language? Try 'I prefer white policemen to black', and note the inevitable reply: 'Why do you hate blacks?') So the saying in general means: 'If you prefer your own interests to the interests of others, you will go astray; if you prefer the interests of others to your own, you will be safe.' And the Gospel applies this maxim to life *in this world*, and the hope of *eternal life* (see p. 37). Hence the death and resurrection of the Son of Man is not out of line with shrewd human experience. (*c*) Finally, *'If anyone is to serve me, he must follow me'* (v. 26). Jesus has already said that 'No follower of mine shall walk in darkness' (8.12), and has pictured the sheep safely following the good shepherd (10.4f., 27); but now he must say that disciples will follow him into danger (a warning to be repeated later: 13.36f.; 21.19) if they are to be his servants – though with the promise that *'Whoever serves me will be honoured by my Father'*. In Mark 10.45 Jesus says that 'the Son of Man did not come to be served' (the same Greek word *diakoneo*). *Diakonos* does not come elsewhere in the Gospel, though the idea is represented by *doulos* in 13.16 and 15.15, 20 where Jesus calls his disciples friends, not servants. If Jesus can properly be called Teacher and Lord, then it is necessary for him to warn his disciples that a *diakonos* or *doulos* cannot expect better treatment than his master: *'Where I am, there will my servant be.'*

If, however, Jesus is to answer Gentile need by displaying the divine glory in crucifixion, he must experience and endure the hour. *'Now is my soul in turmoil, and what am I to say? "Father, save me from this hour"? No, it was for this that I came to this hour. Father, glorify your name'* (vv. 27–28). These words (which could be compared with the Gethsemane prayer in Mark 14.34–36) call to mind Ps. 6.3–6, especially *in turmoil* (*tarasso*) already used in response to Lazarus' death, and used again at 13.21 (betrayal) and 14.1, 27.

> I am utterly distraught (*tarasso*).
> When will you act, Lord?
> Return, Lord, deliver me;
> save me, for your love is steadfast.
> Among the dead no one remembers you;
> in Sheol who praises you?

Jesus is troubled by the destructiveness of death, by human anxiety (whatever the Pharisees may teach about resurrection) that God will be beyond human reach. But unlike the psalmist (who confidently concludes that God will transfer the trouble from him to his enemies), Jesus asks God to glorify his name: that is, to exert his power and show himself the Lord of life and death. He does not ask to be saved from the decisive confrontation with the destructive and alienating power of death because the whole purpose of his life had been to force that confrontation ('I have come that they may have life', 10.10). When the voice from heaven says *'I have glorified it* (the name), *and I will glorify it again'*, the meaning is that the Father validates what the Son has already done and confirms what he must shortly do. Only Jesus grasps the intention and authority of the voice: the crowd took it to be a standard divine threat ('Those who oppose the Lord will be terrified when from heaven he thunders against them', I Sam 2.10), or a second-level angelic communication. If they so misunderstand the voice – the question is constantly asked – how can Jesus possibly say: *'This voice spoke for your sake, not mine'*? (v. 30). Because the voice came for their *benefit* (not their *information*), whether they understood it or not. Jesus is the only interpreter of God's words and actions; and here he makes four announcements: (i) God has glorified and will glorify his name for the benefit of his people; (ii) that the judgment of this world has now been decided (v. 31a), namely that 'the dead shall hear the voice of the Son of God, and those who hear shall come to life' (5.25); (iii) that *now shall the prince of this world be driven out* (v. 31b); and (iv) that *'When I am lifted up from the earth I shall draw everyone to myself'* (v. 32). These are statements of what now becomes *possible*, i.e. the exclusion of the prince and the allegiance of all humanity, not of what is sure to happen. The Gospel does not suppose that the prince of this world has lost his power to inflict damage and destroy faith, or that all hearers of the gospel would promptly believe. But it certainly thinks that the exaltation of Jesus in death and resurrection would claim adherents among Jews and Gentiles, and that God's edict now made it possible to defy *the prince of this world*. It is not an urgent matter to decide whether the prince refers to the destructive-alienating power of death imagined as a terrifying person, or to the malignant pseudo-person called Satan ('pseudo-person' because Satan has no existence independent of those he preys on). In the symbolic world of the Gospel they are one and the same. In 14.30 the prince comes to lead Jesus to his death (though he has no rights over him at all), and in 8.44 the devil is recognised by his bent for murder. The Gospel – rather like the Qumran sect – views the world as subject to contrasting powers – here, life and death, creativeness and destructiveness. When God glorifies his name, death no longer has power to thwart life. That indicates *the kind of death* Jesus *would die*: a lifting up from the earth in crucifixion which would in fact be the beginning of life.

The people, however, are still perplexed: why does Jesus insist on replacing the Messiah by the Son of Man? *'Our law teaches us that the Messiah remains for ever'* – not, it is true, in the Mosaic law, but in the prophets ('my servant David is to be their prince for ever', Ezek. 37.25), the psalms ('I have sworn an oath to my servant David: I will establish your line for ever, I shall make your throne endure for all generations', Ps. 89.3–4); and even 'one like a son of man' in Dan. 7.14 is promised that 'his sovereignty was to be an everlasting sovereignty'. *What do you mean by saying that the Son of Man must be lifted up* in crucifixion? *What Son of Man is this?* To which Jesus, in effect, replies that they are still not seeing their situation correctly. It is not a question of having a Jewish Messiah who will first remove their enemies and then establish his permanent sovereignty, but of realising that *the light* is present *but not for long* (v. 35). By means of the light you can know where you are going and become what you should be – *children of light*. The Qumran sect regarded themselves as children of light and possessed a Rule of War giving (fanciful) instructions for unleashing the attack of the sons of light against the company of the sons of darkness.[40] Jesus, however, invites his hearers, not to assert their identity against others, but to *become children of light*, i.e. enlightened people. Then the darkness will not overcome them, as he will show by his death.

Darkness and Light

12.37–50 The public phase of Jesus' work ends with a qualified admission of his rejection (vv. 37–43) and a lucid summary of his proclamation (vv. 44–50). Despite many references to those who put their faith in him and to the Pharisees' conviction that he had a mass following (12.19), the Jews as a whole *would not believe in him* (v. 37). *Even among those in authority many believed in him, but would not acknowledge him on account of the Pharisees, for fear of being banned from*

---

[40] Community Rule iii.13–iv.26; War Rule i (*DSSE* pp. 64–66, 105).

the synagogue (v. 42). Our knowledge of Judaea before 70 CE (when the temple was destroyed) makes it difficult to interpret that remark. *Those in authority* would be members of the high priestly family and their wealthy associates, who might indeed lose popular support if the Pharisees were against them, but would scarcely run the risk of exclusion from Jewish society. The Pharisees became powerful *after* 70 CE and in fact dominated Jewish life, in so far as the Romans allowed self-government at that time. The significant point is perhaps concealed in the comment that *they valued human reputation rather than the honour that comes from God* (v. 43), cf. the words of Jesus in 5.44: 'you accept honour from one another, and care nothing for the honour that comes from God' (see p. 54). *Reputation* and *honour* render *doxa*, often translated 'glory' – in general meaning your substance, standing, presence. Every human being, made in the image of God, has a right to such 'standing'; and in this Gospel the model is the Son who gains his own standing by devoting himself to his Father's standing. Those who cannot bring themselves to follow his example are fearful of losing their standing, and give themselves to defending it against and promoting it before others. Yet it is by no means easy for any of us to leave all this in the hands of God.

The limited success of Jesus is a familiar story to Jews. Moses reminded Israel of the signs and great wonders they had seen 'but to this day the Lord has not given you a mind to learn, or eyes to see, or ears to hear' (Deut. 29.2–4). *In spite of many signs which Jesus had performed in their presence they would not believe in him* (v. 37). Long after Moses Isaiah encountered disbelief and incomprehension (v. 38, quoting Isa. 53). He fulfilled his prophetic calling among a people devotedly offering sacrifices (Isa. 1.11), yet insensitive to what God required. He was commissioned with savage irony (on the model of the pretended false prophet of Amos 4.4 and I Kings 22.13–23): 'Make the heart of this people fat, and their ears heavy, and shut their eyes, lest they see with their eyes, and hear with their ears, and understand with their hearts, and turn and be healed.'[41] This ironically *says* the opposite of what it *intends*. So also when Isaiah's commission is applied to Jesus: he who said 'It is my Father's will that everyone who sees the Son and has faith in him should have eternal life' cannot have made his appeal to Jews knowing that God had predetermined that they should not believe. Why was it then that *they could not*

---

[41] This is the RSV translation of Isa. 6.10: see the interpretation of O. Kaiser, *Isaiah 1–12*, London and Philadelphia 1983. REB (following NEB) has a different rendering.

believe? Because the comprehensive cultic system centred upon the temple, and the vigorous Pharisaic teaching on purity in the synagogues gave the Jewish people a treasured identity which could not easily be surrendered in the face of Jesus' claim that he was the sole Agent of God. What Jesus did *blinded their eyes and dulled their minds*; to many it had the opposite effect to God's intention, so they did not turn to God to heal them. Isaiah *saw his glory*, i.e. the glory of God which was later displayed in Jesus, but the Jewish leaders lacked Isaiah's perception.

So that nobody should be mistaken there is a summary of essentials. Believing in Jesus and seeing him is believing and seeing God (vv. 44–45). Hence Jesus comes into the world as the divine light, so that faith in Jesus is a movement from darkness to light (v. 46). Rejecting the words of Jesus is rejecting the saving intention of God (v. 47), i.e. this is not a threat of divine judgment (condemnation) but a warning against self-wounding. To adopt the traditional image of judgment on the last day, the indictment at that great assize will be the rejected offer of life (v. 48). For Jesus did not speak independently *'but the Father who sent me has himself commanded me what to say and how to speak.'* And his *commands are eternal life* (vv. 49–50). Just as Jesus does nothing for his own sake but everything for his Father, so God also does nothing for himself but everything for his people's benefit.

Jesus and the Disciples
13–17

In this section the pressure of Jewish hostility, though present, is seen only in the background. All the problems arise from internal tensions – particularly the helplessness of disciples in an unresponsive world, their depression at the absence of Jesus, and their precarious grasp of his teaching. There are hints that some will have to be excluded from the community (15.2, 6); some are in danger of falling away and others may be killed by fanatics (16.1–2). Individual disciples are named: Judas betrays Jesus, Peter is boorishly self-confident, Thomas plaintively baffled, and Philip is simple-minded. The mysterious disciple whom Jesus loved knew the traitor but did nothing about it. As a body the disciples are stupid and rash. So in a dramatic action at supper Jesus visibly portrayed his teaching and then answered their questions, promised them his presence and a way of knowing the truth of his teaching, identified himself wholly with them and they with him, and prayed for them.

It can scarcely be questioned that this was written to help and encourage Christians at the end of the first century. No doubt the arrangement and selection of material reflects their anxieties, at the same time expressing an understanding of the community's nature which is firmly rooted in the words of Jesus. Chapters 13–14 read like a self-contained unit which, at an early stage of the Gospel's composition, may have led immediately to ch. 18. Chapter 17 is also an independent unit which transmutes the anxious questionings *of* the community into the earnest prayer of Jesus *for* the community. Chapters 15–16 are scarcely a unit at all, rather a collection of short statements about various community problems. Chapters 14–16 include five passages about the advocate (*paraclete*) or Spirit of truth: 14.15–17 and 26 (which look like later intrusions into speeches that run easily without them), and 15.26–27; 16.7–11, 13–15. This instruction (in special language) about the Spirit suggests that the community needed particular help in relating the Spirit to Jesus and to the world. When Jesus departs the community is not bereft of guidance: in 'the Spirit of truth that issues from the Father' (15.26) they are in direct communion with the Father and the Son, and are free to ask of them what they will (14.13–14; 15.16; 16.23–24). Yet in ch. 17 that communion is even more confidently asserted without reference to the Spirit at all.

Last Supper and Footwashing

13.1–30 All four Gospels have traditional information about the Last Supper, with references to betrayal by Judas and denial by Peter. Mark and Matthew use the story to define, by the symbolism of bread and wine, the significance of what God will accomplish when Jesus makes the offering of his body and blood. Luke does that also but goes further and uses the occasion to deal with matters of dispute and perplexity among the Twelve (Luke 22.24–38). The Fourth Gospel's account of the Last Supper says nothing about the body and blood of Jesus (indeed *explicit* reference to his death is absent from chs 13–17) but concentrates entirely – and at great length – on the problems of the community and Jesus' intentions for it. When *we* wish to deal with church problems and forward planning we call a synod or church meeting, or appoint a special committee; but this Gospel does it at a meal. The meal in fact was *before the Passover festival* (v. 1) – the festival which gratefully remembers God's past protection, and claims it for the present generation when it too moves from slavery to freedom, from shame to glory, from darkness to light. At a later time, Christians gathered for the Lord's Supper would have an equally powerful symbol of past benefits and future hopes, a reminder of the context in which disputes could be settled and perplexities resolved. Indeed, if (as has been suggested) the main teaching of this Gospel was first disclosed at gatherings for the community meal, it may explain why *this* Last Supper says nothing about the so-called 'institution of the eucharist : the worshippers already knew why they were there and what the meal meant. But that would not explain why the words in 6.53–56 about eating the flesh of the Son of Man and drinking his blood should be spoken in the Capernaum synagogue but omitted here. The perplexing and (to some) shocking invitation is transferred from a small, private group of disciples (as in Mark) to a public gathering of people who are asking 'what must we do if our work is to be the work of God?' (6.28). In other words, the flesh and blood of Jesus is given for the benefit of the *kosmos*, the footwashing is for the instruction of the closest followers.

An elaborate introduction (vv. 1–3) both establishes the supper scene and emphasises that Jesus was entirely aware of what was taking place (see further vv. 11, 18 – and also 16.30; 18.4; and 19.28). He knew that *his hour had come* at last – the hour postponed since his mother's request (2.4) by a series of indicative signs, ending with the raising of Lazarus. It was the hour *to leave this world and go to the Father*; he lived in the knowledge *that he had come from God and was going back to God* (and that had consequences which we learn of in ch. 17). He also knew *that the Father had entrusted* (authority in) *everything to him*. Hence it was within his knowledge and authority that *the devil had already put it into the mind of Judas . . . to betray him*; and, since *betray* means 'hand over to the authorities', those authorities were within *his* authority (see further on v. 27). Granted that awareness, Jesus *loved his own* (cf. the good shepherd, 10.3) *who were in the world, and he loved them to the end*. That coded statement means (as chs 13–14 will show) that Jesus will take the necessary steps for a return to the Father so that they can receive the Holy Spirit.

The meal took place before Passover (v. 1) – confirmed by 18.28 where the Jewish authorities were careful to maintain their ritual purity for eating the Passover meal. This Gospel therefore is in conflict with Mark 14.12–16 where the disciples make preparations for Passover (though Mark's actual account of the meal, 14.17–25, makes no reference to its central feature: the Passover lamb). Mark has the supper on the same day of the week as the Fourth Gospel, but changes the Jewish monthly date by one day (see the diagram on p. 149). The discussion of this difference is a complex technical question, and three views may be held: (i) that John is right and Mark is wrong, or that Mark is right and John wrong; (ii) that Mark uses the official date of Passover, and John a date two or three days earlier of a sectarian group of Jews (but Jesus was not a sectarian); (iii) the Last Supper was a community meal of bread and wine (no doubt with Passover overtones) such as is mentioned in the Qumran writings[1] and perhaps suggested in the Jewish romance *Joseph and*

---

[1] Community Rule vi.4–6; Messianic Rule ii.17–21 (*DSSE* pp. 69, 102).

Asenath.[2] Whatever the correct answer may be, exegesis must pay chief attention to what each Evangelist has decided to tell his readers. In this Gospel Jesus goes many times to Jerusalem for the festivals, but he is never pictured as taking part in the cultic activity. Passover, of course, is primarily a domestic festival: the lambs were killed in the temple but eaten at home. In this Gospel there was no Passover lamb, and the dating suggests that Jesus was put to death at the time when lambs were being killed for the evening meal. But the matter is not plainly stated, and non-Jewish readers may not have made the deduction.

Whatever the meal was, Jesus and the disciples follow Passover custom and eat reclining. That is, in Hellenistic manner, they dispose themselves on three low benches arranged, round a central table, in a rough horse-shoe pattern. Each person reclines on his left arm (and has the right hand free for eating) with legs stretched out away from the table. His head is near the chest of the person on his left, with whom conversation is specially easy. The Gospel does not say how many were present, though the number cannot have been much more than twelve (otherwise the footwashing would have been comically laborious), and probably, in line with old tradition, they were the Twelve. All the named persons traditionally belong to the Twelve, though there is one unnamed person: *the disciple he loved* (v. 23). But the Twelve play a minor part in the Gospel (only 6.67, 70, 71; 20.24), perhaps because they were under the leadership of Peter who may have been regarded in the community as a rival to the beloved disciple (21.20–24).

The customary course of a meal among associates was surprisingly interrupted when Jesus (acting no doubt with the full authority of the Father, v. 3) ceremoniously removed his outer clothing, tied a towel round himself, and *began to wash his disciples' feet* – conveniently available because of their reclining position. Footwashing was a social courtesy, offered by the host to his guests to ease the discomfort of their feet, and by the guests to the host to avoid dirtying the furnishings. Normally, of course, it was done as guests arrived. But Jesus did it in mid-supper. In effect he was saying: 'You are wholly welcome as my guests; but if you wish to prolong your welcome and finish the meal, you must allow me to wash your feet.' Clearly he was performing a symbolic action: its meaning is partly explained in

[2] *Joseph and Asenath* 8 (11) of an Egyptian convert: 'Let her eat your bread of life, and drink your cup of blessing, and number her among your people.' First century BCE–second century CE (*OTP* II, p. 213).

his exchange with Peter (vv. 6–11), partly in his subsequent instruction to the whole company (vv. 12–17). Or, as some would say, he gives two different meanings: the former theological (if the footwashing is a symbol of the crucifixion) and the latter moral (if the company is being warned against pride and encouraged to undertake 'humble service'). It has been said that both footwashing and cross are acts of condescending love.[3] But how could a flamboyant gesture of needless courtesy by abasement be symbolic of the necessary exaltation of the Son by crucifixion? And how could footwashing be an example of 'humble service'? Footwashing could be an example of respect for others (as when a disciple washed his master's feet); but a courteous gesture, which in our society might be represented by a host cleaning his guest's shoes, is scarcely a persuasive model for the stressful, loving service which Christians owe one another. A different symbolic understanding is required. Jesus implies: 'You are welcome as my guests – but something is not right. I show you, on the highest authority, that it can be, and must be, put right.'

And so to Peter. It is usually supposed that he is embarrassed and upset that Jesus should so lower himself: *'You, Lord, washing my feet?'* Embarrassed and upset, yes; but not 'impulsive humility'. He is deeply affronted. He cannot believe that Jesus, of all persons, should think that anything was wrong with him. Jesus replies: *'You do not understand now what I am doing, but one day you will'* (a signal that the reader must find the application in the later community, e.g. I John 5.16–17). Peter truculently answers: *'I will never let you wash my feet'*, to be warned by Jesus: *'If I do not wash you, you have no* (more) *part with me* (and my company)' (v. 8). To which Peter angrily replies: *'Then, Lord, not my feet only; wash my hands and head as well'* (since you think I am unclean). Peter represents those in the later community who say 'we have no sin' (I John 1.8); and the dialogue ends when Jesus, speaking with full authority and careful moderation says: *'anyone who has bathed needs only to wash his feet; he is* (otherwise) *clean all over; and you* (plural) *are clean, though not every one of you'* (v. 10).[4] The members of the community are fundamentally clean, unlike Judas (and those he represents) who betrays Jesus, but they need to be cleansed from impurities acquired by accident and error. According to 15.3, the disciples are already clean by the word he has spoken to

---

[3] Haenchen, *John*, vol. 2, p. 107.
[4] This cites the marginal translation, which is necessary for any sensible exegesis. The technical evidence is in B. M. Metzger, *A Textual Commentary on the Greek New Testament*, London and New York 1971.

them, i.e. his revelatory teaching has transformed their condition and determined their new nature. But they still must live in the world, and their feet (as it were) will bring the world's dirt into the community. In the footwashing, Jesus gives an impressive symbolic demonstration: *'If I, your Lord and Teacher, have washed your feet, you ought to wash one another's feet,'* i.e. they must help one another to remove the defilements of the *kosmos*. In the later community, as we know from I John, there were some who accepted only sinless members, others who found a way back for sinners who had not committed a sin unto death (I John 5.14–17). *But a servant is not greater* (in making demands) *than his master, nor a messenger than the one who sent him* (v. 16). Though expressed in polite language, v. 17 means: 'If you understand that, do as you are told.'

But even if the community is not to be rigorist about the conduct of its members, there are activities (and activists) which threaten the life of the community. Jesus continues: *'I am not speaking about all of you; I know whom I have chosen.'* He means Judas: see 6.70–71, 'Have I not chosen the twelve of you? Yet one of you is a devil'. As previously explained (pp. 67–68), that makes Judas the representative of all disciples who mar the work of Jesus. If Jesus knew that, why did he choose him? When you choose someone to be part of a team, you choose not an independent individual but a person with a history, subject to this and that kind of pressure, a person with drive, abilities, and contacts. The very qualities that decide the choice may make or mar the team (unless you have chosen a dull nonentity). *Judas was in charge of the common purse* (v. 29), responsible for buying provisions and making gifts to the poor – a matter that evoked his protest against the extravagant use of nard at Bethany (12.4–6). He was there because he could handle money; he provided a useful interface between the Twelve and the cash economy, part of the social *kosmos*. That *kosmos* has an acceptable and an unacceptable face. When *the devil put it into the mind of Judas to betray him* (v. 2), when *Satan entered him* (v. 27) – first the thought, then the impulse to act – the unacceptable face of the *kosmos* (which is one meaning of Satan) was dominant. As Jesus knew it could be. *'There is a text of scripture* (bound) *to be fulfilled* at times (because it is not uncommon in experience): *"He who eats bread with me has turned against me* with a sudden, sharp attack" (Ps. 41.9). *I tell you now, before the event, so that when it happens* (and your confidence is shaken) *you may believe that I am what I am* (i.e. the one from above)'. That is to say, the destruction of Jesus by a treacherous friend is not the humiliating end of earthly ambitions, but the necessary release for his heavenly reality. For Judas goes to do what he will do at least with the knowledge and consent of Jesus – so much so that the sending formula can be applied to his mission: *'In very truth I tell you, whoever receives any messenger of mine receives me* (Judas goes to act, as he thinks, against Jesus, but in fact on his behalf); *and receiving me, he receives the One who sent me* (so that the result is determined by God himself)'. Not that this is unimpassioned, cynical manipulation of a disaffected man. It is extremely distressing that one of them should play this part. Others therefore must bear the knowledge: *'In very truth I tell you, one of you is going to betray me.'* That announcement caused bewilderment (which, it must be admitted, is reflected in the account that follows): *which of them could he mean? Simon Peter* tried to find out, but there is no hint that he was better placed than the rest of the company, then or later. Only one person was told the secret (not only that the betrayer was Judas, but also that he went about his work at the command of Jesus), namely the *disciple he loved*. He is told: *'It is the one to whom I give this piece of bread when I have dipped it in the dish.'* To all other members of the company that would be a sign of friendship and trust (precisely what gave Judas the impulse for action). When they heard Jesus say: *'Do quickly what you have to do'* what else could they suppose than that Judas was off about his treasurer's duties? But the beloved disciple knows what Jesus has determined, and keeps it to himself. The *piece of bread* was a stimulus to Judas and a sign to the beloved disciple. He and Jesus knew the fatal consequences; the rest were in the dark. Appropriately *It was night* (v. 30).

THE BELOVED DISCIPLE

Who is the disciple Jesus loved, here making his first appearance (at least under that description)? In 11.36 it is said of Jesus and his friend Lazarus 'How dearly he must have loved him!'; but it is unbelievable that a person so plainly named in chs 11–12 should be so mysteriously indicated here and henceforward. Is he a new character in the drama (such as the unnamed companion of Andrew in 1.40, or the unnamed companion of Peter in 18.15), or is he one of the Twelve? His designation is used only in the final Jerusalem part of the Gospel, and he seems to come off best when compared with Peter: at the supper he discovers the secret, but not Peter; he outruns Peter to the tomb and first believes (20.4, 8); from the boat he recognises the risen Lord before Peter does (21.7);

and in 21.20–22 Peter asks Jesus what instruction there is for the disciple whom Jesus loved, and is told to mind his own business. It seems best to suppose that *the disciple Jesus loved* is used with reference not to a signal expression of love that has gone before but to one that will come after, namely the words from the cross whereby Jesus designates the beloved disciple as his mother's son, and puts his mother in that disciple's care (19.25–27). Significantly the earthly family of the Son of God is entrusted not to Peter but to another disciple. The use of 'beloved disciple' suggests that tension between the two came into the open at the Last Supper when one understood what was going on and the other did not.

It is possible that the beloved disciple was one of the Twelve. The ancient tradition of John Zebedee may be right (suggesting tension between the brothers Simon and Andrew and the brothers James and John, the leading quartet of the Twelve?), but it cannot be confidently asserted. In 21.2 the beloved disciple must be included among Simon Peter, Thomas the Twin, Nathanael, the sons of Zebedee, and two other disciples. 'The fact that the author is so careful to hide his identity makes it more likely that he is intended to be one of the two unnamed, rather than one of the sons of Zebedee.'[5]

Final Instructions

13.31–35   Jesus now uses the keyword 'glorify' (picking up references in 12.23, 28 and anticipating 17.1, 5) to interpret the situation created by Judas' withdrawal (vv. 31–32), and he announces two themes that need explanation: *his own* alarming departure and *their* inability to follow (v. 33, developed in 13.36–14.14); and the new commandment of mutual love (vv. 34–35, developed in 14.15–26). These two matters are of continuing importance to the later community (notice the words *My children* in v. 33, frequently used by the writer of I John). They are still important to us.

In response to Judas' withdrawal which, on later reflection, might seem like a humiliation for Jesus and those who believe in him, Jesus makes a statement memorably phrased and worth remembering:

[5] Lindars, *John*, p. 33.

> *Now the Son of Man is glorified,*
> *and in him God is glorified.*
> *If God is glorified in him,*
> *God will also glorify him in himself;*
> *and he will glorify him now* (vv. 31–32).

'To glorify' means to acknowledge, or display, or enhance a person's pre-eminent standing. In what sense had that happened to Jesus, and why must it be repeated? It has happened because Jesus has taken the necessary step to put himself in the hands of his opponents, and thus to go to his death. The Gospel is not content with that statement but shows Jesus as the dominant person in the scenes of his arrest, examination and crucifixion. It has happened to Jesus not simply as the Son and Agent of God, but as *the Son of Man*, i.e. as the heavenly representative of humanity. He is indeed the Agent of God for *in him God is glorified*. The decision he has taken is God's decision, and the outworking of that decision carries God's approval. That *God will glorify him in himself* means that the display of this pre-eminence is not a novelty, something hitherto foreign to the being of God – but is inherent in the divine nature. *Now* he *is glorified*, God *will glorify him now* (Greek: *euthus*) i.e. in the movement towards and the event of his death. The glory is not deferred until the resurrection or some other return of the risen Lord. In Mark 8.38, for example, Jesus speaks of 'the Son of Man . . . when he comes in the glory of his Father with the holy angels'. But in this Gospel the glory of the Son of Man is displayed in the expected hour when he returns to the heavenly world by crucifixion.

But what of the community of disciples if the glory of Jesus is displayed in his *departure*?, especially as *'where I am going you cannot come'* (cf. 8.21)? The words *a little longer* had already been used as a warning to the Jewish authorities (7.33–34; 12.35); now they expose the disciples to their approaching need (more clearly described in ch. 16). For that testing period Jesus gives them *a new commandment*, also memorably phrased:

> *Love one another;*
> *as I have loved you,*
> *so you are to love one another* (v. 34).

Mutual love within a community is not new. Judaism knew it well: from the Mosaic law ('You shall love your neighbour as yourself' Lev. 19.18); among the Qumran sectarians ('whose works shall be truth, righteousness, justice, loving kindness, and humility'); in popular writings at least a century before Christ ('Now, my children, each of you love his brother'), and in popular rabbinic teaching of the time of Jesus ('Hillel said: Be of the disciples of Aaron, loving peace and pursuing peace, loving mankind and bringing them nigh to the law').[6] The Hellenistic world regarded mutual love as the political imperative of the city state,[7] e.g. the Stoic teaching on *philanthrōpia* (early defined as 'a friendly attitude in the relations of human beings') which was a dominant theme in the moral teaching of Plutarch (contemporary with the Gospel).

Then wherein lies the newness of the commandment? (i) In the Gospel and I John there is no other commandment (cf. 15.12). The love commandment displaces all others, not because other commandments are unnecessary for promoting justice and happiness in social life, but because 'We have crossed over from death to life, because we love our fellow-Christians' (I John 3.14). This is the commandment, beyond all others, which permits those in this world to experience the life of the heavenly world. (ii) It is not simply a commandment of mutual love but love *as I have loved you*. Jesus loved as the Agent of the Father's love, and he carried that love to the point of death knowing that death took him to life with the Father. So the new commandment is that his disciples love as agents of the Father's love, and give themselves without reserve to the needs of fellow-members of the community – knowing that the community provides a supportive network of mutual love. They love knowing that they will be loved in return. *'If there is this love among you, then everyone will know that you are my disciples'*, i.e. that you are learning from me (v. 35). With an assurance of such supportive love, it may then be possible to venture on love to enemies that expects nothing in return (Luke 6.35).

By now Jesus is ready to begin his farewell speech, which (in the biblical tradition) is the proper way for a godly man to end his life. For example, there is Jacob's farewell to his children in Gen. 49 which later prompted the Testaments of the Twelve Patriarchs; and there is Deuteronomy, presented as Moses' farewell. In the NT there is Paul's farewell to the elders of Ephesus in Acts 20.17–38. If the many specimens are compared, something like a common form appears: the great man announces his imminent departure, recalls his previous

[6] Community Rule viii.2 (*DSSE* p. 72); Testament of Gad 6.1 (*OTP* I, p. 816); Aboth 1.12 (Danby p. 447).
[7] Bultmann, *John*, p. 527 n. 2.

actions and sayings, urges obedience of God's commands, commends unity and mutual love, warns of dangers and temptations but holds out the possibility of peace and joy, is concerned that his name should be perpetuated, and prays for his family. Such in general are the themes of chs 14–17.

13.36–14.14   It is *Simon Peter* who asks *'Lord, where are you going?'* It was the same Peter who made himself guardian of the 'words of eternal life' (6.68) when many disciples were protesting at Jesus' statement that they could not have eternal life unless they ate the flesh of the Son of Man and drank his blood. In part he had grasped the significance of that disturbing language: he knew that receiving eternal life depended in some manner on sharing the death of Jesus. He must now learn that Jesus will first die alone before others can follow: *'I am going where you cannot follow me now, but one day you will'* (v. 36 – cf. 21.19). But just as he had found it difficult to accept his need of cleansing (13.6–9), so now it was difficult to doubt his competence to die *with* Jesus and *for* the brethren. If Peter had succeeded in getting himself killed alongside Jesus, that would be a distraction from the death of the Son of Man returning to the heavenly world. If Peter had succeeded in rescuing Jesus from death (even by the loss of his own life), that would ruin Jesus' purpose of falling into his opponents' power. So Jesus stopped Peter by uttering the precise prophetic instruction: *'In very truth I tell you, before the cock crows you will have denied me three times'* – and prophetic instructions are not mere predictions of what is bound to happen, but are effective words that set events in train. When (in 18.17, 25–27) Peter makes his denials he is not simply giving way to cowardice – though no doubt he is overcome by fear and dread – but he is doing what he is required to do. Both Judas and Peter play the parts they are given. Sinners cannot even pride themselves on being the cause of their own wickedness, though of course they must bear the consequences of it. The situation of believers caught up in the saving activity of God is very precarious, and made almost impossibly difficult if Jesus is about to depart and go where they, with all their good intentions, cannot follow.

So Jesus offers three consoling explanations of his departure: (i) he leaves them only to prepare a place for them (vv. 1–4); (ii) his departure discloses the way to God (vv. 5–11); and (iii) it will permit greater things to be done (vv. 12–14).

(i) *'Set your troubled hearts at rest'* is somewhat romantic as a translation of the opening words. Remembering the standard Hebraic meaning of *heart*,[8] 'Let not your resolution be upset' would be better – used again with telling force at the end of the farewell (v. 27) with the added words 'or intimidated' (instead of *and banish your fears*: Jesus is reinforcing their courage, not confirming their anxiety by telling them not to fear). In this disturbing time they are told: *Trust in God* (*always* indeed, but that is an addition to the Greek); *trust also in me*, namely in what Jesus is going away to do. He goes to prepare for their reception in the heavenly family of God. In 2.16 *my Father's house* is the temple, and the author of A Letter to Hebrews envisages heaven as a great cultic complex. But in this Gospel Jesus has no interest in the temple except as a convenient place for teaching. *He* pictures heaven as a great household, a vast extended family, into which those who believe in him can be welcomed and given a secure and permanent place. If *dwelling-places* (*monai*, related to the verb of permanent residence and possession) suggests a visual image – not, of course, to be taken literally – it might be of Windsor Great Park where grace-and-favour houses are at the disposal of the monarch on the recommendation of trusted people. In the Gospel, the Son is trusted by the Father and goes to make his recommendations (*'if it were not so I should have told you'*) for those he is sponsoring. In fact he goes as their *paraclete* (as he is called in I John 2.1, and by implication in v. 16 below) and *'will come again and take you to myself, so that where I am you may be also'* (v. 3). That is what Jesus is doing when he prepares *a place*: assuring God that these are his own, and where he is they too must be. The talk of 'going' and 'returning' sounds at first like the departure of Jesus to heaven after his resurrection and his advent at the end of the age; but this Gospel has revised the older expectation. Instead, Jesus departs for heaven as the *paraclete* of his believers, and returns to them as the *paraclete* who is the spirit of truth (v. 17).

In notable ways this Gospel responds to the need, urgently felt in late antiquity, for human beings to have a secure sense of belonging in the real world, separated from the bewildering changes, disappointments, tragedies, and horrors of the world in which we actually live. To meet that need the gnostic religions put forward their offers, sometimes in serious assessments of the human condition, sometimes in grotesque mystifications. In some, a saviour descended to seek his own who properly belong to the heavenly world, to

---

[8] And English too, e.g. as in 'When told to give him the sack, we had no heart for the matter.'

reveal their true nature, and then to return heavenwards either accompanied by the saved or promising that they would in due course be where he is. Behind this talk of descent and ascent there lies the offer of a new self-understanding (or, as gnostics would have said, the revelation of a true understanding of the self that has hitherto been deceived). Hence what Jesus says in vv. 2–3 is much to the point; so also its continuation in v. 4: *'You know the way I am taking.'* That is something more than the familiar Jewish use of way as a metaphor of behaviour patterns, e.g. 'Lord, teach me your way, that I may walk in your truth' (Ps. 86.11). The vivid picture of Isa. 40.3 whereby a road is made for God to return to his people is interpreted by the Qumran sect as study and practice of Torah.[9] Members of the community 'walk in perfection of way as he commanded'. But this Gospel is not interested in sectarian morality: the meaning of 'way' is nearer to the gnostic search. Ode 39 of the Odes of Solomon pictures the dangerous journey of the soul, the difficult river to cross: 'Put on the name of the Most High and know him, and you shall cross without danger, because the rivers shall be obedient to you. The Lord has bridged them by his word, and he walked and crossed them on foot . . . And the Way has been appointed for those who cross over after him, and for those who adhere to the path of his faith; and who adore his name.'[10] From the middle of the second century CE we have the hymn of a gnostic sect called Naasenes ('serpent-people', from the Hebrew word for snake). It ends with Jesus saying: 'Therefore send me, Father; I will descend, bearing the seals. I will pass through all the aeons (i.e. divisions of the universe); I will reveal all mysteries; I will show the forms of gods; and I will deliver, under the name of *gnosis*, the secrets of the holy way.'[11] People who thought of 'way' like that would find the reference in this Gospel congenial.

(ii) Apart, that is, from the objection by Thomas: *Lord, we do not know where you are going*. We thought you were leading us to God, but apparently you are going to death. *So how can we know the way*, whether it leads to a new self-understanding or to destruction (v. 5)? *Jesus replied: I AM* (from the world above, and therefore) *the way, the truth, and the life* (v. 6a).[12] From the second part of the verse it is clear

---

[9] Community Rule viii.14, 21 (*DSSE*, p. 73).

[10] Ode 39.8–13 (OTP II, p. 768).

[11] Hippolytus, *Refutation of All Heresies* V. 10.2; R. M. Grant, *Gnosticism: An Anthology*, New York and London 1961, p. 115.

[12] See I AM, pp. 61–62; Truth, p. 178; Life, p. 37.

that way means 'way to God'. Hence *truth* and *life* are further explanations of *way*. *Truth* is a newly available way to God by belief in his Agent. *Life* is the inherent quality which the Son possesses by gift of the Father (5.26), of which we·partake and, in partaking, are with God. It would be easier to understand if Jesus said: 'I pioneer the way, and point it out to you (like the Ode quoted above). I reveal the truth (like the saviour of the Naasene hymn). I demonstrate the life.' But he says; '*I AM the way*' as he said 'I AM the door' in 10.7. Involvement with Jesus *is* the way to God. Once we are thus involved there is no further journey *from* Jesus *to* God, but only a journey *with* Jesus in the truth and life of God. Hence *no one comes to the Father except by me* (v. 6b). That statement – which does not express an insensitive imperialism but simply the logic of the situation – has two consequences: (*a*) it can be directed against those in the community who wish to leave Jesus aside and approach God directly by the Spirit; (*b*) if there is access to God by other religions – and that is implied by the use of Jewish and gnostic convictions – then they come to the Father by Jesus as the Logos.

What Thomas says in v. 5 is a real objection, not the silly remark of a dull man. It evokes a rebuke: '*If you knew me,* which clearly you do not, *you would know my Father too.*[13] *From now on,* with the disclosure I have made, *you do know him; you have seen him*' (v. 7). Here indeed is Christian *gnosis*, in fact a knowledge that goes beyond the piecing together of information, impressions, and convictions and arrives at sight. But there is further objection from Philip: '*Lord, show us the Father; we ask no more.* We do not ask you to die; only allow us to see God' (v. 8). In this matter he speaks like a Greek, for Hellenistic religion did not share Jewish reserve in using language about 'seeing God'. The prologue of the Gospel firmly says 'No one has ever seen God' (1.18), and it is said again in I John 4.12. It looks as if some members of the community were of Philip's mind (and of course somewhere on the edge of the community was a seer called John who was caught up by the Spirit, entered heaven, and saw the divine person and his entourage, Rev. 4.2ff.). In the old Jewish tradition no one can see God and live (Exod. 33.20); God may be heard, but not seen (Deut. 4.12). 'To behold the face of God' became a technical term for visiting the sanctuary, and the occasional promises that the righteous shall see God have strong cultic associations. How then does Jesus answer Philip's request, which is also a criticism?

---

[13] The REB margin withdraws the rebuke and turns Thomas into a dullard.

Reproachfully, with this definitive statement of the vision of God: *'Anyone who has seen me has seen the Father'* (v. 9). What had Jesus been doing all this time that Philip should not realise that he was intending exclusively to show them the Father? Did he not believe – this is the essence of believing – *that I am in the Father, and the Father in me?* (v. 10).

That kind of formula ('I in you and you in me') is characteristic of the Gospel and the Epistle (already at 10.38; also at 17.21–23), together with the strengthened form 'he dwells in me and I in him' (already at 6.56; also at 15.4–7). It is usually described, not quite accurately, as an expression of mutual indwelling; but it is neither mysterious nor mystical. It is not uncommon for two persons closely united – in a marriage, or a business partnership, or a piano and violin duo – each to find satisfaction and completion in the work of the other. When Jesus says *'I am in the Father'* we can expand the concise formula by 'I am in the Father's confidence, I am acting in the Father's interests, I am speaking in the Father's place', and so on. Correspondingly *the Father in me* or *who dwells in me* (the addition of dwelling brings in the idea of permanence) is achieving his purposes, doing what he intends should be done. The formula, in fact, is aptly constructed to express the idea of Agency by which, in the work of revelation and salvation, the Father and Son are joined. Even if Philip cannot accept the formula, at least he can make up his mind whether or not the deeds of Jesus are the deeds of God (v. 11).

(iii) The departure of Jesus makes it possible for *whoever has faith in me* to do what Jesus does, and *to do greater things still* (see Work, p. 49). The word *greater* comes as a shock (how can a believer do greater things than the Son of God?), but the shock is obviously intended. The reader is made to think. (*a*) The *greater things* are greater than the *deeds* which Jesus performs, namely the signs (p. 31) which are parables or indications of God's good will towards the Jewish people and his intention to save them by rebirth or resurrection. When Jesus departs, God's good will and saving intention is extended to the greater community of Gentiles (cf. 12.20–23). (*b*) When Jesus departs to obtain for believers a secure place in the divine household, the work of his two hands is placed in many hands. Believers become agents of the Agent of God. Their authorization is pronounced in vv. 13–14: *Anything you ask* when acting *in my name I will do,* on condition *that*[14] *the Father may be glorified in the Son.* This is not an open-ended

---

[14] The translation 'so that' misses the function of *hina* plus subjunctive here.

invitation to demand anything you please, but a promise to honour requests of a believer who hopes to demonstrate the glory of God in Jesus. *If you ask anything* when acting *in my name I will do it* (vv. 13–14; cf. 15.7, 16; 16.23–26).

14.15–26 How can anyone act in his name? By obeying his commands (v. 15) – except that such a translation turns Jesus into a sergeant-major. *Commands* are military orders, and obedience (i.e. 'do what you're told') is the ominous virtue of a police state. Obeying commands may be important in emergencies, but it cannot be the standard requirement of a Christian community. The Greek says 'keep my instructions', meaning: keep them as the acknowledged standard of your community by following their guidance yourself. 'That is what you will do', says Jesus, *'if you love me.'* Love is more than affection and devotion: it is keeping his instructions (v. 21), heeding what I say (vv. 23–24). But he says only one thing, the new commandment to love one another (13.34). To love him is to love one another, as I John 3.11–18; 4.7–12 copiously insists. But that becomes a circular exposition unless it can be assumed that the implications of love are otherwise known – as indeed they are in the relations of the Father and the Son acting as the Father's Agent. Jesus says that 'the world must be shown that I love the Father and am doing what he commands' (14.31). The Agent shows love for the one who sent him in being responsive to his teaching and leading, in being devoted to his interests and reputation. He does not cultivate an absence of self-expression, becoming thus a pure cipher, but uses his self-expression in the service of his agency. Correspondingly the Father loves the Son in sending him to be his Agent, in showing him all that he himself is doing, in entrusting him with complete authority, and in approving his actions (17.23; 5.20; 3.35; 10.17). That loving exchange between Father and Son indicates a pattern of loving for the community: loving Jesus, being loved by the Father and the Son, and loving one another. This community love is another benefit of the departure of Jesus and a compensation for it.

How does the single new commandment of 13.34 (repeated in 15.12) become the *commands* or instructions of 14.15 and 21 (as also in 15.10)? How can the single commandment of love be developed so that it produces the pattern of community loving already described? This Gospel lacks instructions of the kind found in the Sermon on the Mount. Indeed it diverges sharply from the moral tradition (derived from the scribal interpretation of Torah and the

Pharisaic search for purity) found in the sayings of Jesus contained in Matthew and Luke. Instead Jesus promises that *I will ask the Father, and he will give you another to be your advocate, who will be with you for ever – the Spirit of truth* (vv. 16–17). On one level the intention is immediately plain: if believers intend to follow the commandment of love and turn it into instructions for action, God will provide inspiration to work out loving actions that are valid for the community. But on other levels there are questions to be explored.

The Spirit

This is the first of five passages in the farewell speeches which promise the sending of the Spirit of truth as the advocate (14.16–17, 26; 15.26; 16.7–11 (advocate), 13–14 (Spirit of truth)). Only here in the Gospel are these two names used, suggesting that they refer to special functions of the Spirit within the life of the community. But there are previous references to the Spirit, and it will now be instructive to collect them. (*a*) In the widest sense Spirit indicates God in his self-existent transforming energy, not subject to human control, and indeed the very opposite of 'flesh', i.e. dependent and precarious human existence (3.6, 8; 4.24). Consequently there is no access for human beings to the divine sovereignty unless they are reborn from water and spirit (3.3, 5 suggested in part by Ezek. 36) and so come to share the spontaneity of Spirit (3.8b). That is a genuine possibility: the time is coming – indeed with Jesus present is already here – when Jews and Samaritans (perhaps others too) will worship the Father in spirit and truth (4.23). That is, by the transforming energy of Spirit they will be directed along the way to God, newly available by faith in his Son. (*b*) When Jesus appears the Spirit comes down from heaven and comes to rest on him, and John learns from God that Jesus is the one who will baptize in Holy Spirit (1.32–33). But not until he has been glorified when he would become a copious source of living water, i.e. the Spirit which believers in him would receive (7.37–39). For the period of his ministry Jesus is fully equipped with God's measureless gift of the Spirit (3.34), and the words he speaks are both spirit and life (6.63).

When, however, Jesus is in session with his disciples, he instructs them about *the Spirit of truth*. In I John 4.6 it is contrasted with 'the spirit of error' which on first hearing sounds like 'the spirits of truth and falsehood' in the Community Rule of Qumran.[15] But in fact they are widely different. The Qumran phrase expresses a view of human nature: by God's design mankind, created to govern the world, is the battleground of two opposed spirits until the time of God's visitation. But the community of I John is concerned, not with theoretical perceptions, but with the practical consequences of schism (cf. I John 2.18–19). Both sides claimed inspiration and the gift of the Spirit (I John 3.24–4.1). Those who remained in the community confessed Jesus Christ come in the flesh as Son of God, and therefore as the way to God; those who left the community abandoned Jesus Christ after their initiation and claimed direct access to God by the Spirit. It is therefore of high importance that Jesus speaks of *the Spirit of truth*, with the implied warning against a misleading spirit. *The Spirit of truth* is given only to those who love Jesus and obey his commands; is given only when Jesus asks the Father so to act. *The Spirit of truth* is then permanently resident in the community: *with* the community as it faces the world, *in* the community as it works out its inner life, the centre of Christian *gnosis*. With the world it was different – the world into which the inspired schismatics had successfully gone and gained a hearing (I John 4.1, 5). The world, i.e. human society organized according to its own rules of development and self-preservation, could not accept *the Spirit of truth* as the basis of its operations. *The world cannot accept him, because the world neither sees nor knows him* (v. 17). Why not? Because *the truth* is the new way to God made available by faith in the Son who returns to his Father by crucifixion. Thus when Jesus departs, '*I will not leave you bereft; I am coming back to you* as the Spirit of truth' (v. 18). *In a little while* (picking up 13.33; what it implies is explored in 16.16–24) *the world will see me no longer* (because they will suppose me dead and buried); *but you will see me* (when I am risen). *Because I live* (in the world above), *you too will live* in that world above' (v. 19). *When that day comes* they will no longer see Jesus as the visible Agent of the Father, but the principle of agency will be fully operative and they will know it: *I am* acting in the name of my Father, *you are* living *in me and I am* at work *in you* (v. 20). All this is made possible by the Spirit of truth to those who accept and carry out the instructions of Jesus and are bound up in love with him and his Father (v. 21).

[15] Community Rule iii.18 (*DSSE* p. 64).

ADVOCATE/PARACLETE

One more question must be asked: why is the Spirit of truth introduced by the word advocate (v. 16)? The Greek *paraklētos* (not a common word, and certainly not the name of a legal officer) is someone brought in to provide help and support, especially an influential friend who eases the way for you to succeed. Even his mere presence at the right moment, indicating that he is interested, may be sufficient. In *The Last Chronicle of Barset* by Anthony Trollope (Vol. I Part 2) Mr Crawley, a clergyman, has been sent to the assize, unlikely as it may seem, on a charge of theft. Years before he had been a fellow-student with Dr Arabin, now Dean of Barchester. Can the Dean help? (He is now abroad.) One of Mr Crawley's friends says: 'If we can do nothing else but bring him back, it will be a great thing to have the support of such a friend in the court. A Barchester jury won't like to find a man guilty who is hand-in-glove with the dean.' They wanted the Dean as a *paraclete*, i.e. a sponsor or patron (fortunately not necessary when the charge, based on surmise and missing information, was withdrawn). Anywhere in the world, throughout history, most people would recognise why the Dean was needed to play an informal but effective social role. In late antiquity a *paraclete* was *not* an advocate in the sense 'professional pleader in courts of justice'; possibly (though not commonly) 'one who speaks in favour of a plaintiff or applicant' – better 'one whose presence and involvement tells in favour of plaintiff or applicant'. It is notoriously difficult to find a suitable English word. The American 'counselor' is open to the same objections as 'advocate'; so is 'intercessor'. 'Helper' and 'protector' are on the right lines; and the AV 'Comforter' would not be bad if its Latin origin could suggest 'one who strengthens your hand' rather than 'one who consoles'. The word 'patron' is still familiar, and 'sponsor' is well known. They have the additional merit that someone who relies on patron or sponsor will, if sensible, keep in line with the aims and standards of the *paraclete*. In I John 2.1, 'we have in Jesus Christ one who is acceptable to God and will plead our cause (*paraklētos*) with the Father.' In John 14.16 Jesus says 'I will ask the Father, and he will give you *allon paraklēton*, i.e. another sponsor in place of me', namely *the Spirit of truth*. (REB adopts the possible but awkward translation 'another to be your advocate', perhaps suggesting that Jesus did not regard himself as their chief *paraclete*.) The primary function of the Spirit-paraclete is to commend believers to God, only secondarily to support their confrontation with the world. (See therefore 14.26; 15.16; 16.7–11. See also pp. 137–138.)

But all is not yet well. An objection comes from the other Judas who belongs to the last quartet in the Lukan lists of the Twelve, namely: James son of Alphaeus, Simon the Zealot, Judas son of James (unknown to Mark and Matthew), and Judas Iscariot (Luke 6.14–16; Acts 1.13) – one of the several indications that this Gospel had contacts with the Lukan tradition. Judas is worried that Jesus' promise to disclose himself to those who love him will make no impression on the *kosmos* (v. 22). Whereupon Jesus defines more amply what disclosure will mean for the community, and what it cannot mean for the *kosmos*. Once more the phrasing is memorable:

> *Anyone who loves me will heed what I say;*
> *then my Father will love him,*
> *and we will come to him*
> *and make our dwelling with him;*
> *but whoever does not love me does not heed what I say.* (vv. 23–24).

Thus 'disclosure' is not demonstration at a distance but demonstration from within. Since the divine indwelling comes in response to heeding what Jesus says, there cannot be a demonstration to those who do not love him (for loving and heeding see pp. 119–120f.). This Gospel is not interested in alarming symptoms of the end of this age – the sun darkened, the moon not giving her light, the stars falling from the sky – of Mark 13.24–25. Even if they happened they would not be the promised disclosure of God. And that, says Jesus, is not his own word, but God's (v. 24). The promise is that *we will make our dwelling* (*monē*, a permanent dwelling as in v. 2) *with him*. Clearly therefore Jesus' preparation of dwelling-places in the heavenly household is now rephrased as the arrival of Father and Son to dwell in the community. The imagery of *this* world and the *heavenly* world must not mislead the reader into thinking that a journey in space is required – not a journey in space but a journey from one frame of mind to another, from flesh to spirit, from competitive self-regard to a supportive network of love (see p. 112).

The indwelling of God is known in the OT, chiefly to express the divine presence in the temple, e.g. Solomon's prayer at the dedication of the temple, I Kings 8.27; Ezekiel's prophecy of a new cultic community: 'I shall put my sanctuary in their midst for all time. They will live under the shelter of my dwelling; I shall be their God and they will be my people' (Ezek. 37.26–27); and the post-exilic hopes of Zechariah: 'Shout aloud and rejoice, daughter of Zion! I am coming, I shall make my dwelling among you, says the Lord. Many nations will give their allegiance to the Lord on that day and become his people, and he will dwell in your midst' (Zech. 2.10–11). That cultic, communal and (in the end) supra-national expectation is transformed, in the Hellenistic Judaism of Philo (the Alexandrian philosopher contemporary with Jesus), into something individualistic and universal, e.g. 'Be zealous therefore, O soul, to become a house of God, a holy temple, a most beauteous abiding-place; for perchance, perchance the Master of the whole world's household shall be thine too and keep thee under His care as His special house, to preserve thee evermore strongly guarded and unharmed.'[16]

The promise that Jesus makes is not concerned with the human soul but with the Jewish and Gentile community which offers itself as the dwelling-place of God without the necessity of a sanctuary (cf. 4.21–24). The reader must not be misled by the wording of v. 23 into thinking that the promise is made to individuals and to men only. Of the thirty-one verses in this chapter, twenty-seven are addressed to *you* in the plural. Jesus is talking to the community, the people at the supper table, and in effect the community for whom the Gospel was written. It was customary for that later community to formulate their rules of belief and conduct in one of two forms (very prominent in I John), both present in this chapter:[17] (a) 'anyone believing . . . will do such and such' (v. 12); 'anyone receiving my commands . . . *he* (i.e. that person) *it is who loves me*' (v. 21); 'anyone not loving . . . is unheeding' (v. 24). (b) 'If anyone loves me that person *will heed what I say, and we will come and make our dwelling with him* (i.e. that person)' (v. 23). The lack of a personal pronoun meaning 'her or him' accounts for the conventional masculine forms in both Greek and English. If pressed, readers have always known that they mean both. The personal formulation of *community* rules makes sure that the community's business is everybody's business. And Jesus has made this known while he is still with them (v. 25) – that is, he has pressed upon them the commandment of mutual love in its new form (see p. 113). '*But the advocate* (sponsor), *the Holy Spirit whom the Father will*

---

[16] Philo, *On Dreams* I, 149.
[17] See Grayston.

send in my name, will teach you everything and remind you of all that I have told you' (v. 26). That statement adds to the promise of v. 16: 'The Father . . . *will give you another* sponsor' becomes *'the Father will send* the sponsor *in my name* – standing in the place of Christ and acting in his name (the agency principle again in operation). In v. 17 it is said that the Spirit-paraclete will dwell *with* the community as it faces the world, *in* the community as it works óut its inner life (see p. 121). That second part is now expanded: the sponsor will instruct them in all matters (relating to the love commandment) and – because he stands in place of Jesus – will bring to mind all that Jesus told them. Under the stress of hardship, some part of his teaching could be pushed aside; under the excitement of success, some part could gain undue dominance: the Spirit will preserve the whole. Members of the community came from diverse backgrounds – varieties of Jewish (and Samaritan) practice – prophetic, priestly, Pharisaic; varieties of Greek popular, gnostic and philosophical religion. Each would seize on some part of Jesus' teaching and try to shape it to their own understanding. The Spirit-paraclete would remind them of the totality and unity of what Jesus had said.

The Blessing of Peace

14.27–31   Jesus ends his farewell by giving the blessing of peace as his parting gift. This is something more than peace as the absence of conflict – it at least suggests the Hebrew *shālôm*, well-being – and something other than the common use of *peace* in farewells ('go in peace', Mark 5.34) and greetings (John 20.19, 21, 26). Elsewhere Jesus speaks to the disciples 'so that in me you may find peace', though they will have suffering in the world (16.33). Throughout this speech he has been strengthening their resolution (see on v. 1), and now he does so again. He leaves them with the assurance that all is well – with his own assurance (knowing what he knows about his forthcoming death) that all is well. There is another reason for his departure, and for the confidence of his peace: *'I am going to the Father, and the Father is greater than I am'* (v. 28). And for that the disciples should be glad, for he who is not only the Agent of God but also their representative now goes to the Father, the source of all life, for their benefit. Yet because of the manner of his going they need to be

forewarned *'so that when it does happen you may have faith'* (v. 29, cf.
13.19).

Throughout the Gospel Jesus insists that he is the Son and Agent
of God. To see and hear his words is to see and hear God, in so far
as God can be seen and heard. Yet what he says and does derives
not from his independent decision but from his knowledge of,
dependence on, and authorization by the Father (see Awareness of
God, pp. 15–16). In 13.31–32 Jesus announced that 'the Son of Man
is glorified, and in him God is glorified'; in 17.1 he says 'Glorify your
Son, that the Son may glorify you'. It is the glory of Jesus that he both
proclaims 'the Father is greater than I am', and knows that he is going
to him.

At this moment, however, he knows that *the prince of this world
approaches*. What in fact happens (in 18.2–3) is that Judas appears
with soldiers and temple police; but they are no more than uncomprehending representatives of the demonic destructiveness of this
world. *'He has no rights over me'*, says Jesus, even though he has put
himself into the hands of Judas (see p. 109). At 12.31 Jesus had said
'Now shall the prince of this world be cast out' meaning that by God's
edict it is now possible to defy that prince (see pp. 100–101). *But the
world must be shown that I love the Father and am doing his commands*. On
his Father's instruction he goes to meet the enemy, and invites the
disciples to go with him: *Come, let us go!* (v. 31 – cf. Mark 14.42 in
Gethsemane).

Dramatically, the reader now needs to move immediately to the
garden across the Kedron ravine. But the action is held up by further
exploration of the difficulties attaching to community love when
Jesus is absent (chs 15–16) and by a long prayer in which the Son
renders to his Father an account of his work and how it is to be
continued (ch. 17). Nobody can easily suggest that, having said *'Let
us go'*, Jesus actually went on talking where he was; or perhaps left
the supper room and discoursed as he walked along, ending up with
an elaborate prayer in public – with someone busily memorizing
what he said, or even making notes. That kind of suggestion trivialises
the placing of these chapters. It must first be observed that the Gospel
places discussions between Jesus and his opponents in chs 5–12,
between Jesus and his disciples after ch. 13 and before ch. 18. If the
tradition of the community included more material of the second
kind than is found in 13–14, then it had to be placed between 14 and
18. Granted so much, many exegetes re-arrange the material, for
example placing 15–16 (and perhaps 17) before 14. But such proposals

fail to give weight to the distribution of the word *kosmos*. It occurs throughout the Gospel, but rather sparsely until ch. 14 is reached. Then it becomes very frequent and is usually hostile. 'God so loved the world' in 3.16, but much less obviously in chs 15–17. Thus when *the prince of this world approaches* and Jesus says *'Let us go'*, it is an invitation to journey not in space but in thought. And the reader of the Gospel will be aware that the unacceptable face of the *kosmos* (not its damnation) is to be endured with the footwashing on one side and the crucifixion on the other (see World, pp. 17–19).

Instruction about Love

15.1–17   In 13.34–35 Jesus gave the new commandment of love and in some measure developed it in the second part of his farewell speech (14.15–24). Now he develops it at length, first by using the figure of a vine. The text as we have it runs together the figure and its interpretation; but it is not difficult to see them apart.

1. *I am the true vine,* (see v. 5)
   and my Father is the gardener.
2. *Any branch of mine that is barren he cuts away* (see v. 6);
   and any fruiting branch he prunes clean,
   to make it more fruitful still.
3. *You are already clean*
   because of the word I have spoken to you.
4. *Dwell in me, as I in you.* (see v. 7)
4. **No branch can bear fruit by itself,*
   *but only if it remains united with the vine;
   No more can you bear fruit
   unless you remain united with me.
5. **I am the vine;*
   *You are the branches.
   Anyone who dwells in me,
   as I dwell in him,
   bears much fruit;
   apart from me you can do nothing.
6. *Anyone who does not dwell in me*
   is thrown away like a withered branch.

6. *The withered branches are gathered up,
   thrown into the fire, and burnt. (see v. 2)

If we read in sequence vv. 1, 2, 4*, 5* and 6* we are presented with a well-devised figure (even more effective rhetorically if 5* and 6* are interchanged). Its emphasis lies clearly on the production of specially strong fruiting branches from the genuine root-stock and the removal of non-fruiting growth. The figure can be interpreted in two complementary ways. According to v. 1 *the true vine*, identified as Jesus, is the means by which *the Father* conveys true life to the world, ensures its abundance, and protects its quality. According to v. 5* the vine, again identified as Jesus, is the means by which a community of people is given its constitution and made aware of its discipline. Since all the commentary added to the basic figure is to do with disciples, it is clear that its chief purpose is to instruct the Christian community.

I am the true vine is the seventh of the special I AM sayings (see pp. 61–62) which fundamentally serve to identify not so much the nature of Jesus as the nature of the salvation he brings. He is food and light for God's people (bread, light), the way and door to God, protection and leadership (shepherd), and life from the dead. If the vine is interpreted in the first way suggested, then it becomes another symbol of life, the mythical 'tree of life' by which divine energies are conveyed to the healing of the creation. In the Third Apocalypse of Baruch (possibly a Jewish writing from the first to third century CE, with Christian reworkings) it is said that a sprig of the original vine from Paradise was planted by Noah with the promise that 'Its bitterness will be changed into sweetness, and its curse will become a blessing, and its fruit will become the blood of God, and just as the race of men have been condemned through it, so through Jesus Christ Emmanuel in it they will receive a calling and entry into Paradise.'[18]

That is not remotely like this Gospel. The second interpretation is better: the vine symbolically is Jesus who indeed feeds life to a community of believers so long as they remain attached to him and are fruitful in the way that he was. In the OT the vine is much used as an admonitory symbol for God's people: God brought a vine from Egypt so that it struck root and filled the land, but now God cares for it no more (Ps. 80.8–16); God planted Israel as a choice red vine, a wholly pure strain; but now they are turned into a vine that has

[18] III Baruch 4.15 (*OTP* I, p. 669).

reverted to its wild state (Jer. 2.21); their mother was a vine that grew fruitful and luxuriant, but it was torn up in anger (Ezek. 19.10–14); Israel is like a spreading vine with ripening fruit, but the more fruit the more idolatry (Hos. 10.1). To which may be added the love song of Israel as God's vineyard which for its injustice must be left derelict (Isa. 5.1–7). When therefore Jesus calls himself *the true vine* he represents himself as the root-stock of the genuine people of God – from whom the Jews are not excluded, within whom the Gentiles *are* included.

That *my Father is the gardener* (v. 1) is a necessary feature of the imagery. As in the quotation from Jer. 2, the growth of this choice vine must not be allowed to degenerate and become wild, covering everything with abundant foliage and little fruit. A vineyard carries a managed crop: the plants are trained, barren shoots are cut away, fruiting branches are strengthened by shortening. This can have a bearing on the Christian community which is not intended to be an uncontrolled luxuriant growth, but a social arrangement that produces good *fruit in plenty*. Hence the cutting and pruning of v. 2 can be applied to discipline within the community, and indeed may have been specially appropriate to the Christians for whom I John was written. The words *he prunes clean* call forth a comment in v. 3 which insists that the disciples (and hence the later community) are *clean because of the word I have spoken to you*. Against any thought that cleanness derived from Jewish methods of purification (including baptism) and reception of the Spirit apart from Jesus, it is laid down that Christian cleanness comes from the revealing and saving message of Jesus who himself said: 'the words I have spoken to you are both spirit and life' (6.63).[19]

The main application, however, is announced by the preliminary comment *Dwell in me, as I in you* (v. 4). The imperative *dwell* translates the permanence-verb (*menein*, 'to remain', traditionally 'to abide') which is highly important in Gospel and Epistle (partly in response to those who had *not* remained in the community). It raises the question: where in our lives do we find some kind of permanence? – assuming that we are not permanently in the dark (12.46). The

---

[19] Cleansing is not a leading concern in the Gospel. 'Clean' (*katharos*) occurs only here and 13.10–11; cleansing (*katharismos*) only at 2.6 and 3.25. The standard NT verb 'to clean' (*katharizō*) is never used; its alternative *kathairō* appears only here in the NT. It can be used for cultic and moral cleaning, and for cleaning work on a farm. But it does not properly mean 'to prune'. It looks as if word-play has taken over, since *cuts away . . . prunes clean* in Greek is *airei . . . kathairei*.

answer: we find permanence when we remain willingly, loyally (and sometimes courageously) in that which holds us. *Dwell in me, as I in you* is not a simple surrender but a willing co-operation – a persistence in the life of faith.[20] Nor, despite the form of the words, is the relation truly reciprocal as was already made clear in 6.56: 'Whoever eats my flesh and drinks my blood dwells in me and I in him.' It is *he* who offers benefits and makes the gift of his life; it is *we* who receive the benefits and in some measure share his death. Those are true disciples who stand by (i.e. remain in) his teaching (8.31); or, to put it the other way round, *if you dwell in me, and my words dwell in you* (v. 7) you are indeed agents of the Agent of God (cf. 14.13–14). *You dwell in me* means that the secure basis of your life is provided by him who is humanity's representative in the world above; *my words dwell in you* means that his instruction is permanently effective on your will as you live in this world below.

What instruction? That is made plain when Jesus says *Dwell in my love* (v. 9). When the vine imagery mentions fruit-bearing (vv. 2, 4) and its application urges the disciples to bear much fruit (vv. 5, 8, 16) it is thinking of fruitfulness in *love*, of producing that supportive network of mutual love (see p. 112) which is to mark out the community. The word 'love', of course, has a wide range of meanings, so it needs some definition; and friendly relations within a closed community are much in demand but difficult to maintain. So the vine imagery is used to draw out some formative and critical thought which can guide the community. (In vv. 5–6 the sentences beginning *Anyone who* are good examples of the community style found in I John.) The carefully repetitive, patiently developed teaching of vv. 4–10 can be summarized thus:

The Father has loved me (v. 9a), and I have loved him by heeding his commands and dwelling in his love (v. 10b). *I have loved you* (v. 9b). *If you* love me and *heed my commands, you will dwell in my love* (v. 10a). *Anyone who dwells in me, as I dwell in him, bears much fruit; apart from me you can do nothing* (v. 5b). You cannot bear fruit *unless you remain united with me* (v. 4b). *Anyone who does not dwell in me* is discarded as a productive member of the community (v. 6a) for my Father is glorified if you *bear fruit in plenty* and so remain *my disciples*, i.e. those who learn from me (v. 8).

From that four things are plain. (*a*) Jesus is the sole guaranteed

[20] Bultmann, *John*, p. 535.

access to God's love – his recognition, protection, and approval; (*b*) hence Jesus cannot be thrust aside for other inspirations and aspirations; (*c*) what he offers is love of the kind that he himself showed; and so (*d*) if that kind of love is not acceptable there is nothing else on offer. It is a severe but proper warning: if people refuse the truth, i.e. the true way to God newly available by faith in his Son, it is useless to hope or pretend that they can charitably be rescued by something inferior. Yet it must also be said that what is offered to them is not bitter and self-denying: it is joyful (v. 11). What Jesus did he did for joy, that *my joy may be in you, and your joy complete*. Every sign he performed ended in rejoicing; and when 'he showed them his hands and his side . . . the disciples were overjoyed' (20.20). Of course not everything can be joyful but 'your grief will be turned to joy' (16.20).

Since Jesus knows himself to be under his Father's commands he can properly require disciples to *heed his commands* (v. 10; cf. 14.15, 21) which can be gathered together in the instruction to *love one another as I have loved you* (repeating in vv. 12 and 17 what has previously been said in 13.34). But what relation does that imply (beyond teacher and learners) between Jesus and his disciples? In the middle of the supper, when Jesus had washed their feet, did he not say that they were right to call him Teacher and Lord? (13.13). A 'lord' (*kyrios*) is the master of slaves (*douloi*). In 13.16 Jesus uses the stock Jewish sentiment 'a servant (*doulos*) is not greater than his master (*kyrios*)' – at that point meaning that a slave must not be more demanding than his master. He uses the words again in 15.20 meaning that a slave cannot expect better treatment than his master. Jesus nowhere actually calls his disciples 'slaves' – to translate *douloi* as *servants* is no help nowadays – but is there not an underlying assumption that Jesus is master and that disciples do what they are told? – since *a servant does not know what his master is about* (v. 15). A non-Jewish reader might well draw that conclusion, though it would not be safe anywhere in early Christian tradition. Paul sometimes calls himself a *doulos* of Christ Jesus (e.g. Rom. 1.1; Gal. 1.10; Phil. 1.1) but no one was less given to doing simply what he was told. In the other Gospels, Jesus says that 'whoever wants to be first must be slave of all'; but explicitly says that the Son of Man did not come to be a slave master (Mark 10.45). Luke, sensitive to Greek feeling, changes the expression though not the thought: 'the greatest among you must bear himself like the youngest, the one who rules like one who serves' (*diakonōn*, Luke 22.26). Luke was fully aware that in the formalities of Semitic courtesy master and slave language was fully acceptable (the *Nunc Dimittis* in Luke 2.29 begins with a *despot* and his *doulos*) but not so to Greeks – so he used the language of *diakonia* (service). In this Gospel, however, the shift from Semitic to Hellenistic feelings is made by changing slave to *friend*. In Semitic life your close companion, supporter and helper is usually called your 'brother'; in Greek life he is your *philos*, the person you love (*phileō*), your friend. Friendship appears occasionally in the OT (e.g. David and Jonathan, I Sam. 18), more frequently though rather suspiciously in the Hellenistic period (e.g. Ecclus. 6.5–17); but it is a dominant feature in accounts of Greek life. And, in writers four centuries before Christ to four centuries after, it is agreed that the supreme duty of the friend is self-sacrifice even to the point of death.[21] At that point Jesus begins (v. 13). He will lay down his life for friends who do what he commands them out of friendship, not servitude. They know what he is doing: *I have disclosed to you everything that I heard from my Father* (v. 15), and so are his friends. But this is not the friendship of mutual attraction, of equal give and take: *You did not choose me: I chose you*. Friendship is a gift, offered by him and accepted by them. Indeed it is both gift and responsibility. Jesus knows what it is to be Son in the Father's house: 'the slave has no permanent standing in the household, but the son belongs to it for ever' (8.35). When therefore Jesus prepares a place for them in his Father's house (14.2), that is the *gift* of friendship. And when he discloses that he has chosen them out of the world (15.19) that points to the *responsibility* of friendship.

Instruction about Hostility

15.18–25 By contrast, the disciples are now warned about the hatred of the world. Readers should not hastily assume that 'hatred' carries the commonest modern meaning (namely a strongly emotional repugnance) especially in the contrast of loving and hating. The idea has a range of meaning: in *The Concise Oxford Dictionary* 'hatred' is defined as 'intense dislike, enmity, rejection and ill-will'. When (as Jesus says) the world loves its own, a great deal is demanded of love. Anything less than total, uncritical support is treated as enmity,

---

[21] G. Stählin, *'phileo* etc.', *TDNT* IX, p. 153: from Aristotle to Iamblichus.

criticisms as hatred. Hence *the world hates you* means that the world interprets your withdrawal from it as a deliberate threat, and so defends itself by enmity, rejection and ill-will. It is true that any social system (for that meaning of *kosmos* see pp. 17–19) will defend itself against attack, and rightly so. If the *kosmos* was brought into being by the Logos and is loved by God, it can be expected to maintain itself. How the Judaean social group thought to maintain itself is displayed in John 5–12; how the Christian social group tried to counter such threats appears in I John. But all social groups are tempted to maintain privilege by using force and to show maximum hostility to any who question their conventions and symbols. That is precisely what Jesus did, and the *kosmos* showed its enmity. Using again the old tag *'A servant is not* to expect *greater* consideration *than his master'* (v. 20, from 13.16), Jesus gives the warning: if the world is hostile to my servants, much more will it ill-treat my friends. *If they persecuted me, they will also persecute you* (v. 20). The word *persecute* is not too strong: on the Jewish side, the threefold use of 'banned from the synagogue' (9.22; 12.42; 16.2) suggests some hostility against Christians by the time the Gospel was complete; but more seriously on the Gentile side there is ample evidence of civil disabilities (e.g. in I Peter) and official violence (e.g. in Revelation). Not all is rejection: *if they have followed my teaching* (as some have), *they will follow yours* (v. 20). But *all this will they do to you on my account, because they do not know the One who sent me.* That refers explicitly to the Jews. It must not be read as a general condemnation of Jews and Judaism: old Jewish tradition had a very rich awareness of God, as this Gospel fully admits (cf. 5.18 where the Jews defend the sole authority of God; 8.41 where they claim him as their only Father; 9.29 where they rely on what God said to Moses). But many (especially leading) Jews lacked or rejected the Christian *gnosis* (awareness) of God as *the One who sent me* (v. 21). If Jesus *had not come and spoken to them,* if he *had not done such deeds among them as no one else had ever done, they would not have been guilty of sin,* (vv. 22, 24; cf. what Jesus said to the Pharisees in 9.41). Their sin was not disobedience to the God they worshipped and defended, but their refusal or inability to listen and perceive the Father's new initiative in the Son. They rejected the Son and thereby – against their intention – rejected the Father. It is exceedingly difficult for any social group to build into its system of defences a mechanism for recognising the benefits, indeed the imperatives, of change. Not that Jesus was surprised: such a response was already indicated *in their law* (no doubt suggesting 'the law they claim to defend', though the expression distances Jesus from fellow-Jews; and *law* has the wider sense of accepted scripture, namely the Psalms). A group of psalms contains the complaint of a devout and suffering worshipper who says 'they have assailed me without cause' (Ps. 109.3). 'Unprovoked they have hidden a net to catch me . . . May the net which they hid catch them' (Ps. 35.7–8, cf. v. 19) which explains why Jesus puts himself in his enemies' hands. 'Those who hate me without reason are more than the hairs of my head' (Ps. 69.4; cf. v. 9 'Zeal for your house has consumed me', quoted at John 2.17). Thus *They hated me without reason* prepared Jesus for hostility and marked the path of his disciples.

Support from the Paraclete

15.26–16.15   There is more to be said about the hostility of the world which will press hard upon the community. There are two ways of dealing with it. One is to surround the threat of death with promises of support from the Paraclete (in this present section); the other is to promise that grief will be overcome by joy (16.16–33).

In 14.17 the Spirit of truth 'dwells with you and will be in you'; so here the Spirit is *in* the community and its witness, and *with* the community in confronting the *kosmos* (see p. 17). *The Spirit of truth* is not a projection of our human search for the divine or of our true self-fulfilment. He issues from the Father, is sent by Jesus to be our *advocate* (or sponsor) and *bears witness* to him – namely as Agent of the Father. When Jesus himself (on whom the Spirit came to rest, 1.32) was no longer among them to present himself as the divine Agent, *the Spirit of truth* maintained that witness in the community – in agreement with the testimony of 'you who *have been with me from the first* witness of John' (vv. 26–27). The departure of Jesus makes it necessary for all members of the community to give their witness to him, and the presence of the Spirit of truth makes it possible.

Nevertheless, the faith of the community is under threat. The way to deal with that is to tell them the worst: *they will ban you from the synagogue* (cf. 9.22; 12.42); indeed, *the time is coming when anyone who kills you will suppose that he is serving God* – though without knowing the Father or properly assessing the threat posed by Jesus (vv. 1–3). On two grounds modern readers cannot respond with shock to that possibility: in our own time we are familiar with religious fanaticism, and we too must sometimes have thought that a few murders would put things right. But in the early days of Christianity the evidence for Jewish violence is slender: according to Acts, the killing of Stephen by councillors, with Paul assisting (Acts 7.54–59), and of James b. Zebedee by king Herod (Acts 12.1–2). According to the Jewish historian Josephus,[22] in 61 CE the high priest had James the brother of Jesus and some others stoned, though fair-minded Jews protested and had the high priest deposed. In the middle of the second century Justin, in his imaginary dialogue with Trypho,[23] accuses Jews of putting Christians to death when they had the power; and at the martyrdom of Polycarp[24] Jews were said to have been active in building the fire. There is no doubt that Christians suffered, and had good reason to be fearful; but not much damage was done by Jewish hostility. So Jesus tells them the worst – namely, that they may have to suffer death at the hands of devout people, and will have to cope with it themselves, with him not present. *'I am going away to him who sent me.'* Unlike Peter's earlier enquiry (13.36) and Thomas's probing comment (14.5), *None of you asks me 'Where are you going?'* They are too frightened. *You are plunged into grief at what I have told you* (vv. 5–6). These words of Jesus have a vocabulary of sadness that is absent from the farewell speech in ch. 14, and suit a rather different situation.

So there is need of consolation. *It is in your interest that I am leaving you. If I do not go, the advocate (paraclete) will not come.* Why? Because while he is with them, Jesus himself is their paraclete (I John 2.1; John 14.16) and himself has total command of the Spirit of truth (cf. 7.37). Therefore the actions of his disciples are responses to his physical presence rather than to the situation in which they find themselves – somewhat as a medical student, on the wards with the professor, responds to the teacher rather than to the patient. So if Jesus goes he will send the *paraclete*, and the community will have the proper freedom of making decisions. In vv. 8–11 that freedom is described, but the verses are difficult to interpret. It is worth discovering what the problems are.

(*a*) *Prove . . . wrong* is an attempt to translate a Greek verb which occurs 17 or 18 times in the NT (its noun form appears in the *Concise Oxford Dictionary* as 'elenchus' meaning a logical refutation) in the following senses: (i) to expose, as in John 3.20; (ii) to convict or

---

[22] Josephus, *Antiquities* 20.200.
[23] Justin, *Trypho* 95.4; 133.6.
[24] *Martyrdom of Polycarp* 13.1.

convince, as in John 8.46 REB; (iii) to reprove, as 8.46 can be translated: 'which of you reproves me concerning sin'; and (iv) to punish. In general it is a moralist's verb. So then is the *paraclete*, through the Christian community, rebuking the world, or dramatically convicting 'all the godless of every godless deed' in the manner of Jude 15?

(*b*) Whichever it is, it is *about (peri) sin, justice and judgment*. What do those three words mean? In this Gospel sin (*hamartia*) is the opposite of truth, wilful ignorance of the Logos, living entirely in *this* world, enslavement to impermanence, refusal to respond when words are spoken and signs are given by the Agent of God. In the Gospel *justice (dikaiosynē)* occurs only here; three times in the Epistle (I John 2.29; 3.7, 10). It means 'what is morally right and proper'. Finding a suitable translation for it is notoriously difficult: *justice* will do if the reader realises that a connection with law and legality is at best indirect. In this Gospel *judgment (krisis)* is an important theme. It is always a process of separating the good from the bad, of distinguishing what is true from what is false, of commending and strengthening the good and true and of condemning the false and bad. The word *krisis* sometimes concentrates on condemnation (self-imposed by the unbeliever, 3.19), but more often it refers to that distinguishing judgment by which the world can be saved, by which it can pass from death to life (5.24). When therefore Jesus said 'Now is the *krisis* of this world; now shall the prince of this world be driven out' (12.31) he was indicating the critical decision, the make-or-break point for human social existence. To sum up, it is the *paraclete*'s function to confront the *kosmos* with its deplorably self-destructive condition of sin, to hold before it what is morally right and proper, and to present the word and work of Jesus as the critically decisive factor.

(*c*) That would be satisfactory if the statement ended with v. 8; but it continues with comments on *sin, justice* and *judgment* in a standard form (*about . . . because*) though oddly varied in content (*because they refuse . . . ; because I go . . . ; because . . . he stands condemned*). The comment on *sin* is a brief indication of what has been said above. The comment on *justice*, however, is perplexing. How could the world be proven wrong about what is morally right and proper by the departure of Jesus from sight and the assertion that he had returned to his Father? Or should *justice* be read as the Father's vindication of his Son (as it might be in Paul) with the world being persuaded that it had misjudged the crucifixion? The comment on *judgment* is easier; but what was it the world had got wrong about *judgment*, and how would it change its mind if it was told that the prince of this world stood condemned? The best sense that can be made of this is to suppose two stages of composition: first vv. 8 and 11b, then the addition (not too happily) of vv. 9, 10 and 11a. The proposal may be written out thus:

8a *When he comes he will prove the world wrong*
 b *about sin,*
 c and about *justice,*
 d *and* about *judgment:*
9a [8b] *about sin,*
 b *because they refuse to believe in me;*
10a [8c] *about justice,*
 b *because I go to the Father,*
 c *when I pass from your sight;*
11a *about judgment,*
 b *because the prince of this world stands condemned.*

Thus the *paraclete* is to convince the world about *sin* and *justice* and about the possibilities of *judgment* at the critical moment when *the prince of this world stands condemned.*

This may be more comprehensible if the imagery is not rejected but translated for our own circumstances. The imagery has a group of disciples who rely on an eminent person called the *paraclete* to maintain their favour with God and to give them terms for existing in the *kosmos* ruled by its prince (sometimes bearing the archaic name Satan). So it follows that (*a*) the Christian community must not abandon the world but live in it, and therefore relate to the world below as well as to the world above. (*b*) The dominating forces of this world stand condemned by what the Father does in and through his Son. (In Britain today one of the names of the prince of this world is 'Value for Money'.) (*c*) The Christian community's orders are to expose the world's perpetual enslavement to eagerly sought but miserably destructive illusions, and to display what is morally right and proper in terms of Jesus who achieved glory after crucifixion.

So much for what the disciples can bear now! (v. 12). They cannot be prepared for every likely situation; and if they were, they would still be unprepared for unforeseen situations. *However, when the Spirit of truth comes, he will guide you into all the truth* i.e. the full scope of the truth. That famous promise will be misinterpreted if *the truth* is thought of as a vast collection of information and knowledge, or even as a repository of orthodox theology. *Truth* is the way to God newly available in his Son (see p. 78). When the need arises, when new circumstances demand a novel response, the *Spirit of truth* opens up the resources of this way to God. *He will not speak on his own authority,* independently of what we have been taught by Jesus. *He will speak only what he hears* from God as the necessary instruction for our need. *He will make known to you what is to come* (v. 13) – not in the sense of giving information about the course of future events, but of disclosing occasions on which the glory of Jesus can be displayed. *'He will glorify me, for he will take what is mine* – what service is due to me – *and make it known to you'* (v. 14). And of course by thus relating to Jesus they are related to the Father.

It is now possible to bring together the special sayings about the paraclete or Spirit of truth (see also pp. 120, 122–23). They are distinct from anything else in the Gospel tradition, certainly in expression and partially in content. It is probable that they correspond to certain developments in the Gospel community, whereby at first the breakaway group overemphasised the power of the Spirit and diminished the influence of Jesus, whereas the remaining members insisted on the essential importance of Jesus but underemphasised the work of the Spirit. When the Gospel reached the later stages of composition it was able to incorporate important sayings about the Spirit as the 'other *Paraclete*', Jesus being the first and primary *Paraclete*. The Spirit-*Paraclete* is not received or perceived by the world but relates the community firmly to God – in the name 'Spirit of truth' developing the community's inner life; in the name '*Paraclete*' defining the community's relation to the world. The Spirit issues from the Father, the *Paraclete* is given or sent by the Father. More precisely Jesus sends the Spirit-*Paraclete* from the Father, the Father sends the Spirit-*Paraclete* in the name of Jesus. Hence no one can suppose that the Spirit displaces Jesus. Moreover, in teaching all things, the Spirit reminds the community of what Jesus said, bears testimony to Jesus, takes what belongs to Jesus, makes it known and glorifies him. When the prince of this world stands condemned the Spirit, through the community, proves the world wrong about sin and justice – precisely because Jesus has returned to the Father and the Spirit has come as *Paraclete*.

Instruction about Grief and Joy

16.16–33 This section is deliberately repetitive. It begins with questions about the *little while*, already mentioned four times in the Gospel (7.33; 12.35; 13.33; 14.19), because that was obviously a nagging worry (vv. 16–19). It concludes in vv. 23–30 with detailed promises, previously recorded three times (14.12–14; 15.7, 14–16), that God will grant them what they ask in the name of Jesus. Thus the question is put beyond doubt and the answer is plainly given and plainly understood, in a context of grief and joy.

The perplexity (set out in vv. 16–19) arises from the apparent threat hidden in the saying of Jesus that they will see him for only *a little while* longer, though *again a little while* and they will see him. The shortness of the time is worrying. Between now and then what has to be done? Before he appears again what has to be decided? When Jesus spoke of *a little while* to the Jews, it was an urgent matter for them to become children of light, with the hint that, if they would not, the Greeks would. When he spoke similarly to his disciples it was urgent that they should establish the rule of mutual love and look to the *paraclete*. It is easy enough to say that there should be no perplexity: Jesus simply meant that in *a little while* he would be dead; *again a little while* and he would be raised from the dead. But it is not as if Jesus were going into hospital for a minor operation, after which all would be much the same as before. Within a very short time, an event of unimaginable consequence was to take place, as the disciples knew when they puzzled over *'Because I am going to the Father'*. The physical presence they could see was to be removed, yet then they were to see him again. They were not asking for an explanation of that strange possibility (*that* after all was God's affair, not theirs); they were worried about the time. Given the shortness of the time, what were they to do?

They were to *weep and mourn* at the death of Jesus (for this was to be a real, not a mimed death), and they were to bear the world's consequent rejoicing. But *your grief will be turned to joy* (v. 20). They were to understand their expected distress by means of the traditional image of a woman in labour (so, with more or less confidence in a new birth for God's people, in Isa. 26.16–19 and 66.7–14). She *is in pain because her time has come*. Already in this Gospel the appointed time carries great weight: the time or hour (both translating *hōra*) for true worship, for the dead to hear the voice of the Son of God, for

139

the Son to be glorified, for plain speaking and – to temper excitement
with realism – for the disciples to be scattered and killed (4.21, 23;
5.25, 28; 12.23 and 17.1; 16.25; 16.32 and 16.2). *But when her baby is
born she forgets the anguish (thlipsis*, a characteristic word in prophetic
visions of the end of this age, as in Dan. 12.1; Zeph. 1.15; Mark 13.19)
in her joy that a child has been born into the world. Just as there cannot be
new birth without pain (at least that is a woman's common experience, even if it should not be necessary) so there cannot be new life
for God's people apart from resistance, hostility and anguish. The
traditional language of the end of this age is appropriated for the
consequences of the death and resurrection of Jesus. The *kosmos* of
course goes on, and at the last day will come to its end (6.39, 40, 44,
54; 12.48); but disciples living in this world below can already be
transported into the world above. *For the moment you are sad; but I shall
see you again* (as the Son of Man welcoming those who are his), *and
then you will be joyful, and no one shall rob you of your joy* (v. 22).

That joy is also experienced by disciples living in this world
and (as agents of the Agent of God) representing Jesus here. The
community is authorised to do exactly that in two complementary
statements, vv. 23–24 and vv. 26–27. Their meaning is plain if the
reader understands that the repeated words *in my name* imply not
that the disciples are begging favours by using the name of Jesus,
but are asking instructions when acting in his name. This is not a
formula for gaining benefits (not even the answers to theological
questions), but a way of discovering what they must do. A small re-
arrangement (placing v. 23 inside v. 24) will help the reader:

> *So far you have asked nothing*
> (acting) *in my name.*
> *When that day comes*
> *you will ask nothing of me* (more is an invention).
> *In very truth I tell you,*
> *if you ask the Father for anything*
> (acting) *in my name,*
> *he will give it you.*
> *Ask and you will receive,*
> *that your joy may be complete* (vv. 23–24).

The promise is explicit: they will have the same access to the Father
that Jesus possesses. Till now Jesus has used *figures of speech*, almost
riddles *(paroimia)*, expressions that tease the will and the imagination
into activity – such as the shepherd and the sheep, the woman in

travail, the 'little while' (remembering 'For *a passing moment* I forsook you but with tender affection I shall bring you home again', Isa. 54.7). But now I *tell you of the Father in plain words* (v. 25). *When that day comes* they will make their request (for instruction) directly to the Father. Not that they can dispense with Jesus – for the Father's love for them corresponds to their love for Jesus and their belief that he came from God (v. 27); but in him they have direct access to the Father. In that understanding, Jesus gives to the disciples the definitive statement of his coming into the world and his departure from it (which will occupy his prayer in ch. 17). Whereupon *his disciples said, 'Now you are speaking plainly, not in figures of speech'* (and indeed he is providing the answer that will be needed to a later dispute within the community: namely, that believers have direct access to God in the Spirit but are thereby wholly dependent on Jesus). And they proceed to declare their understanding of *come from God*, not in the figurative language of a descent from heaven, but in terms of knowledge (*gnosis*):

> We are certain now
> that you know everything,
> and do not need to be asked (v. 30).

Since he knows everything he does not need to ask; since he is in command of those who are his agents, he has no need to rely on their request for instructions (with reference to v. 24a). Now they believe, and know what they mean by believing – and for that very reason a warning must be renewed. At the very moment when their conviction is strongest, Jesus must tell them that he will be supported by his Father, not by their conviction. Like him, and in him, they *may find peace* because he has *conquered the world*. Not that the *kosmos*, the social world of human life, has been transformed or overthrown; but that Jesus has opened the way to living both in this world and the world above.

The Son Reports to the Father

17.1–26   If chs 15–16 describe how disciples endure the world, ch. 17 sets out the definitive condition of their existence. The Agent of God tells the Father what he has done, what he has arranged for his disciples to do, and what consequences he has planned. This is the charter of the community. It is spoken publicly this side of the crucifixion, with the intention that its words should apply on the other side. It may be divided as follows:

1–5   A prayer for Jesus to be glorified.

6–8   A statement that the Agent has done what he was sent to do.

9–19 A prayer for the agents of the Agent of God in this world below.

20–23 A prayer for those who believe because of what the agents do.

24–26 A prayer relating the agents to the world above.

Granted that the whole prayer is exactly suited to the situation, it presents two major surprises. (*a*) It says nothing about the death of Jesus and nothing about the Spirit of truth. No one, it is true, can read the prayer in its context and ignore either; but it is equally true that the reader does not expect them to be taken for granted in the charter of the community. Why were they not explicitly mentioned? Probably because there was dispute in the community about emphasis on the blood and emphasis on the Spirit (I John 5.6–8). If both parties could consent to the words of this prayer, then each might welcome what the other was stressing. (*b*) The wording of the prayer brings it remarkably close to Hellenistic religions of *gnosis* (or religious awareness). In vv. 3, 7, 8, 23, 25 the emphasis is on knowing, and on the disclosure of the divine name (vv. 6, 11, 12, 26). This knowledge is brought (it seems) by an originally glorious precosmic being (vv. 5, 24) who enters the world in order to reject it and then to return whence he came. But certain people in the world belonged to God and were given to Jesus. He therefore gave them God's words, which they received; they knew that he came from God, that God had sent him, that everything God gave him was indeed from God (vv. 6–8, 10). Therefore Jesus asks that they may be with him where he is (in the world above) and may see his glory (v. 24). Does the definitive prayer of Jesus complete the shift from 'kingdom of God' to 'rebirth' (see p. 35 on 3.3) by adopting the form of gnostic religion; or is the genuine quest of gnostic religion brought to a point where the knowledge it helplessly seeks can become truth?

17.1–5 *The hour has come* for displaying the glory of God, thus finally affirming the repeated theme of Jesus' conflicts (7.39; 8.54; 11.4;

12.23, 28; 13.31–32). He had finished the work that was given him to do, namely glorifying God by performing the signs (see pp. 32–33) and by giving eternal life to an indicated group of people. God had *made him sovereign over all mankind* with the intention that he should exercise his sovereignty by the agency of people possessing the gift of eternal life. Clearly therefore eternal life is not a gift for private enjoyment but for public benefit; and since it is here mentioned for the last time in the Gospel, it is (as it were) defined: *to know you the only true God, and Jesus Christ whom you have sent* (v. 3).

KNOWLEDGE[25]

Words for *knowing* appear in every chapter of the Gospel, and some of the most effective story-telling depends on knowledge and ignorance, on recognition and mistaken identity (e.g. chs 9 and 21). It could be said that the Gospel is about knowing, though knowing is parallel to believing (which is not an inferior form of knowing): cf. 'we *believe* and *know* that you are God's Holy One' (6.69); and set 17.3 alongside 3.15 'everyone who has faith may in him have eternal life'. *Knowledge* is not simply useful information but has a measure of engagement; *faith* is not simply devotion but has a measure of understanding. Moreover it is worth observing that religious knowledge springs naturally out of everyday knowing. It includes possessing information; knowing that something has happened, is taking place, or is about to happen (13.11); knowing the right way (14.4, 5); knowing where somebody is, and who somebody is – recognising them and giving them recognition (4.42; 10.4, 5, 14, 27; 13.35). Such recognition is the key to many statements about knowing the Father and the Son (8.19; 10.15, 38; 14.7, 9, 20, 31; 15.21; 16.3) culminating in the disciples' confession in 16.30, which is taken up in 17.7–8. And there is more: knowing the origin of somebody (in that last reference, and also in 3.2; 7.29; 8.28; 13.3) leads to the basic statement of self-awareness: 'I know where I come from and where I am going', (8.14). There is also knowing the condition of people (2.24, 25) and knowing one's own mind – hence, knowing the mind or will of God (especially 'his commands are eternal life', 12.50; and knowing that the hour had come, 13.1; 19.28). Finally there is knowing (comprehending)

---

[25] The passages mentioned in this note use the Greek verbs *ginōskō* and *oida* (without observable distinction of meaning). REB usually translates 'know', but sometimes 'recognise, understand, be shown, be convinced'.

teaching or action (especially 7.17; 13.7, 12, 17) and knowing the truth (8.32).

Knowing *the only true God* has its root (often as a protest against the many gods of paganism) in the prophets, e.g. Jer. 31.33–34 'all of them, high and low alike, will know me, says the Lord'; and Hab. 2.14 'the earth will be full of the knowledge of the Lord's glory'. It is much developed in the Wisdom literature, e.g. Wisd. 15.3 'to know you is the whole of righteousness, and to acknowledge your power is the root of immortality'; and forcefully asserted by the Qumran community, e.g. 'from the source of his knowledge he has opened up his light and upon his wonders mine eye has gazed and the illumination of my heart is in the secret of what shall be and of that which is, for ever.'[26] But for Christians knowledge of you *the only true God* is inseparable from knowledge of *Jesus Christ whom you have sent* as is made plain in the famous 'Johannine' verses in Matt. 11.27, Luke 10.22.

If then Jesus had already glorified God on earth, why was it necessary for God to glorify him *now*? Not for the Son's honour, but for God's honour. In obedience to the Father, the Son was about to die; and death by crucifixion – universally shocking to the ancient world – scarcely seems to display God's glory. So Jesus prays that in dying he may display not (or not only) the cruel humiliation of God's Agent but the majestic, all-redeeming, transformative power of God – indeed the precosmic power of God who has life in himself (5.26). The imagery behind *the glory which I had with you before the world began* (vv. 5, 24) is of Jesus as a precosmic, divine being; the *significance* of the imagery, however, is that the glorious death of Jesus arises from the original creative purpose of God. Like the divine Wisdom, it is 'a clear effluence from the glory of the Almighty . . . the flawless mirror of the active power of God, and the image of his goodness (Wisd. 7.25–26).

17.6–8 What Jesus had done was to make known the *name* of God to those who already belonged to God. He did not (as a gnostic teacher might have done) persuade them of their *own* divinity, but he disclosed the divinity whose they were. If an actual *name* is implied it must be 'Father' (cf. 12.28 'Father, glorify your name') which Jesus

---

[26] Community Rule xi.3–4 in A. R. C. Leaney, *The Rule of Qumran and its Meaning*, London and Philadelphia 1966, p. 235.

disclosed by behaving as Son – as, for example, the meaning of the name Yorkshire is disclosed by the activities of Yorkshiremen. But perhaps the very word NAME carried a sense of mysterious power. A prayer from the Hermetic writings, widely known in antiquity (though probably later than this Gospel), gives thanks to 'the undisturbed name, honoured with the name God and praised with the name "Father" for . . . giving us mind, speech and knowledge: mind, so that we may understand Thee, speech, so that we may expound Thee, knowledge so that we may know Thee . . . We rejoice because while we were in the body, Thou hast made us divine through Thy knowledge.'[27] But for the Gospel, that moves in the wrong direction: the familiar thought (commonplace in the OT) that name discloses nature fits better. To *act* in somebody's name is to act as their authorised representative. To *believe* in somebody's name is to believe that they have effective power. To *make known* their name is to disclose that power (v. 6, repeated in v. 26). To *keep* them in that name is to keep them believing and acting in the power of the name (vv. 11, 12). That must be the meaning of *they have obeyed your* word: wider than *command* (as in REB), implying everything included in vv. 7–8. Here the disciples stand for the later community of the faithful.

17.9–19   The petition for the disciples in vv. 11b–19 is preceded in vv. 9–11a by the reason for the prayer and its object. Jesus is to be *no longer in the world*, but is returning to his Father; whereas *those whom you have given me are still in the world*. Through them the glory of Jesus is to be revealed. *All that is mine* (i.e. all my reliance on them to promote my glory) *is yours* (i.e. is your concern also); *and what is yours* (i.e. your power to direct them) *is mine* (i.e. is what they expect from me). Therefore Jesus prays God to instruct them for their new task in the world. He does not pray for the world, because his work *for* the world will now be done *in* the world by his instructed disciples (cf. vv. 21, 23 'that the world may believe . . . and know'). If we remember 'God so loved the world' (3.16), it is a shock at first to hear *I am not praying for the world*; but that is because we too readily assume that praying for somebody is praying for their well-being. But since God always intends our well-being, our intercessions should properly ask for a sense of the presence of God, and for instructions about what to do in adverse circumstances and the resolution to carry them out.

[27] The Prayer of Thanksgiving VI.7 in *The Nag Hammadi Library in English*, Leiden 1977, p. 298.

The intercession is addressed to God as the *Holy Father*, thus introducing at the beginning the theme of consecration with which this section will end. In a very early manual of Christian morals and church practice, the post-eucharistic prayer begins: 'We give you thanks, Holy Father, for your holy name, which you have made to dwell in our hearts . . . which you have made known to us through Jesus your servant.'[28] His intercession corresponds very closely to the possibilities and anxieties of a small community experiencing the pressures of the world.

(i) Jesus has established them in the *name*, i.e. the effective power of God; he prays that God will *keep* them in it (see above p. 144 – *protect* is an REB invention). *We are one*, i.e. God validates what Jesus says; *that they may be one*, in the same sense: each one living *by the power of your name* is validated by other members of the community (v. 11b).

(ii) Living in the world is risky. Even when Jesus *kept them safe*, someone was *doomed to be lost* (v. 12). That is a sensible translation of the Hebraic idiom 'son of perdition', which occurs again as 'the man doomed to destruction' in II Thess. 2.3, where Paul presents vivid images of the catastrophic ending of this age. Common to the two passages is the observation that life in the world is neither endlessly stable nor irreversibly progressive, but is involved in periodical ruin at the hands of people who overreach their powers and thus doom themselves (and many others) to be lost. It happened in the circle around Jesus, and this is a tacit prayer that it should not happen again.

(iii) Even so, life in the world can be joyful, and Jesus prays *that they may have my joy within them in full measure*. According to v. 13 that depends on the words that Jesus speaks while *still in the world*: according to 16.24 on being agents of the Agent of God; according to 15.11–12 on practising mutual love.

(iv) Yet they are inevitably *strangers in the world*, as he is; and therefore are objects of hatred or rejection – as British-born Pakistanis are in some English towns. So Jesus asks God, not to remove them from the world (i.e. not to permit them to live in an enclosed, self-regarding community) *but to keep them from the evil one* (vv. 14–15). The translation of that last phrase (no doubt because of the prince of this world in 12.31; 14.30; and 16.11) is modelled on 'save us from

---

[28] *Didache* (*Teaching of the Twelve Apostles*) 10.2 in E. J. Goodspeed, *The Apostolic Fathers*, London 1950, p. 15.

the evil one' in the Lord's Prayer (Matt. 6.13). But unlike Matthew, this Gospel lacks interest in demonic powers: '*keep them from the* (inevitable) *evil* (of the world)' would be better. I John 5.19 says that 'the whole world lies in the power of the evil one'; but the writer has said plainly what he means in 2.16: 'all that panders to the appetites or entices the eyes, all the arrogance based on wealth'.

(v) Strangers as they are, like Jesus himself (v. 16) what are they to make of their 'separation-but-not-withdrawal'? They are to treat it (if God so wills) as their consecration, i.e. their separation for the sacred task of following and demonstrating the way of truth, which is the true way to God, which is God's word as indicated in vv. 7–8 (v. 17). *As you sent me into the world, I have sent them into the world* (v. 18). That is, into the world below. How then can they remain consecrated in the world below and at the same time belong to the world above (see p. 141)? By the self-offering of Jesus; *for their sake I consecrate myself, that they too may be consecrated* in the service of (not *by*) the truth. 'To consecrate oneself' is not a common expression: it belongs to the priestly instructions (e.g. Lev. 11.44; 20.7–8),[29] and it means to put yourself in the proper condition for performing sacred duties and for encountering God. Jesus will consecrate himself *for their sake* as the good shepherd lays down his life *for* the sheep (10.11), as one man expediently dies *for* the people (11.50), as someone lays down his life *for* his friends (15.13). In each place *for* is *hyper*, meaning 'for the benefit of'. Jesus regards his death as a cleansing from the world so that, as Son of Man, he can represent in the presence of God that humanity which pursues its consecrated task in the world.

17.20–23   This section of the prayer looks to the situation that will be created when the disciples bring others to faith, when other sheep listen to the good shepherd and become one flock (10.16), when Jesus dies not for the nation alone but to gather together the scattered children of God (11.52). The *one* flock dominates the intercessions, with unity explained entirely as interdependence. This part of the prayer is often compared with the community of Qumran, which used the Hebrew word *yaḥad* as a self-designation meaning 'unity'. Those who joined the sect agreed 'to separate themselves from the congregation of the men of falsehood in order to form a *yaḥad* with respect to the Law and possessions'.[30] But the Qumran *yaḥad*

[29] REB translates 'make yourselves holy', 'hallow yourselves'.
[30] Community Rule v.1f. (*DSSE* p. 87).

separated itself from the world, and insisted on a rigorous unity of convictions, behaviour and hierarchy. Not so the community of the Gospel. This prayer makes plain the manner, the means and the purpose of unity. *May they all be one: (a) manner – as you, Father are* relying on me, *and I* am dependent on *you*. May their life be modelled on us; *(b) purpose – that the world may believe that you sent me* (v. 21). But that might imply no more than imitation of the divine life, so the prayer turns to *(c) means*. The community relies on the gift of glory, not to be exploited but to be mutually experienced. *The glory which you gave me I have given to them, that they may be one, as we are one* (v. 22). Nor is the community assisted simply from outside, but by internal activity: *I* (doing my work) *in them and you* (doing your work) *in me*, that *they may be perfectly one; that the world may know* that God sent his Son and has shown his love (v. 23).

17.24–26   Finally Jesus prays that the disciples, still in the world, may look upon his glory and be where he is, i.e. may see his crucifixion and thereby be lifted into the world above. He expresses *my desire* and, since the disciples were *your gift to me*, he addresses God as *righteous Father* and knows that God will grant his request. Knowledge of God is offered by Jesus through the disciples to an unrecognising world; and it is clear to Jesus and the disciples that knowledge of the name (i.e. the effective power) of God (see p. 143) is knowledge of his love which predates the creation (see p. 144). Two points need comment. When Jesus presents 'my desire' to God it is clear not only that the Son carries out the Father's intentions but also that the Father responds to the Son's desires. The Agent of God is not a mere administrator of the Father's instruction, but a creative exponent of the Father's love. When Jesus addresses God as *righteous Father* some meaning must be attempted for the word *righteous*. It has long fallen out of use among English speakers, and the meanings given in the *Concise Oxford Dictionary* (morally right, just, upright, virtuous, law-abiding) are unsuitable. When applied to God it consorts with faithful, true, gracious and merciful (I John 1.9; Deut. 32.4; Ps. 116.5).[31] It means that God behaves properly as a father should, that he can be relied on to show his love.

---

[31] In REB I John 1.9 *just*, can be trusted; Deut. 32.4 *just*, faithful, *righteous*, true; Ps. 116.5 gracious, *righteous*, full of compassion.

John: Dating the final days

		THUR
6 pm	14 Nisan ———————————————————————	
	Last Supper (13.1)	
	Arrest of Jesus (18.1–12)	
Midnt	— —	
6 am		
	Examination of Jesus before Pilate (18.28–19.16)	
	Condemnation of Jesus (19.14)	FRI
	Passover lambs killed	
	Death of Jesus (19.31)	
	Burial of Jesus (19.42)	
6 pm	15 Nisan/Sabbath ———————————————————	
	Passover meal (Lev. 23.5)	
Midnt	— —	
		SAT
6 pm	16 Nisan ———————————————————————	
	First day of the week	
Midnt	— —	
6 am	Mary Magdalene at the tomb (20.1)	
		SUN
6 pm	17 Nisan ———————————————————————	

Mark has the same days of the week as John, but alters the Jewish calendar by one day: John's 14 Nisan becomes Mark's 15 Nisan and the Last Supper coincides with the Passover meal.

The Passion and Resurrection:
Jesus, the Jewish authorities, and the
Roman state
18–20

The narrative can conveniently be divided as follows:

18.1–14 the arrest	cf. Mark 14.43–53
18.15–27 the denials	14.54–72
18.28–19.16a interrogation and verdict	15.1–20a
19.16b–30 the crucifixion	15.20b–41
19.31–42 the burial	15.42–47
20.1–18 at the tomb	16.1–8
20.19–29 in a closed room	
20.30–31 conclusion	

If these sections are compared with the roughly corresponding Markan passages, it appears that this Gospel is using old tradition which it sometimes confirms, supplements, modifies or even contradicts.

The Arrest

18.1–14   Jesus goes to meet his betrayer (perhaps by arrangement, 14.30–31) in *a garden* (for herbs and vegetables, no doubt with an olive-grove) east of the city *across the Kedron ravine*. He knows everything that is going to happen (v. 4): the story concentrates on the encounter between Jesus and the prince of this world. There is no anguished prayer (though 12.27–28 may be a memory of the story in Mark 14.32–41); there is no betrayer's kiss (Mark 14.45). The disciples are marginal figures (including Judas), and even Peter's attempted resistance is curtly rejected.

The prince of this world is represented by *a detachment of soldiers* (a Roman cohort of six hundred men under its commander (v. 12), a tribune) with temple police supplied by the Jewish authorities (the officials who had acted so feebly in 7.32, 45–46). That was an enormous force (including the whole Jerusalem garrison) to make a single arrest. It helps little to suggest that the number was really much smaller; for, if the arrest of Jesus was important to the Romans, why was he handed over to Annas? Various explanations can be devised, but they miss the point, namely that all the king's horses and all the king's men could not arrest Jesus unless he wished to be arrested. The Pharisees saw the danger, the chief priests supplied the temple police, the Romans turned out in force; but Jesus was in command – necessarily, because the operation was incompetently organised (*lanterns and torches* would have warned desperate men to flee). So Jesus brings them to order and identifies himself: *'I am he'* (see I AM, pp. 61–62). But that throws them into grovelling confusion (cf. Ps. 27.2 'it is my adversaries, my enemies, who stumble and fall', and passages such as Dan. 10.9; Rev. 1.17 where people collapse in the presence of divine beings). So he takes a firmer grip on the situation, and demands (*not* requests) *'If I am the man you want, let these others go'* (so carrying out the promise that 'no one will snatch them from my care', 10.23; cf. also 6.39; 17.12). Simon Peter has as little understanding of what is going on as the soldiers and police: he inflicts a minor injury on the high priest's servant! (The name *Malchus* is not a sign of first-hand knowledge but of first-rate sensitivity: if in defence of Jesus you intend to injure someone, you had better know that he has a name, that he is a human being known to God and presumably loved by him.) Jesus stops Peter's aggression: *'This is the cup the Father has given me; shall I not drink it?'* (v. 11 – cf. 'It is for this that I came to this hour', 12.27; 'No one takes my life away from me; I lay it down of my own free will', 10.17–18). There is no request for the cup to be taken from him. So Jesus makes the arrest easy, and is taken away to Annas, the formidable 'godfather' (as it were) of the ruling high-priestly family. He had been high priest from 6 to 15 CE, but was deposed by the Romans. After three temporary appointments he was succeeded by his son-in-law Caiaphas, 18–36 CE (and at various times between 16 and 62 five sons of Annas held the high priesthood).[1] Caiaphas had already agreed at a meeting with his advisers (11.47–53) *that it would be to their interest if one man died for the people* (v. 14).

---

[1] Information in Schürer II, pp. 230–232.

The Denials

18.15–27   For whatever reason, Peter follows Jesus to the high priest's house (hence *the girl on duty at the door*; cf. Rhoda, Acts 12.13), accompanied by *another disciple known to the high priest*. This person cannot and need not be identified. The Gospel is intended for Levantine readers who would know that there is always somebody who can arrange things. The narrative function of this person is to tell the reader that each party to the confrontation is capable of finding out what the other is up to. So Peter gains access to *the high priest's courtyard*, mingles with *the servants and the police*, perhaps hears the questioning taking place and sees the blow struck, and is a witness when Jesus is led away. Once before the interrogation, once afterwards he denies being a disciple and (to ward off the relatives of the injured man) denies having been with Jesus in the garden. Doubtless he was still smarting from Jesus' rebuke (v. 11), but anybody could now see that Peter would cause no further trouble. *It was cold*, and the denials strike a chill.

There is no suggestion of a large gathering or of a formal session of 'the sanhedrin' (the phrase is not used in this Gospel – see p. 93 n. 33). The old high priest Annas (cf. Luke 3.2; Acts 4.6) is not putting Jesus on trial or even preparing a preliminary case against him. He already knows sufficient about him, and is now sounding him out. He questions him *about his disciples and about his teaching*. About his disciples, Jesus makes no reply. Therefore Annas can conclude that Jesus will not use them as a threat (and with Peter's example on the other side of the courtyard, he is right). About his teaching, Jesus refuses to make claims or assertions, saying merely '*I have said nothing in secret . . . Question those who heard me.*' To later readers that reply is an astounding example of Jesus' confidence in his hearers, but to Annas it is evidence of weakness. Even when Jesus is smacked on the face for insolence to the high priest (allegedly in defiance of Exod. 22.28 'you must not . . . curse a chief of your own people'), he utters only a dignified protest – and nothing comes of it. Annas therefore concludes that Jesus has lost confidence and support and so sends *him bound to Caiaphas* – presumably with the implication 'Do as you see fit. There will be no trouble.' Some commentators utter squeaks about the illegality of interrogating a prisoner and of ill-treating him. Do they not realise that Jesus was simply helping the temple police with their enquiries? Do they not realise that when an individual threatens society or those who have power within it, legality commonly preserves society and the powerful?

In this piece of narrative, however, more than usual demands are made on the reader. It must be realised that (ex-)high priest Annas is at work in the background, and that high priest Caiaphas acts in the foreground in a shrewdly calculated operation. And it must be remembered that Caiaphas had already decided, at a meeting of advisers, what ought to be done (11.47–53). Jesus attracted great attention by his signs and gathered supporters, but he had also made enemies: the temple priesthood and business interests, the nationalists (he was pro-Samaritan, 8.48), the Pharisees, and no doubt God himself (since he claimed equality with God, 5.18). His claims and the objections to them had been publicly discussed. Competent authority had decided that he was a danger to the nation and must die. The only question for Caiaphas to decide was how to put formal accusations against him to the Romans. This is entirely plausible, even though at this point it gives no account of a meeting of 'the chief priests and the whole Council' such as is provided in Mark 14.55–65. It must be admitted that Mark's account does not closely follow the admirable but perhaps imaginative rules of Tractate Sanhedrin of the Mishnah; and English readers need to remind themselves that the peculiar adversarial system of English law courts is not widely regarded as either sensible or just.

Pilate's Interrogation and Verdict

18.28–19.16a   This section and the next make even more demands upon the reader. The narrative of Pilate's interrogation of Jesus is more impressive for its dramatic power than for its historical plausibility. It is not a neutral account of an ancient trial, but a theological presentation in the form of a story. Nor is it, however, a pretext for discrediting the Jewish authorities and thereby blaming the whole Jewish people. It is not open for Christians to dishonour Jews because they are Jews. Paul made that quite plain in Rom. 9–11, and in John 4.22 it is explicitly said that 'it is from the Jews that salvation comes'. Even if Jesus could severely reproach his fellow Jews (in chs 7–8), when on trial he utters not one word of complaint – indeed he says that his kingdom is no threat to Jewish rule (18.36).

What then is the theological purpose of the trial story? The Jewish authorities are determined to make the Romans do what (according to their law, 19.7) they want done but cannot themselves do. To avoid defilement they stay outside the Roman headquarters (18.28). They are insolent to Pilate (18.30), demand the release of a bandit (18.40) and crucifixion for Jesus (19.6), and they threaten Pilate with an official complaint to Caesar (19.12). They get their wish, but only by admitting that they 'have no king but Caesar' (19.15). When God's people, regarding the pagan state with contempt, nevertheless use the state for their own ends, they have their reward – but lose their purity and surrender the sovereignty of God. That is as much a theological lesson for the church as for the synagogue – and it has consequences for the state. The governor Pilate, carrying full military, juridical and financial responsibility on behalf of the Roman state, tells the Jewish authorities to try Jesus by their own law (18.31), finds nothing against him and offers to release him (18.38–39). Yet he has Jesus scourged, permits him to be humiliated and uses him to mock his accusers (19.1–5); but then, giving way to panic, bluster and self-interest, concedes the accusers' demands and hands Jesus over to be crucified. Nobody could seriously believe that this deplorable account was written to ingratiate Christians with the Romans, or to deflect responsibility for the crucifixion from the Romans to the Jews. This is the *kosmos* at work – the scene in which God's will is performed by his Agent.

The story is told in seven dramatic scenes, placed alternately outside the headquarters and inside. This makes a dramatic separation between Jews and Romans, except for the fifth and seventh episodes when Pilate shows Jesus to the Jews. Jesus speaks only inside the headquarters (second and seventh episodes) and it is not possible to be confident in suggesting how the words of Jesus and Pilate could have been heard and reported.

(i) 18.28–32. The Roman *governor's headquarters*, normally at Caesarea, were established in Jerusalem during the great festivals.[2] The governor would usually do official business as soon as possible after dawn. Why entry into his headquarters should cause defilement to Jews is not entirely clear, even if later Pharisaic purity rules were already generally accepted (which is unlikely); but it is entirely clear that the passover lamb had not yet been eaten (v. 28). Pilate was

---

[2] Either in Herod's palace or less probably in the Antonia fortress. See J. Wilkinson, *Jerusalem as Jesus knew it*, London and New York 1978, pp. 132–144.

prefect of Judaea from 26 to 36 CE. His contemporary Agrippa I, in a letter to the emperor, referred to Pilate's briberies, insults, robberies, outrages and wanton injuries, executions without trial, his ceaseless and supremely grievous cruelty, his vindictiveness and furious temper.[3] By contrast, in the Gospel he is patient, willing to listen, and no match for the Jews. He asks what charge they bring against Jesus (v. 29) and gets an insolent answer (v. 30). Of course he knew the charge (as the reader does) but he wishes the Jews to make it – so that it is *they* who denounce a Jewish messianic claimant. The Jews intend that Pilate, using information that they must have given him, should make the charge of sedition. So Pilate directs the Jews to *try him by your own law*; whereupon they admit that they want Jesus put to death by saying: *'We are not allowed to put anyone to death'* (v. 31), possibly 'at this festival time' but probably 'at any time'. This explicit statement has been strongly attacked (in view of other evidence, such as the death of Stephen, Acts 7.54–8.2) but 'if the Sanhedrin exercised an accepted capital jurisdiction in the first century, this was an exception rather than the rule for a local authority in a province'.[4] The Gospel statement is even more plausible if the high priest's council was simply his advisory body, and if the Gospel writer was addressing himself to Syrian readers. The result was that Jesus was put to death not by stoning (like Stephen) but by the Roman method of crucifixion. That death was not only agonising but shocking to all observers, a dreadful warning and an abiding shame to the dead man's family and supporters. But in fact this ensured *the fulfilment of the words by which Jesus had indicated the kind of death he was to die* (32, cf. 3.14; 8.28; 12.32) – the death by which he would be 'lifted up from the earth'. It was the ancient Passover theme: from shame to glory.

(ii) 18.33–38a. Inside the headquarters, Pilate questions Jesus about a claim to be *king of the Jews* (v. 33). That is a Roman way of putting it (Jews would have said 'king of Israel' as in 1.49 and 12.13); so Jesus, speaking at least as an equal, asks whether the question came from Pilate or elsewhere (v. 34). Pilate concedes that he himself has no information except the Jewish accusation; and asks Jesus *'What have you done?'* (v. 35). He could have replied that in Galilee he had evaded attempts to proclaim him king (6.15) – thus admitting that he could be a focus for political disturbance. Instead he refers to his recent arrest when his followers did not fight *to save me from the clutches of*

---

[3] In Philo, *Embassy to Gaius* 302. See Schürer I, pp. 383–387.
[4] Schürer II, p. 220 n. 80.

the Jews – implying his repudiation of directly political kingship (which word is better here than *kingdom*). If Pilate wishes to use the word *king*, then Jesus will admit to kingship of a kind. It is a kingship which does not derive its authority and effectiveness from *this world*, from the struggle for power and self-interested aims of human society as we know it. The translation *My kingdom does not belong to this world* is unsatisfactory if it implies that it has no effective exercise in human society. Precisely because eternal life (the concept preferred to kingship in this Gospel) is livable both in the world below *and* the world above, Jesus can lay claim to a kingship derived from *elsewhere*, a kingship displayed in total mastery of *the truth*, i.e. the true way to God (see p. 78). The whole purpose of Jesus' life, the whole aim of gathering followers was to discover those *who are not deaf to truth* (v. 37).

(iii) 18.38b–40. By asking '*What is truth?*' Pilate excludes himself from that company, and very properly turns to the necessary question: What is expedient? He finds no case against Jesus to justify the death penalty (so also in 19.4, 6), so how can the matter be resolved? – since anyone in custody must have done something wrong! 'There is a custom to your advantage',[5] he says, '*that I release one prisoner for you at Passover*' (v. 39). So he proposes to use the custom and release this harmless *king of the Jews*. But the Jews, prompted by the offer of release, attack Pilate by demanding another prisoner *Barabbas, a bandit*, i.e. someone accused of robbery with violence. If it is implied that Barabbas was released though Jesus was condemned, that is more like a parable of the gospel than a pretext for moral outrage.

(iv) 19.1–3. Pilate must find another way, so he tries a familiar Roman practice: give the prisoner a beating to teach him a lesson for being a nuisance, and let him go (cf. Luke 23.22). It becomes something more than a beating when the soldiers add crude mockery of Jesus' alleged kingship. They dress him up as minor Hellenistic royalty, with a mock radiate *crown* and *a purple cloak*; they hail him as *king of the Jews* and, pretending to offer him reverence, strike *him on the face*. It is possible that this spiteful buffoonery was copied from coarse popular plays of the period, and it is recorded that something like it took place to humiliate the Jewish king Agrippa when he visited

---

[5] Taking *hymin* as a dative of advantage, with Schnackenburg, *John*, vol. 3, p. 252. It is quite unknown whether this custom existed elsewhere or was peculiar to Judaea, whether taken over from the previous Hasmonean priest-kings or as a concession by Pilate.

Alexandria in 38 CE.[6] In Mark the beating and mockery took place (as one would expect) *after* Pilate's decision to have Jesus crucified. Here they precede it, and make the next episode possible; but this placing has theological as well as dramatic significance. Not only the kingship of Jesus but kingship in general is derided. Or, to put it otherwise, kingship is seen in its true colours when a representative man is hurt, humiliated and threatened. That raises the question whether kingship is any longer acceptable imagery for the divine being; and we remember that Jesus has already abandoned 'kingdom of God' for 'eternal life' (see p. 37). In the continuing encounter between Pilate and the Jewish authorities, Pilate supposes that they object to Jesus calling himself 'king of the Jews', but he is wrong. They reject his claim to be 'Son of the Father'.

(v) 19.4–7. Again Pilate publicly announces that he finds *no case against him* (requiring the death penalty) and brings Jesus out to show them a man badly beaten and grotesquely mocked – as much as to say: 'If you want a messianic king, this is what you can have.' In the famous words *Here is the man* (*ecce homo*) Pilate is saying 'He is a man, not a king. As you can see, there is no evidence of sovereignty or divinity about him'; though, in Pilate's words, Christian readers may well hear an unwitting description of Jesus as representative mankind, and may remember 'When you have lifted up the Son of Man you will know that I am what I am' (8.28 – see p. 77). *The chief priests and the temple police*, however, demand that the governor should deal with him as Romans treated rebellious slaves. If he were crucified he would become an outcast from Israel, a social non-person, an object of universal shame. But for the third time Pilate says *'for my part I find no case against him'* – and what is said three times is an unbreakable decision. So the Jews change their ground: Jesus may not be defying Caesar, but he is defying God. *We have a law* (Lev. 24.16 'Whoever utters the name of the LORD must be put to death. The whole community must stone him'); *and according to that law he ought to die* (so that Pilate's sarcastic *Take him yourselves and crucify him* is in fact a shrewd thrust against the community trying to push its own duty on to the Romans) *because he has claimed to be God's Son* (cf. 5.18; 10.33–36). We do not know today, and Pilate would not have known then, how the chief priests interpreted the law of blasphemy – uttering the name of the LORD. It has been argued that in claiming divine sonship Jesus corresponds exactly to Hanina ben Dosa, the

[6] P. Winter, *On the Trial of Jesus*, 2nd ed. Berlin and New York 1974, pp. 148–149.

first-century Galilean miracle-worker;[7] but what was acceptable in Galilee may have horrified Jerusalem. In any case the chief priests insist that Jesus had violated Jewish religious law – with the implication that Pilate must needs avoid the accusation that he failed to respect Jewish custom.

(vi) 19.8–12. To us Pilate's response is surprising, but not to the ancient world (something similar happened when the contemporary religious philosopher Apollonius of Tyana was on trial before a Roman court):[8] the governor 'shared the superstitious regard entertained by many pagans for the *divine man*, the adept or mage, credited with occult powers, who often claimed divine origin'.[9] Hence the anxious question *Where have you come from?* Hence also Jesus' refusal to reply: how could he answer an entirely proper question based on totally wrong assumptions? So Pilate threatens Jesus with his power to *release* or *crucify* him – at the very moment when he is no longer free to exercise that power but is caught in a political trap. Both Pilate and Jesus know it, and Jesus goes as far as he can to help Pilate in his need. He says two things: first, *You would have no authority at all over me if it had not been granted you from above* (i.e. not merely from Caesar, but from God). Hence what Pilate will be forced to do arises essentially not from his own weakness or the Jewish animosity but from the divine will. Second, that what he will do is an evil thing for which he is guilty (for guilt is bearing the consequences, even if not the blame, for what you have done) but *the deeper guilt* belongs elsewhere – to whoever denounced him to the Romans. By that verdict the prisoner has become the judge. That Pilate accepts the verdict is shown by his further attempts to release Jesus; but he is foiled by the Jewish cry: *If you let this man go, you are no friend to Caesar* (possibly an honorific title); *anyone who claims to be a king is opposing Caesar* (i.e. is guilty of treason). Now the Emperor Tiberius had withdrawn to Capri in 26 CE and was moving towards the madness that clouded the last six years of his life (he died in 37 CE). He was hypersensitive to treason, in part because his chief minister Sejanus had corruptly used the law of treason to get rid of enemies. Pilate was a protégé of Sejanus,[10] who however fell from power and was put to death in 31 CE. That year must be somewhat close to the date of Jesus' trial, but in any

[7] G. Vermes, *Jesus the Jew*, London 1973, New York 1974, p. 209.
[8] Philostratus, *Life of Apollonius* IV.44.
[9] C. H. Dodd, *Historical Tradition in the Fourth Gospel*, Cambridge and New York 1963, p. 114.
[10] Implied in Eusebius, *Ecclesiastical History* II.5.7.

case Pilate would not want a Jewish report to Rome that he had released a prisoner suspected of treason.

(vii) 19.13–16a. The governor therefore *took his seat on the tribunal*. In a defence of Christianity from the middle of the second century it is said that 'they tormented him and set him on the judgment seat, and said "Judge us"';[11] and some modern interpreters have supposed that Pilate symbolically placed Jesus on the tribunal. But that would scarcely be plausible as the act of a Roman prefect, however apt the symbolism. Nor would it match the solemnity of the occasion which is formally identified by day (*the day of preparation for the Passover* – as vv. 31, 42; see p. 149) and by hour (*about noon*, when the killing of Passover lambs would begin – in Mark 15.25 Jesus was crucified at nine in the morning; at midday a darkness fell over the whole land) and by place (*The Pavement*).[12] Pilate then explicitly transfers responsibility to the Jews: he uses their accusation (which he has three times rejected) and presents Jesus to them: *Here is your king*. When they demand crucifixion he asks *Am I to crucify your king?* Their scarcely credible reply is *We have no king but Caesar* – except that this is said by the chief priests, and there are circumstances when priests will do anything to preserve their power. Pilate bought their loyalty to Rome by the death of Jesus, though by the time this Gospel was written both temple and priesthood had been destroyed in a disastrous war with Rome.

The Crucifixion

19.16b–30   In this Gospel the account of the crucifixion differs greatly from other accounts. In comparison with Mark there is no mention of Simon of Cyrene, of the offer of wine and myrrh, of the reviling and jeering by the crowd and by those crucified with him, of the darkness, of the explicit loud cry to God, or of the confusion about Elijah. Not only are some episodes chosen rather than others, but

---

[11] Justin, *Apology* I.35.6. The Greek verb *ekathisen* could be translated 'sat' or 'caused to sit'.

[12] 'The Pavement' (Greek *lithostrōton*): paved with stones, possibly a tesselated or mosaic area. Nobody really knows what 'Gabbatha' meant. A paved area has been found in a building that may have been the Antonia (see p. 154 n. 2), though possibly from a century later.

the whole impression is changed. Whereas Mark presents a scene of shouting, malice, confusion, distress and mysterious dread, this Gospel has a quiet, well-ordered scene. Everyone present does whatever has to be done with unhurried competence, including Jesus' carrying of his own cross. What happens is under control; each episode is instructive.

That Jesus *went out, carrying the cross*(-bar) *himself* focuses on his self-determination. When 'Abraham took the wood for the sacrifice and put it on his son Isaac's shoulder' (Gen. 22.6), the boy scarcely knew what he was doing; but Jesus knew exactly what he was doing, and willed himself to do it. *The place was called . . . in Hebrew, 'Golgotha'* (v. 17) – another Semitic name (like 'Gabbatha' in v. 13) to keep this fact before the reader's mind that Jesus was a Jewish man dying in the Jewish land for more than the Jewish people, and dying *with two others, one on either side* (v. 18). Those two appear again in v. 32 to be contrasted with Jesus; but however different Jesus may be, here he shares this dreadful death with two anonymous Jews. Crucifixions were performed in various ways. The least cruel method was to tie or nail the prisoner's outspread arms to the cross-bar, then to hoist him up and fix him to the vertical post so that the body rested on a peg jutting from the post, to which the feet were nailed or fastened with rope. (A few years ago a tomb was discovered just north of Jerusalem, containing the skeleton of a youngish man who had been thus crucified.) The contemporary Roman moralist Seneca describes a man 'fastened to the accursed tree, already weak, already deformed, swelling with ugly weals on shoulders and chest and drawing the breath of life amid long-drawn-out agony'.[13] That would be understood by any ancient reader – but not one word of the narrative calls attention to it.

Instead, two dramatic episodes involving the Romans are developed. *First* the *inscription written and fastened to the cross*, using the local, the official and the commercial languages of the country, *read by many Jews* (so presumably in large letters, on a large board – requiring eighty-one characters if written out in full – so forming a major feature of the scene). If Jesus was condemned for treason (see v. 12) this inscription was an oblique way of indicating his crime; but Pilate refuses to withdraw what he said (v. 14) when the charge was made. Nor will he pretend that Jesus had claimed what in fact he had denied ('My kingdom does not belong to this world', 18.36). The

---

[13] Seneca, *Epistle* 101 to Lucilius.

inscription is a public statement (no doubt intended to be insulting) that, if the Jews want a messiah, this is the best they will get. *What I have written, I have written* (v. 22). And if Pilate's written words cannot be changed, how much less can the words of God! In the *second* episode, the soldiers follow custom and appropriate the prisoner's clothing. The outer clothes they divide among themselves; the seamless inner tunic (worn next to the body) one of them acquires by chance. So the words of Ps. 22.18 come true: *They shared my garments among them, and cast lots for my clothing* (v. 24). This psalm of the indignant sufferer includes many pictures of misfortune: here somebody has been set upon by robbers who are stripping their victim and dividing his clothing (cf. the man on the Jericho road in Luke 10.30). That sort of thing can happen to the godly person, and here it is happening to Jesus. The psalm is not predicting what must be fulfilled but what can all too easily take place, on the principle ascribed to Rabbi Akiba (a younger contemporary of the Gospel): 'All (i.e. every possibility) is foreseen, but freedom of choice is given.'[14] Many commentators are entranced by the seamless tunic. They refer it to the high priest's vestment (Exod. 28.32 – though garments woven in one piece were familiar in Palestine)[15] with the description in Josephus and the compulsive allegorising of Philo. So Jesus is allusively represented as the high priest, or the tunic represents the unity of the church. If so, why is the symbol of Christ's priesthood, or of the church's unity, in the hands of Roman soldiers who will sell it to advantage in the market? The symbolism is simpler and more powerful: even in these deplorable circumstances, something intimately belonging to Jesus is not destroyed but preserved and goes – it seems by chance – into the ruthless world of the Roman empire.

Near the cross (v. 25 – though Mark 15.40 says 'watching from a distance') were four women (though the list *could* be read as meaning only three, or even two): the mother of Jesus, her sister, Mary wife of Clopas, and Mary of Magdala (as well as the beloved disciple).

---

[14] Aboth 3.16 (Danby, p. 452). For poetic emphasis the parallel lines of Ps. 22.18 make the same statement in complementary language about the psalmist's *himatia* and his *himatismon*. The Gospel speaks of two separate items: Jesus' *himatia* and his *chitōn* – clearly not invented from the psalm (as some suggest), because the Gospel does not reproduce the two Greek words from the psalm. It fits plausible tradition rather fortuitously to the psalm's complaint.

[15] In the fourth century Theodore of Mopsuestia says that such methods of weaving were common in the time of Christ, although in his day they had died out except for soldiers' uniforms. M. F. Wiles, *The Spiritual Gospel*, Cambridge and New York 1960, p. 25.

With these four women as witnesses (two of them have no other function) Jesus makes provision for his mother and for the beloved disciple. Once more Jesus addresses his mother with grave courtesy as he did at Cana (2.4, see pp. 30–31). From that previous episode we know that she is a mother in Israel (i.e. she leads the Jewish component of the future Christian community), she can detect a YES within a daunting NO, and she tells people to obey Jesus. Therefore he points to the beloved disciple and says *There is your son*, i.e. he commends to faithful Jews the kind of discipleship which he chiefly approves. *To the disciple* he says: *There is your mother*, and so that disciple becomes heir to the family tradition (very important in the Near East) and can outrun Peter to the tomb in 20.4.

Having thus performed his last acts for his own people and for his disciples (with at least equal responsibility given to women and men), Jesus has one final group to consider: those who are crucifying him. *Aware that all had now come to its appointed end*, he behaved as a devout Jew and *said in fulfilment of scripture, 'I am thirsty'*. It is usually supposed that Ps. 22.15 is meant: 'My mouth is dry as a potsherd', or Ps. 69.21: 'When I was thirsty they gave me vinegar to drink.' Yet neither fits well, and a better interpretation is possible. A passage in the Talmud[16] explains that wine was given to numb the senses of a man led to execution, and justifies this charity to a public enemy by quoting Prov. 31.6: 'Give strong drink to the despairing and wine to the embittered of heart.' What is more, such kindness is a way of gaining merit for 'If your enemy . . . is thirsty, give him drink . . . and the Lord will reward you' (Prov. 25.21–22, used by Paul in Rom. 12.20). So Jesus gives his executioners an opportunity of gaining merit, i.e. he forgives them by accepting the wine they offer. And there is yet more. *They soaked a sponge with the wine, fixed it on hyssop*,[17] and held it up to his lips. Hyssop is 'marjoram that grows out of the wall' (I Kings 4.33), nothing like the stick of Mark 15.36. But a stick was not really necessary if the feet of a crucified man were only just above the ground: his head would be in easy reach. What the soldiers did was to soak a sponge with wine, put it on a wad of hyssop to prevent the wine running down their arms, and hold it to his mouth. But to a devout Jew hyssop has significance

[16] Sanhedrin 43[a].
[17] The NEB translation was 'fixed it on a javelin' on the evidence of one thirteenth-century Greek manuscript which reads *hyssō* (javelin) instead of *hyssōpō* (hyssop, or marjoram). This contradicts sound textual principles in order to make John say what Mark says, and is abandoned in REB.

in ritual cleansing, e.g. Ps. 51.7 'Sprinkle me with hyssop so that I may be cleansed'; in particular it was part of the cleansing rite for outcasts of society (Lev. 14.4, 6 – this is more significant than the use of hyssop to spread the protective power of Passover blood, Exod. 12.22). So, as the soldiers gain merit by giving wine to a dying man, unwittingly they offer him a symbol of cleansing and restoration. Anyone who is sensitive to symbolic indications will realise that Jesus at the end performed an act of unmerited love for his enemies and was not without consolation.

Having received the wine, he said 'It is accomplished!' (v. 30). In vv. 28–30 there is a strong impression of completion: Jesus has completed the work given him by God (as in 4.34; 5.36; 17.4), a work of the divine love (as in 13.1 and I John 2.5; 4.12, 17, 18), so that the disciples may be perfectly one in experiencing the divine glory (17.23). It is notable that the words from the cross in this Gospel are composed and confident. They are somewhat similar in tone to the words in Luke 23.34, 43, 46, though entirely different in wording; and totally different in both tone and wording from the cry in Mark 15.34. It could be thought that the final single word in this Gospel (even shorter in the possibly original Aramaic forms) corresponds to the loud cry in Mark 15.37. However these differences are to be explained, it is clear that this Gospel testifies that Jesus was in command of the situation to the end of his life, when *he bowed his head and gave up his spirit*. That expression probably reflects an earlier saying of Jesus that he lays down his life of his own free will (10.18); it does not imply his handing over of the Spirit, which takes place later (20.22).

The Burial

19.31–37   It was Roman practice to leave executed criminals hanging, as a warning to others; though the Jewish writer Philo knew of festival occasions when relatives were allowed to remove the bodies and bury them.[18] But Jewish custom was more sensitive (in accordance with Deut. 21.22–23: the body must not remain overnight), and in any case the authorities require a hasty conclusion to the crucifixion to avoid polluting the high festival day (in this Gospel's chronology

---

[18] Philo, *Flaccus* 83.

sabbath and Passover happened to coincide – see p. 149). So soldiers are sent to break the legs, thus hastening death by shock or arterial bleeding. But this was not done to Jesus who appeared to be already dead (v. 33) when a soldier *thrust a lance into his side* (v. 34). Presumably there was no muscular reaction to the weapon's stab; but something very strange happened instead: *at once there was a flow of blood and water*. Cautious statements by medical authorities that such an effusion is physiologically possible are irrelevant: the Gospel is not merely reporting medical information. The report perhaps implies that Jesus was really dead, that his human body had ceased to live – though in the very condition of being dead his body produced a symbol of the benefits secured for mankind by the death of Jesus: first cleansing from all sin by his blood (I John 1.7), and then the gift of the Spirit (7.38–39). This meaning may have been intended to counter views in the later community which accepted baptism and the Spirit but not the death of Jesus (cf. I John 5.6–8). At least the fact *is vouched for by an eyewitness* (perhaps the beloved disciple – or had he departed at v. 27?), *whose evidence is to be trusted*. He indeed *knows that he speaks the truth* which is integral to the community's believing. In John 6 there is no feeding unless the death of Christ is fully accepted; here there is no refreshment unless the blood of Christ has flowed.

And yet the violence done to Jesus is not without explanation in the intention of God foreseen in scripture. By dying quickly Jesus was spared protracted suffering and the indignity of having the legs broken. Does that not suggest the Lord's protection of the righteous sufferer: 'He guards every bone of his body, and not one of them will be broken' (Ps. 34.20)? And is not the purpose of Jesus' suffering indicated by the instruction that no bone of the Passover victim should be broken (Exod. 12.46; Num. 9.12)? In other words the death of Jesus protects the people of God and makes possible their journey from slavery to freedom, from shame to glory. And not only the existing people of God, for *they shall look on him whom they pierced* (v. 37). That recalls, though it does not exactly quote, a mysterious comment in Zech. 12.10; and v. 37 would better be translated and understood thus: *they shall look* (for salvation) *to him whom they* (i.e. the Romans) *pierced* (cf. the Gentiles in 12.20–21 who wanted to see Jesus).

19.38–42   Among those who were disciples secretly (because they feared the hostility of the Jewish authorities; cf. 12.42) was Joseph from Arimathaea (probably in Judaea, not Galilee; perhaps Rama-thaim, the birth-place of Samuel, I Sam. 1.1). He was of sufficient standing to approach Pilate and ask *permission to remove the body of Jesus*, which was granted and done (v. 38). Then with Nicodemus, a Pharisaic member of the ruling Jewish group, who once defended Jesus against unfair hostility (3.1–2; 7.50–51), he took an enormous quantity of spices to give Jesus a respectful, devout burial in *a new tomb, not yet* polluted by being *used for burial* (vv. 39–41). The body was not left to the vultures (as was usual with Roman executions), or consigned to a common grave provided by the Jewish authorities for executed criminals. Jesus was buried according to *Jewish burial customs* (cf. the 'Jewish rites of purification' in 2.6) on *the eve of the Jewish sabbath*. In a short while it would be possible to leave the private garden (cf. 18.1) and eat the Passover (see p. 149).

That narrative has no hostility towards the Jews, either to rulers or to Pharisees, only an ironic display of undoubted Jewish devotion as uncomprehending, inappropriate and ineffective. For thirty-six hours Jesus is dead and decently disposed of.

The Resurrection

In 20.1–29 the Gospel develops and modifies traditional resurrection narratives: the early morning visit of women to the tomb, but confined to Mary of Magdala (vv. 1–2) and supplemented by an appearance to her (vv. 11–18; there is an appearance to the women in Matt. 28.9–10); the discovery that the tomb is empty, though made by Peter and the other disciple (vv. 3–10); and an appearance to the body of disciples (vv. 19–23; contrast Luke 24.36–43), with a supplement on the response of Thomas (vv. 24–29). These stories are related more to help the Christian community understand itself than to provide evidence of the resurrection.

At the Tomb

20.1–18   This section contains three stories, originally independent; if read as a continuous, connected report it shows numerous awkward features. But when it is realised that the stories, placed side by side, are leading up tò a carefully designed conclusion, all is well.

(i) In vv. 1–2 *Mary of Magdala came to the tomb* (presumably to mourn; cf. what was expected when Lazarus died, 11.31) and found the tomb open. Without further enquiry or discovery, she presumed that the body had been removed by grave robbers (a great nuisance in those days, as is shown by an edict of the Emperor Claudius 41–54 CE, found near Nazareth, against tomb robbery).[19] So she *ran to Simon Peter and the other disciple, the one whom Jesus loved,* told her discovery, and expressed her distress: *'We do not know* (implying herself and other women?) *where they have laid him.'* Thus the discovery of the open tomb serves only to confirm the deadness of Jesus.

(ii) In vv. 3–10 the two disciples ran to the tomb. (Peter's visit may be confirmed if Luke 24.12 is an original part of that Gospel; REB puts the verse in the margin.) The beloved disciple ran faster and arrived first; Peter arrived second but entered the tomb first (perhaps a hint of rivalry between the two – certainly visible in 21.20–22 – or between the Christian communities attached to them). The beloved disciple *peered in and saw the linen wrappings lying there* – and clearly realised that there was something wrong. Peter entered the tomb, *saw the linen wrappings lying there, and the napkin which had been round his head . . . rolled up in a place by itself* (v. 7). So it was not tomb robbery, but some neat and orderly proceeding (note the contrast with the haste and agitation of the disciples). Yet Peter drew no conclusion, though the beloved disciple entered the tomb, saw what Peter had seen – and realised not that something was wrong but that everything was right. *He saw and believed* (v. 8). Thus it appears that haste and rivalry were inappropriate, that observation of an empty tomb was ineffective, and that entry into the tomb and the sight of indicative signs was unreliable (for the beloved disciple believed though Peter was unmoved). There was, however, one reliable method: the testimony of scripture. Not of course that any passage of scripture says in so many words that the Christ must rise from the dead, not

[19] In C. K. Barrett, *The New Testament Background: Selected Documents*, rev. ed. London and New York 1987, p. 15.

even Ps. 16.8–11 which Peter quoted at Acts 2.25–28; but the general sense of scripture that establishes the pattern of ascent and descent (as Gen. 28.12 is used in John 1.51). If Jesus was indeed the Son of Man who descended from heaven, then of course he must ascend into heaven where he was before (3.13; 6.62) – recognising that this Gospel scarcely separates resurrection from ascension – as the third story shows.

(iii) At v. 11 a new story begins: we discover Mary weeping over the theft of the body. *She peered into the tomb, and saw two angels* (according to the rule of two witnesses, 8.17) *in white sitting there, one at the head, and one at the feet, where the body of Jesus had lain* – thus marking out the sacred space of his absence. Modern readers must realise that in old Jewish culture an appearance of angels was real evidence of divine presence or, to put it otherwise, that was sometimes the manner in which divine presence presented itself. Even so, a vision of angels was not effective in removing Mary's preoccupation with death. Even an appearance of Jesus, and his question to her, could do no more: she supposed him to be *the gardener* who had removed the dead body. Only when Jesus addressed her by name ('he calls his own sheep by name', 10.3–4) did she respond to Jesus alive (v. 16). Thus the woman who in a few moments is authorised to deliver the ascension message is convinced not by an empty tomb, nor by angels, not even by an appearance of Jesus – but by his living words. But first she must cease detaining Jesus on earth: *Do not cling to me*[20] – because Jesus alive is not the restoration of the pre-crucified teacher. To cling to him is to prevent him from returning to the Father; or (put otherwise) to detain Jesus is to prevent the devout imagination from rising with him to God. So Mary was bidden to tell *my brothers* (and it is significant that a woman was chosen for this revelatory task) *that I am ascending to my Father and your Father, to my God and your God*. It is precisely because the divine being *is* their Father and their God that Jesus is ascending. In the simpler imagery of 14.2 he goes to prepare a place for them. But it must be realised that this Gospel has no room for the natural but misleading imagery of a resurrection, a period of life in the resurrection body, and then an ascension that removes Jesus from earth to heaven until he returns at the second advent. In this Gospel the process of ascension indicates

---

[20] Verse 17a is well known in the AV translation 'Touch me not', and the famous Latin words *'Noli me tangere'*. But modern translations carefully observe the grammatical form of the prohibition (negative with the *present* imperative of *haptomai*) which means 'stop what you are doing'.

the permanent identity of Jesus. *Tell them that I am ascending* – so that, when Jesus again appears, he is the risen, ascending Lord who confers the gift of the Spirit as he had promised (16.7).

In a Closed Room

20.19–29   The tomb visitations took place on Sunday morning, the communal gathering (perhaps resembling an early Christian church's apprehension of the Jews) on Sunday evening (compare the gathering to break bread in Acts 20.7) in Jerusalem. How many disciples were present is not clear: possibly only the Twelve (v. 24), less Judas and Thomas, possibly more. *They were behind locked doors for fear of the Jews* (v. 19). Hence normal access was excluded, but not abnormal access. By some means that cannot be known to us, *Jesus came and stood among them*, and calmed their fears with the divine blessing *'Peace be with you'* (cf. 14.27 'Peace is my parting gift to you . . . such as the world cannot give'). He was the identical Jesus who had been crucified, displaying the wounds in hands (actually wrists, since nails through the palms would not bear a body's weight) and side, in what to all appearance was a normal and familiar body. It would be sensible to abandon the much-used but inept statement that the risen body could pass through closed doors (why not through a window? and why was the stone removed from the tomb?), and simply state that the risen Jesus could present himself to disciples as he wished and convince them that resurrection cancelled neither the memory nor the effect of crucifixion – to the joy of the disciples (v. 20).

The purpose of this appearance, however, was not only to produce conviction but also to extend the doctrine of agency (see p. 15 and p. 59). As a function of the divine blessing, the disciples are made agents of the Agent of God: *'As the Father sent me, so I send you'* (cf. the pre-arrangement in 17.18). *Then he breathed on them* – as the Lord breathed into Adam's nostrils the breath of life (Gen. 2.7; Wisd. 15.11), and breathed new life into the dry bones of ruined Israel (Ezek. 37.5–10). This metaphor of inbreathing is only one among several expressions that are needed to compass the experience of the Spirit: remember also rebirth by the Spirit (3.5–8), the inner spring of living waters (7.38–39), and the Spirit of truth as personal sponsor in the paraclete sayings. (The Lukan Pentecost, depending on the metaphors of mountain storm and divine outpouring (Acts 2.2–3, 33) is a special demonstration or set-piece rather than the occasion when the Spirit was bestowed by Jesus.)

From what the Gospel has already said the benefits of possessing the Spirit are plain: access to the divine energy, worship of God in truth, sharing in the life of the world above, and entering into the truth of what Jesus has said and done (see pp. 120–123). Nothing whatever has been said about the forgiveness of sins.[21] It is true that the paraclete 'will prove the world wrong about sin' which is unbelief (16.8–9) – but that does not *forgive* sin: it exposes it and rubs in the accusation. The connection between the gift of the Spirit in v. 22 and forgiveness in v. 23 follows from the fact that the Spirit of truth is given only to those who love Jesus and obey his instructions relating to the world and the inner life of the community (see p. 121). Against the conviction that Christians cannot sin and that anyone who does sin must be excluded (a view considered in I John), Jesus says – to the Spirit-endowed community: *'If you forgive anyone's sins, they are forgiven* [by God]; *if you pronounce them unforgiven, unforgiven* [by God] *they remain'* (v. 23). Into a formal instruction Jesus puts the teaching of the footwashing (see pp. 107–108). This interpretation is confirmed by the similarity between v. 23 and two passages in Matthew: in Matt. 18.18 community disputes are in the end resolved by the instruction that 'whatever you forbid on earth shall be forbidden in heaven, and whatever you allow on earth shall be allowed in heaven'. In Matt. 16.19, in almost identical terms, Peter is given the keys of the kingdom of Heaven, i.e. like the major domo of Isa. 22.22 he can admit to the royal palace or exclude from it as he sees fit. Thus one function of the Holy Spirit is to discern whether the disorderly behaviour of Christians carries them beyond the boundaries of the church, or whether they can be welcomed back as repentant sinners.

A case in point is immediately provided when Thomas (speaking unwittingly for some future Christians) insists on seeing *the mark of the nails on his hands*, on putting his *finger into the place where the nails were* and his *hand into his side* before he will believe in the resurrection (v. 25). This demand must not be rebuked as crude disbelief: it indeed labours under the conviction that the sense of touch is more convincing than other senses, but it is also a form of identification with the sufferings of Jesus (which dissident members of the later

---

[21] 'Forgive' occurs only here in the Gospel (twice also in I John). In Mark 10 times, Luke 15 times, Matthew 17 times. For the meaning of 'sin' in the Gospel, see p. 000. I John says much more about sin and sins.

community rejected). It leads to the demand that the risen Jesus must possess a physically touchable body – no other kind is allowable – if the resurrection is to be truly asserted. *A week later* Thomas was present when, in similar circumstances, Jesus again appeared and gave the divine blessing. He does not deny Thomas' demand but allows it, though implying that it arises from unbelief. How does Thomas respond? By hearing and seeing certainly, but by touch – who can say? Thomas' confession – which brings the Gospel story to a triumphant climax and fills out the meaning of 'God the only [Son]' in 1.18 (see p. 15) – is spoken and heard. 'Touch' is significant when we wash one another's feet (see pp. 107–109), and sight is dealt with in v. 29.

First, however, we must consider the confession: *My Lord and my God* (v. 28), one of the rare occasions in the New Testament when Jesus is called God. It is true that the word *god* was widely applied in Hellenistic culture to emperors and other important persons, and that the Emperor Domitian 81–96 CE (in the period when the Gospel was being written) expected to be called 'Our Master and our God';[22] but Jesus was not an important person in that sense, and his story lies within – if only just within – the stricter circle of the Jewish conception of God. When Jesus defined the ascension message in v. 17, he distinguished himself from God: 'I am ascending . . . to my God and your God.' But Thomas found God so fully present in Jesus that his confession erased the distinction – precisely because the confession expressed personal devotion. If we consider the relation of Jesus to God, he is God's Agent and Son; if we consider the believer's relation to Jesus, he is more than God's Agent – he is the Logos, the one in whom God speaks and makes himself known to us. If we follow the example of Thomas, we may usefully reflect on the conviction of Philo (the Jewish philosopher who spoke to the Hellenistic world). For him the Divine Being was unknowable deity, that which really exists: what could be known were his activities, past and present. The name *God* alludes to his activity in creating the world, the name *Lord* to his activity in ruling the world.[23] It is no wonder that Jesus confirmed Thomas' faith (v. 29 expresses approval, not gentle mockery like 1.50 and 16.31), but yet more strongly approved those *who find faith without seeing me* (v. 29). The story in vv. 19–29 implies that the disciples experienced appearances of

---

[22] In Barrett (see p. 166 n. 9 above), p. 20. More generally J. D. G. Dunn, *Christology* (see p. 52 n. 5 above), pp. 16–17.
[23] S. Sandmel, *Philo of Alexandria*, (see p. 5 n. 1 above), pp. 91–92.

Jesus that were visual, auditory and tactile. In days to come such appearances would be replaced by seeing, hearing and touching fellow believers.

Conclusion

20.30–31 This paragraph looks back over the whole Gospel, and indicates that its course is complete. Of the *many other signs that Jesus performed in the presence of his disciples* a selection had been made (see p. 31). Presumably they have been chosen with care, and are to be interpreted not individually but as a group. They are not merely striking marvels, intended to demonstrate that Jesus has access to supernatural power and so is himself a divine being: they are *signs* which signify the generosity of God in offering joyful reconciliation, rescue from acute dangers of many kinds, and in the end – when these benefits are refused – the judgment that Judaism must die before it can live. The signs *written here have been recorded* to make faith possible when the resurrection is known and properly understood (contrast 12.37): *that you may believe* (see p. 37) *that Jesus is the Christ* (a Hellenistic Jewish title; see pp. 27–29), *the Son of God* (a more Hellenistic title; see pp. 52–53), *and that through this faith you may have life* (see p. 37) *by his name* (see pp. 10–11).

For what readers was the Gospel intended? Was it intended to arouse faith among devout and thoughtful Greeks or among potential Jewish converts in the Hellenistic world? Or was it intended to develop and strengthen the faith of an existing Christian community? The answer cannot be decided from the wording of the concluding paragraph; but from an exegesis of the whole Gospel – in relation to the First Epistle – it seems most likely that it was composed in and for a Christian community whose inward life was both enriched and complicated by Jewish, Baptist and Samaritan traditions, and whose relations with the world were both fruitful and dangerous because some members had upped and gone. Given such taxing circumstances, the theological impetus behind the Gospel persuaded those who composed it not simply to repeat the tradition in safe, remembered phrases but to re-affirm it by finding innovative expression for it.

A Resurrection Supplement
21

This supplementary chapter is awkwardly composed and enigmatic in meaning. The writer could manage the Johannine style reasonably well, but the interests he displays – the direct concerns of the later community – take him outside the main scope of the Gospel. There are the following items:

(a) a third appearance of the risen Jesus (vv. 1–14);
(b) a solemn restoration of Simon Peter (vv. 15–17);
(c) a designation of Peter's martyrdom (vv. 18–19);
(d) a revised expectation about the beloved disciple (vv. 20–23);
(e) an affirmation of his written testimony (v. 24); and
(f) a conventional ending (v. 25).

21.1–14   This is exceptional in being both a miracle story (similar to the marvellous catch of fish, with Simon Peter the dominant figure and his partners the two sons of Zebedee, in Luke 5.1–11) and an appearance story which interests the writer most (v. 1). If the appearance is understood literally it could have been the *first* appearance to a group of disciples after 20.9, but most improbably after 20.17–18 and quite impossibly after 20.19–29 (since the disciples had been given their commission in 20.21; and v. 29b rules out further 'seeing').[1] Thus the story must be understood symbolically.

'I am going fishing' means that Peter encourages his fellow-disciples to set about their apostolic work as 'fishers of men' (as Mark 1.16–17 puts it). The recognition theme is suggested by John 6.16–21: 'they saw Jesus walking on the sea(-shore)'.[2] The feeding on bread and fish in v. 9 reflects the feeding in 6.11, and Peter's satisfactory prominence at 6.68 is qualified by his actions in 21.7, 11. Above all, the location

[1] The third time (v. 14) may perhaps be understood as 'the third (definitive) time'.
[2] Both 6.19 'on the sea' and 21.1 'by the sea' use the same Greek words, *epi tēs thalassēs*.

172

is the same: *the sea of Tiberias* (21.1 – see 6.1, 23), identified not merely as a site in Galilee but as in the neighbourhood of Tiberias – the splendid new town of the Greek *polis*-type, founded about 20 CE by Herod Antipas, named out of respect for the Roman emperor, a thriving centre of the farming and fish-salting industries. The disciples had symbolically moved out of the closed room into the world of Roman enterprise culture. The story begins in failure and ends in success, begins in uncertainty and ends in recognition – and that, of course, is the gospel. The people concerned (v. 2) are *Simon Peter* (also in vv. 15–16, 18–19), *Thomas the Twin* (see 20.28), *Nathanael from Cana in Galilee* (see 1.49), *the sons of Zebedee* (nowhere else mentioned in the Gospel, but according to Mark 1.19 partners in Simon's fishing business), and *two other disciples* presumably including the beloved disciple (see v. 20 and pp. 110–111). That is seven in all, not the traditional Twelve[3], combining two types: the 'activists' Peter and the sons of Zebedee, the 'recognisers' Thomas, Nathanael and the beloved disciple. To Jesus they are *Friends* (really 'children' which is how the community members are addressed; see I John 2.13, 18) and he says to them: *Have you caught anything?* (v. 5) – much better rendered in the gently mocking words: 'You haven't caught a sprat, have you?'[4] But when they obey the directions of Jesus they make an enormous catch of big fish, *a hundred and fifty three in all*[5] – recalling the enormous generosity of God in giving wine and bread – though *the net was not torn*, i.e. the unity of the Christian group was not broken by so great an influx (v. 11). But more is needed than the great catch, namely recognition of him who made the catch possible. At first *the disciples did not know that it was Jesus* (v. 4) until *the disciple*

[3] Biblical numbers are often used for their symbolic value rather than their actual size. Seven is a totality number, perhaps suggesting all the nations, and so more striking than twelve signifying Israel. Cf. the seventy in Luke 10.1, and the seventy nations in Gen. 10; and perhaps the seven in Acts 6.3; 21.8.
[4] The question expects the answer No. The word *prosphagion* means a bite, a snack, a morsel on a plate of *mezes* (which every visitor to Greece knows) – rather than the big fish of v. 11.
[5] 153 is simply a large number. In a symbolic story it can scarcely be an actual fish count (like a preacher counting his congregation). Why would that be interesting? Nor is it the number of fish recognised by ancient zoologists (as Jerome, it seems wrongly, said). Nor is *three* the Trinity if something else can be found for 150. Nor is it the total when numerical values are given to each letter in a group of words, e.g. 'sons of God' in Gen. 6.2, giving Hebrew consonants their conventional values:

$$b(2)n(50)y(10) \ h(5)-'(1)l(30)h(5)y(10)m(40) = 153.$$

That may be a game for bored old men at the festival of Purim, but it has no other value. (Example from *Expository Times* 100, March 1989, p. 217.)

whom Jesus loved said, 'It is the Lord!' (v. 7). Then Peter was prompted into action – respectful (*he fastened his coat about him* to cover his nakedness) and vigorous, though without much effect until he went back on board to help with the net (v. 11). With the others he is invited to breakfast, and *none of the disciples dared to ask 'Who are you?' They knew it was the Lord* (v. 12). The beloved disciple had already recognised the Lord in the greatness of the catch; others recognised him when he offered them food. At this point the dream-like quality of the encounter is accentuated: *when they came ashore they saw a charcoal fire there with fish laid on it, and some bread,* and they are told *Bring some of the fish you have caught* (vv. 9–10). The Christian community does not feed on its own success. Of course, success contributes to its happiness and confidence; but basically it feeds on what Christ has prepared for it. We already know, from the discourse of John 6, that feeding on bread and fish implies the food of God's instruction and wisdom given through his Son. Although that is not directly eucharistic teaching – since eucharistic imagery required feeding *on* the Son of Man – it is teaching that should be kept in mind at every eucharist, for both 'activists' and 'recognisers'.

21.15–17   For this separate scene *after breakfast* the imagery changes from the fisherman to the shepherd. The conversation between Jesus and Simon Peter is dignified and formal. Three times Jesus uses not the nickname Peter, familiar in the apostolic band, but the proper family name: *Simon son of John* – the kind of thing that happens in the legal part of our marriage service. It is a solemn occasion, and a change of social standing is taking place. It is a triple formula with repetitions (common in the language of worship, e.g. 'Lord have mercy; Christ have mercy; Lord have mercy') and variations: *feed* and *tend, lambs* and *sheep*, two words for *know*, two words for *love*. This is not a realistic conversation where two speakers try to evade the point or gain an advantage by shifting the words. It is a liturgical question and response which must have come from the Greek-speaking community, not in the earliest days when they spoke Aramaic (since Aramaic had only *one* word for *love*, and *one* word for *know*). It marks the point at which Peter becomes the shepherd (i.e. leader) of the community, and so suggests a shift in the teaching of the Gospel about how Christians are looked after. The main teaching is simple: they look after one another, and wash one another's feet (13.14). 'Love one another as I have loved you' (15.12) – with the stress not on 'love' but on 'one another'. The Christian community is self-regulating and self-caring. It had a vivid belief that Jesus was alive. He did not hand over his authority to someone else. He had been the good shepherd, and still was. All others claiming authority over the flock were thieves and robbers. There is one flock, one shepherd. Now that is changed by the authorisation of Peter: a self-regulating, self-caring group is replaced by a flock with a human shepherd. And a very fallible one: the threefold authorisation recalls the threefold denial. If *Peter was hurt* that his love was questioned three times, it cannot be helped. Given the history of Israel's shepherds – and Christian shepherds too – the question must be insistently asked.

21.18–19 Presumably a proverbial saying on the lines 'A young man can do as he pleases, an old man is helpless' has been adapted to signify the manner of Peter's death. *When you are old you will stretch out your arms*[6] (on a cross-bar), *and a stranger will bind you fast* (to a cross), *and carry you where you have no wish to go* (namely to death), so fulfilling what Jesus had said: 'You cannot follow me now, but one day you will' (13.36). Well before this Gospel was published Peter had glorified God by a martyr's death.

21.20–23 Here are more hints of a mild rivalry between Peter and the beloved disciple. It is no business of Peter's if Jesus intends the beloved disciple to remain until he comes (a striking example of the expectation, otherwise lacking in this Gospel, that Jesus would soon return to his followers on earth). Yet it is wrong to conclude that Jesus intended that the beloved disciple would not die. This rather embarrassed argument suggests that he had in fact died, to the distress of the brethren; or possibly that he was still alive at a great age but was likely soon to die.

21.24 *It is this same disciple* (i.e. the beloved disciple referred to in vv. 20–22) *who vouches for what has been written here*, namely the interpretation in v. 23 of what Jesus intended, or the traditions contained in ch. 21, or the whole Gospel. To claim the beloved disciple's authority for v. 23 is scarcely supported by *He it is who wrote it*. To claim his authority for formal Petrine leadership which overthrows the main teaching of the Gospel is implausible. Hence it is being stated, by a member of the later community, that the

---

[6] The stretching out of hands is so interpreted by early Christian writers; see also Epictetus (55–135 CE) III.26.22.

beloved disciple is the authority for this Gospel's interpretation of the traditions about Jesus. When the community says that *we* (cf. 1.14, 16) *know that his testimony is true*, they are not rejecting other ways of telling the Jesus-story but confessing that their self-regulating, self-caring life as Christians is wholly supported by this theological understanding. The words *He it is who wrote it* most probably imply that, as Pilate caused the inscription to be written (19.22), so the beloved disciple was the indirect author and necessary authority for the Gospel.

The Beloved Disciple and the Editor

But to account for the compositional questions mentioned on pp. XIX–XXII it is necessary to think not simply of *an* author but of some such sequence as this: the original bearers of the tradition; the beloved disciple as the theological reviser of the tradition; a composing editor; and the we-group of the community. The name of *the beloved disciple* has not been disclosed, perhaps because he did not wish to be set in competition, or even comparison, with the Petrine claim to authority; more probably because he wished to subtract nothing from the name of Jesus, the one shepherd. The style of *the composing editor* puts him closer to Mark than to any other NT writer. His stock of words is characteristic of the Greek OT, and has only a modest affinity with the Hermetic writings and the gnostic Gospel of Truth. He makes use of OT imagery as developed in the story-telling tradition of Judaism, not its law-making tradition. Hence, despite the interesting parallels, he is remote in spirit from the Qumran writings. 'Men with capital, landed property, business and position hardly occur in John, and none of his illustrative remarks is drawn from the world of power and wealth.'[7] Among second-century Christian writers he is nearest in thought to Ignatius of Antioch; his Gospel is tentatively used by Justin from Samaria; is first put in a collection of writings by Tatian in northern Syria; and is first ascribed to John by Theophilus of Antioch. He looks like a Hellenistic Jewish Christian who knew Jerusalem as a festal pilgrim and wrote for a marginal Christian community in Syria.

21.25   In a sense the ending is conventional. Cf. the end of Philo's

[7] G. D. Kilpatrick, 'What John tells us about John', in *Studies in John, Novum Testamentum* Supplement XXIV, 1970, pp. 76–7.

very long treatise *On the Special Laws*: 'If one should wish to tell in full all the praises of equality the time would fail him, be his life the longest' (IV. 238). In this case, however, it is something of an apology for having added ch. 21 to the Gospel. There is much else, indeed, to be said about Jesus but all of it can be said in relation to John 1–20.